Al

The author has long been writing poems & prose-poetry inspired by his birding and nature in general encouraged from an early age by J. A. Baker's seminal book The Peregrine. Some of the author's work has been published online in 'Birdforum's' thread 'Your Birding Day'.

When a pair of Hobbies bred on his patch near Lymm, Cheshire, returning each spring from Africa, they became something of an obsession. The birds and the words they inspired with their aerial prowess and beauty became the beginnings of this book.

Years of observation accumulated and condensed to form this volume.

Following his retirement last year (from the Civil Service) he was able, finally, to complete the novel.

Dedication

To my wife, Mandy: my Bobby Dazzler.

Richard Hargreaves

RAZOR IN THE WIND

AUSTIN MACAULEY PUBLISHERS™

LONDON • CAMBRIDGE • NEW YORK • SHARJAH

A CIP catalogue record for this title is available from the British Library.

ISBN 9781528919982 (Paperback)
ISBN 9781528922852 (ePub e-book)

www.austinmacauley.com

First Published (2020)
Austin Macauley Publishers Ltd
25 Canada Square
Canary Wharf
London
E14 5LQ

Acknowledgements

To Mandy, my wife, for the encouragement, patience and advice during the years of this book's research and writing.

Thanks, too, to my stepdaughter, Jai Lane, who has given hours of technical assistance to my computer-illiterate self.

Contents

PRO-PROLOGUE

'Zen Birding' or 'The struggle between infinite semiosis and the path to Nirvana'

BIRDS, like all things, are signs. More so, much more so, to a birder. As each sight, each sound, reaches our perception a cacophony of meaning, relation, reinterpretation, significance, recognition (non-recognition!) explodes in our consciousness, at the same time that pattern, colour, contrast, volume, pitch, speed and timbre of the actual things seen or heard. (This process is semiosis.)

As birders a bird's significance in every sense, is enhanced. Can we even see or hear a bird without its name blooming within our heads? Try it. Difficult towards impossible. (And, if we do not recognise a bird the blossoming of thought is much the louder.) Each feather tract, each pattern of colour, each sound brings to mind a catalogue of abstract text, of meaning, of emotion, of memory. And each continues along the threads of thought; and still we continue to observe and renew afresh these processes in an infinite multi-dimensional swirl.

This then would seem to crowd the head in exactly the wrong way required for the non-attachment needed to approach Nirvana. Yet there comes a feeling, almost simultaneously, sometimes, of calm.

Almost counter-intuitively (since a conscious effort is required) we can latch onto this path and allow the world to melt away while observing it.

Perhaps because we are birders and know birds and their place in our world, because they have significance, are emotive, this allows us some detachment, perhaps, and peace is inevitably a part of the process occasionally.

The Gestalt principles of perceptual organisation so automatic to us that, though the brain is really busy, it is still, well...still.

That euphoric other-world state begins to pervade and warm the spirit, the world melts away and we stand alone in a bubble of birdness: a place familiar and true – a place without place. We stand outside ourselves within our head. For perhaps an instant the wind blows through our spirit and we are gone.

Then an alarm call, like a starter pistol's crack, starts the infinite semiosis again and we are birders once more.

PROLOGUES

FROM October until April, these northern skies hold no Hobbies. Spring arrives and life blossoms again, and the final migrants return from an African winter, flying impossible distances to their summering grounds. The Hobby follows the Swallow on these migrations, running with the Swifts across continents.

As each spring begins again the memory of others is brought back with the warmth of the sun, and the hope of a successful season for the Hobby is renewed. Even predators have an unpredictable life, their success depending on so many things, and they are not without their own predators, and summer storms can be devastating.

A Weasel runs gingerly across my path, tail fluffed out, feet wetted by rains beginning to dry in the lengthening grasses of a new season.

The clouds drift apart...

Sunlight shafts shine down my memory and the breeze blows between my youth and the now, as a Cuckoo casts a line that snags my heart – two notes tripped from bars on a breast – and pulls taught the line of my years.

My feet lift from the lane, careless on the sound; place and time blurred and gone. My soul borne with the bird's song back to somewhere remembered; landing me later on the path.

Along and along in sunlight and shadows, floating home...

WINTER TURNS TO SPRING

A HARE springs up from furrows beyond the dazzle of a backlit puddle. There, amongst the Lapwings, a Redshank picks, and pauses to call a soft, worried, plover-like "teoo", stretching its neck and strutting. The sun catches its legs to incandescence.

At the field's top, by the canal, two territory-returned Oystercatchers in pied livery fly off, piping loudly. Buzzards fill the gaps between earth and heaven, rolling circuits in the warming air.

Under the humpback bridge a Kingfisher's call echoes against the arc of brickwork as it exits to fly the curve of the canal.

Away and along the calming river: crocuses and snowdrops on the turf. New molehills pepper the levees like sun-drawn freckles. A Kingfisher calls again.

A calm, like sleep, slows the soul; peace invades; the world of nature envelops, takes hold, walks the banks: becomes.

A flash of azure and aquamarine, a splash and plish, and a fish is bashed on a bough. The fisher turns its foxy belly, bright orange feet beneath, and eats.

And, as this is happening, a Green Woodpecker yaffles over a deer's bark, a Great spotted Woodpecker alarms and bounds away, but the Lesser spotted Woodpecker remains to hammer gently at the alder. In one instant.

On the bank of the ox-bow the Kingfisher sits, the white triangle of his throat beneath his dagger-like bill, and above, the woodpecker flicks up the tree and shows off his red crown, ladder-backed black and white, tiny.

The percussive tapping of this little woodpecker is underscored: lesser notes pitched high: two Treecreepers, horn-coloured curved mandibles pressing into creases, probing and teasing, calling softly, sliding along and dropping down tree trunks to start again.

Two Mistle Thrushes undulate through the copse and a Wren twists its song from a twiggy tangle by the pond, the water zebra-striped by shadows. Lesser celandines burn bright on the bank under the ripple of Goldfinches amongst the dangling lambs' tails of catkins.

And under water hides a Moorhen, perfectly still, breathing through the periscope of its bill, just protruding from the murky shallows, scarlet forehead-shield sunlit, wetly red like a secret sin.

A sloped verge of pale translucent crocus swarms with Honey Bees, a little torpid in the too-early air, and a fat and furry Bumblebee, buzzing, bombs the blooms. Four beautiful Bullfinches blink pinkly in the hedge and almost outdo all the splendour of this splendid day.

Standing brazen on the field's shallow crest, a Grey Partridge, black-hearted belly pushed out in a showy challenge – calls to a rival who backs off, but answers over his fleeing shoulder.

And at the hedge edge a female watches the contest, crouched and creeping to keep pace as the suitors chase.

At a run they take off over the hawthorns to the field beyond and the bout continues; but the battle is won and the victor returns to crouch in wheat, with his mate.

From the west, a Curlew spirals a helter-skelter to the wet field, calling once and settles. Lapwings watch. A Hare continues to nibble at weeds. The much-reduced Fieldfare flock, dark in the gloom of the glowering sky, moves from stubble to sycamores.

The Kestrel stays on her pole top, head-down, curious. But the Little Owl is more wary and flies to melt away in his camouflage. Under the hedge two more partridge, already paired, court in a snaking path.

Out along the river into the shelving sun, temperate air serenading serenely. Sparkles from waters jabbing and the glistening of dew.

The Kingfisher's call now splinters the quiet. He is perching bolt-blue in the dapple of the pond. Still. The morning holds its breath. For a while he sits, statuesque, then he flashes away, and the clocks restart.

A pair of Greater spotted Woodpeckers hammer into rotten tree trunks, splintering chunks from yellow wood which fall beyond their fiery bellies. A Treecreeper, mouse-like, runs up the alder. Tiny sounds: Reed Bunting and Meadow Pipits overhead, then the clear loud call of a Lesser spotted Woodpecker, close but invisible against the sun.

There he is: low on a trunk, pecking and prising at bark edges, slowly stalking upwards, an exquisite jewel in the bright light, red cap colouring the wonderful piedness of him. Under a rotten limb, the white of his black-and-white bar-code back catches the light. His mate on the upright spar of an alder watches; he flies and calls from a nearby tree.

Time passes like the torpid river behind. He calls again and drums a long, quiet roll which barely reaches beyond his own tree. Only he exists, all else has gone in the halted, unending moment.

Suddenly the sharp sound of a Green Sandpiper cracks the meditative reverie, splits the soft solitude to shards. Against the dazzling reflection of the pool, now the white rump swerves down to land. Simultaneously a movement just to the left – a Redwing has flown in to perch low in the tree.

As this happens the fizz of a Sand Martin overhead flies at the sun, and the blinding is complete: light explodes and both birds are gone. Back at the shade of the alders the woodpecker, too has disappeared. Somewhere in the dark distance he calls his soft "hee hee hee".

Cumuli accumulate as the day warms further. And with them Buzzards by the dozen are up in the billowing air. Along the canal two Redpolls come down to the trees to the right of the path and, for a short while, sit obligingly.

Above the settling beds clouds of flies boil off the trees like smoke; their mating shoal tightens and spirals, darkening inkily; relaxes and disperses, blanching; condenses and collides, just to dissipate and dissolve again.

A Chiffchaff sings, just once. He remains invisible somewhere in the willows. But now there are two Sand Martins sailing high up amongst the Buzzards and clouds.

And, below, by the river, another Kingfisher sits, impossibly blue.

A female Kestrel sways slowly on a blackthorn's top, eyes on the meadow. Her subtle beauty – barred brown-and-black back, soft brown head, dark moustachial and streaked underparts – enhanced by the brightening and blowing day. Her mate, against the wind, slowly sails in, and, halting in the air, gently lands on her back, and they briefly mate. A soft keening call blows down the wind.

They sit side by side, matching only in eye and claw, his dove-grey head handsome: they part to hunt.

Frost-whitened fields of early April: a gossamer shroud of mist hanging over the pond, the sun through a milky sky, low, and, as yet, cold.

Ribbon-eared Hares squat in hard-frozen furrows where a Linnet flock twitter and Lapwings stretch. A chevron of Cormorants heads west. Then the Kestrel pair vacate their telegraph pole perch, the Little Owl a dark silhouette in the distance.

Sixty Fieldfare move in frosty stubble. Somewhere a Redshank calls, perhaps.

Along the eddied mercury river under the still-weak sun, a Goosander is already off, body bowed and wings whirring, over the heronry and away. Herons sit – already with eggs, still amongst the bare trees bulky with their nests.

Two young Rabbits scurry back to a burrow amongst newly-pushed primroses – the first of spring.

Down in a little valley cuckoo flowers in tight, pale-purple bud are ready to open, bluebells and campions push past celandines lying yellow in jagged yellow sun patches, and the wood's new leaf trembles. Blackbirds' mellow songs overlap invisibly.

A quick whisper of Sparrowhawk from a dozen quiet voices, then silence. A Hare, from dewy underfoot, breaks away to sprint a circuit back to her form. Somewhere a crouching newborn lies hidden for her anxious return.

Along the canal two Blackcaps now sing rival warbles from blackthorns across the narrow water's gap. Chiffchaffs too mark territories. Down on the river Sand Martins prospecting sand banks loop along meanders and rise for risen flies. A Swallow sings and a House Martin skims warming air for aerial plankton. A Kingfisher's call appears from under the bridge, the bird itself invisible.

But, in the near distance, a Wood Pigeon bomb has gone off. Birds scatter in panic. And there: a tiercel Peregrine, rakish and powerful, powers up to the pylon's apex to sit, brightly pied in the sunshine, swivelling his head as a Mallard goes under him. One spellbound minute and he's off. Rising and accelerating to the north-east. Distance melts him as he stoops.

Alarmed birds begin to resettle, amongst the finches three Siskins approach closest, a Bullfinch pair to the right, three Reed Buntings left. A Jay, like a first-time swimmer completing a width, makes it to an isolated tree and screeches.

Sun-warmed Bumblebees stumble along the lane, and gorse flowers, coaxed by spring, fill the air with the coconut of their scent, enough to eat. A Chiffchaff 'chiff-chaffs', and buoyed Buzzards rise and cross the canal. A pair of bright Bullfinches, gorging on fat buds, balance among bush tops.

Willows, doubled in the mirror of the water, meet their reflections along a line indiscernible, and from them the blade-thin calls of two Kingfishers slash at the calm. Their mating couplets, bouncing from bank to bank across the cut, shining from the steely surface, as each flies a speedy parallel to its reflection, then rocket up to perch.

Overhead a Sparrowhawk, undersides uplit, draws alarm notes from a Greenfinch and sails away.

It was on a gusty, cloud-scudding day at the end of April when the first Hobby returned, suddenly appearing between cumuli chasing across the dazzling sky, as newly-opened leaves bent to the breeze.

At first just a dark boomerang, tiny in the long-searched distance, but getting closer: becoming itself instead of a memory, the long winter wait at an end at last.

At the old nest the Crow was still her on eggs, sitting tight, gently swaying with the wind. The Hobby approached, seeing the nest again, re-occupied by its owner, and swerved away to land on a nearby treetop to survey the familiar scene: seven months away in Africa, its huge journey done.

Now the Hobby season had begun.

It has been almost seven months since their return to Africa, seven months of Hobby-empty skies, seven months of waiting and hoping.

A Himalaya of cumulus on the horizon sends occasional clouds over, like irregular Zeppelins, otherwise the sky holds only a smear of vapour trails.

Four-eyed Peacock butterflies chase each other and a Chiffchaff flits around the adjacent hawthorn. A trio of Song Thrushes compete in song with Wrens, Dunnocks, Goldfinches and a Goldcrest – like a jazz jam session without a lead. A Greenfinch like a lemon-edged mangetout sings on the fence and a dozen denizens of the briar come and go.

Through the wood: Willow Warblers' songs everywhere. Cowslips flowering in pale patches push above the still-wet grasses.

There: a Whitethroat sings from the stream-side alders, under whose branches Badgers' paths meander on the bank. Dandelions, like myriad suns, shine on the ditch edges.

Along the lanes the Wheatear still perches proudly on clod tops, showing off in the spring light, pausing on his northward journey. A Little Owl, until now part-of-the-tree stock still, stretches up and twists its head, yellow eyes following a Buzzard that over flies its tree, calling to a rival.

The Buzzards meet up downwind with another five, and pirouette in the clear air, marking invisible territory boundaries. Skylarks' songs ripple down to earth where a Hare's ears show from a furrow.

To the canal: Blackcaps sing and a Green Woodpecker's yaffle reaches across the water from the wood. Twelve Mallard chicks, day-old and downy, bob on ripples, trying to grip the water as they blow about.

A pair of Kestrels circle each other over the field and a Jay's brightness gives itself away at a sycamore's base.

At the ox-bow lake a Kingfisher defines a blue line obliquely away, piping a whistle along the water, splitting the sitting Gadwall pair with electric shine. A solitary Redpoll heads north into the deer park.

At the roadside a limply dead Polecat lies.

In the hedge gap by the lane, corn and barley crops split by set-aside, bright with poppies and ox-eye daisies, thirteen half-grown Grey Partridges crouch, cryptic and still: watching, silent under the wind.

Two sharp calls of unseen and high House Martins prick the ears, cause a scrutiny of the sky, thick with clouds. And, sure as a promise, the Hobby drives the spirit to sprint before it, splits the before and after. In a thin slice of silence, it is gone.

At the corner the young Little Owl looks down from its oak, pale and unblinking. Around the Swallowy farm the path leads on. Down in the creek banks the purple and lilacs of loostrife and thistle, and pinks of late ragged robin crowd the eye. One Damselfly offers a dot of neon.

Past Barn Owl boxes and over a hump of hillock thick with crops, and in the descent a sound freezes the feet: distant, half-heard, a Grasshopper Warbler has just sung for a second or so. Again! Just once more, but it remains invisible.

Along the river, forested with thick vegetation, with a hog-weed canopy ten feet tall, Yellowhammers sing half-songs and Whitethroats flit away. Striped snails, like bent humbugs, cling calmly unstung to nettle stems, where Banded Demoiselles, torpid in the cool, allow close approach: glinting steely-blue and blue-black.

At the stile, an impulse urges a turn, and there is the Hobby, skimming wind and advancing. Beating upwind and then drifting down, fly-catching with easy grabs, lazily keeping station above the haymaking.

Swifts approach, seeming to know they are safe, and the falcon ignores them. The Hobby continues hunting for many minutes, then crosses the river, circles, gains height, slips into a different mode.

Suddenly, using the wind, it accelerates to a shocking speed and is gone eastwards.

A minute later a world full of Swifts heads west overhead, knowing now they are prey. In seconds they have cleared this part of the sky and somewhere in those depths the cloud-high Hobby is following.

Around the meander, towards the bridge, a Stonechat bobs beautifully, then swerves over the wheat tops away. Back along the lane a Wren skims the tarmac like a small brown Kingfisher, watched by Linnets on the wire, clutching at the cable, crab-like in the wind. A Hare crouches, rock-still on the verge, with faith in its camouflage. A Kestrel, ragged in moult, takes a mouse to the pylon.

Early next morning and a Goldfinch sounds an unusual triple-note alarm. In the distance a dot grows: it is an Osprey, heading north towards breeding grounds. As it closes to one field distant, it circles on a thermal and gains height. As it ascends a female Sparrowhawk joins it in the upwelling and, a little way off a Peregrine too is in sight.

The Osprey is quickly up and accelerating, gone too soon, away.

Out at the Hobbies' possible nest site they are screeching: they are attacking a Buzzard – looping around it and stooping at it as they drive it off their tree, cries filling the air. The Buzzard takes off and the male falcon dives at it, almost touching the larger bird, forcing it to roll and present its talons to the Hobby. The task done the falcon turns and rises high, disappearing up amongst the clouds, to hunt.

Half an hour later he's once again visible – speck-high and going for a singled-out Swift. He flies at it with lightning speed in a looping dive, forcing his prey towards the ground, closing right up on it, almost within snatching, but no. He spins away and goes for a Swallow just below him, but this attack misses too.

For several minutes he is circling, and making half-hearted attempts at prey, when, suddenly he stoops and makes straight for a copse. He sits and preens, and for a while the world is calm.

Then he's off once again. House Martins alarm and bunch together in the air, trying to rise above his approach, but the female streaks in from the other side of the copse and lands in a nearby tree, calling the whole way in. But he is continuing upward, heading east, fast. He is soon lost to distance. Once more peace settles. But only for a minute.

She comes out from her tree and towers rapidly. Within seconds she is two hundred feet high, still twisting up in a remarkable show of power. Then she sees her mate. He has a Swift in his sights and is diving at it – missing twice narrowly. But she is now with them and joins the hunt. She tries for the Swift and misses. He goes for it again – and this time he has it – a blur of claw as hunter and prey merge.

The Hobbies now perform an aerial pass – he giving up his catch to his mate. She scoops her wings back against her body and drops, the Swift tucked neatly under her tail. She descends to three feet above the meadow, and makes for the nest site. It has taken her seconds, but her mate has already got there.

Before long he is up in the air again – searching out a meal for himself. As he rises a Sparrowhawk goes underneath him, hunting a flock of Starlings. It almost catches one – just missing by a fraction.

SUDDENLY IT WAS SUNNY

A YACHT race of white clouds chases across the blue, scudding to the horizon. A wet world reawakens from a drowning.

Lapwings fight in the quick air – broad wings catching gobs of wind and flicking to turn in the light, calls lost in the howls of the westerlies. Beneath, keeping low, a party of Linnets skims the furrows and re-settles.

A horse puts up a Grey Partridge pair to sail over the hedge, and on its tree, the Little Owl bends away from the trunk to look balefully into the lee.

At the canal's embankment huge spinnakers of wind smack and flutter, sucking air from lungs and stuffing nostrils, slamming the trees in a long roar. And spinning through, five Sand Martins swim loops above the water, white flashes in the sun.

A Kestrel hangs on the crashing wind, spilling air from its quivering tail, against a towering sky now darkening again to the west.

But, down in the sheltering copse, the sun: bright and warm. Anemones in snowy drifts under bursting leaf, nod their pinky-white petals. A score of thin sounds spin silky threads, stitching the wood. Treecreepers, Robins, Long-tailed Tits, like escaping air: hissing. The Chiffchaff loud above, the Wren, silent below: a bobbing chestnut cork along the fallen mossy log.

Low, by the murkily churning river, hunches the Kingfisher – head bobbing – while, above, the Buzzards wheel in the strong air. On cue two Bullfinches come down to the blackthorn where a Goldfinch pair are already nest-building.

At the partly-drain pool a Green Sandpiper takes flight with a "kweel-weet" and speeds away, white rump showing between a blur of arced rapid wings.

A Sparrowhawk, as low as a Fox, slinks along the hedge across the river, lands behind an oak watched by a pair of Crows – put up from their nest by a young Buzzard, now sitting on top of it. Then off she goes again, hugging the contours of the field, over the rise and gone.

A dozen Linnets along the hedge, picking by the lane's edge. And around the corner stands a cow, apart from the herd, new-born calf at her feet. She licks its raised head.

From the canal, the river below rushes into the howling wind, and between the trees a white something flashes briefly on the water. There, again: a Goosander has just surfaced. It dives repeatedly, approaching all the time, working his way upstream. His scarlet hooked-tipped bill and glossy head showing both bronzy-brown and green as it moves, the salmony sides of this drake show pale and bright as he dives again, fish-like beneath the dark, oily flow of the river, as he fishes the shallows, just showing beneath the surface.

Then a silver fish rises, desperately wriggling along the river's surface, half-in, half-out of the water, running downstream, away from danger. But a red bill jabs out from below, grasps the fish and the Goosander rises and swallows his catch.

As this happens a female Goosander surfaces, then another, and a second drake: two pairs are hunting together now. They fish for a while then haul out on a silty bank downstream – pushing a Mallard from his resting place. One of the drakes begins to preen – a huge red, webbed foot scratching his neck.

Sheltering from winds in the spring wood, Chiffchaffs sing. A Mistle Thrush churring angrily, chases Blackbirds away from a fruiting ivy. Spears of bluebell leaves push palely grey-green amongst closed anemones.

Footprints in muddy pool edges crisscross and circle: Heron and Moorhen, and a brief line of Badger. A Treecreeper, almost close enough to touch, backs off to the back of an alder, peeking from the rear.

Back across darkening meadows, the sky blackening, as hail slams in a stinging squall.

The large stubble field, grown weedy lately, dressed in strawy manure, is alive this morning. Two hundred Starlings, alternately pecking and flying off in a shoal to another patch; and more coming in – porpoising over the hedges against the wind, under a restless sky.

Amongst them, and moving with them, thirty or so Fieldfares, twenty Linnets and a few Skylarks. A single Yellowhammer, calling, flies downwind.

Beyond, showing out in their tree, the Little Owls watch, impassively. But a closer movement, just beyond the hedge, has the eye. A Wheatear. Two, three. Two females and a male are hunting in the stubble – sometimes perching on top of the short, sharp straw.

Flashes of white rumps show them, otherwise the females are stubble field-coloured, and disappear each time they stand.

In the paddyfield-green winter wheat hunches a Hare, his haunches as patterned as a Woodcock's back. Above, on the wire, a Kestrel, horizontal in the howl, spies on the field below.

A bank of daunting grey clouds expands in the west, like a cresting wave in slow motion, fronted by a rainbow, the promise of a downpour to come. For now, the sun shines.

The Wheatears are all gone from the field, moved on to breeding grounds further north, and replacing them, seven spangled Golden Plover, rest in the wheat. The Little Owl, like a branch stub, on his usual perch.

To the south a large Sparrowhawk circles slowly east, drifting with the breeze, puts up Wood Pigeons to swirl.

By the farm three Swallows at once – circling and calling, like they've never been gone. And at the canal a Blackcap sings his spring warble to the rainbow. Dark skies close in: dawn reversing, bringing drizzle and six Sand Martins merely passing.

The Kestrel pair, on the wire, their backs to the disappearing sun, and a Stock Dove flies a display on raised wings back to its Barn Owl box nest on the tree.

Down by the sheltered river a Willow Tit calls. A Kingfisher, just visible on a riverside branch, sits. The rainbow is finally extinguished. A cold draught falls with the soft rain.

There are two Willow Tits in the hedge trees and bramble bank. They make their way slowly. Small sounds: "tsee" and "tsisisi" reach out from them, their passage known from moving weed stems, they only show occasionally – sometimes one will hover briefly before clinging to a bramble leaf-cluster. Chiffchaffs, now more numerous, compete around them and Long-tailed Tits come and go, but the Willow Tits still progress infinitesimally along the bank.

Spring turns to summer with the final arrivals: Swifts are one of the last.

Grey on grey, pearl on slate, smoke on charcoal: clouds torn on the wind, blowing ragged over the ridge. A watercolour sun slips under frothy waves, dowsing itself in foam: extinguished.

And, above the defiance of the just-leaved trees, shifting in the tide of the wind, a single Swift slices straight and true, lately in from Africa, picking food from the ebbing day. Behind and beneath, by the kelp of the beeches, the Martins twist and jink: white rumps like fish eyes in the shadow.

The Swift the Shark, the Barracuda, circling darkly beneath the rolling breakers, lifting on the rising rush. The Martins a shoal of smaller fry, bunching and rolling with the current, above the reef of the trees.

On the horizon a cold sun sets and the dark greys darken: the Swift swims on into the night.

In the low and grey skies and a cold, cold morning, in from the east like a dream and at pace they come, the female in front, male some fifty yards behind. A streak, a blur of blue-grey wings. She goes behind the trees, he to the front of them. Around the treetops she arcs, swerves to an oak and lands; he sweeps a circle and back to another oak and lands, mis-judging his speed, and, as he lands, tips forward, his tail braking in air over his back, then settles. He sits: orange vent and yellow feet brighter, head swivelling – and showing pale nape patches – black moustachials against white cheeks. For a restless minute he sits, waiting for his mate to move. She does.

Off she goes, accelerating a loop out over the fields and back over the trees, higher now, looking for prey. He follows as she scythes back over the copse again, and they hunt in tandem for a minute and are gone.

For over an hour, as Swifts come past and Buzzards and a Sparrow-hawk entertain, the falcons remain invisible.

Early morning and the low sky remains leaden, like a hangover, but the day begins to brighten with the rising sun, and fills with promise.

Smell the grass. Wet verges lush with warm spring – pink campions and white stitchworts jostling with dandelions and daisies. New molehills thrusting through turf are still moist in their crumb.

Saturated air stalled and warm: no lift for Buzzards, which have to flap for purchase. A Sparrowhawk gets out of the trees, skims the wheat and beats along the hedge base, hiding at speed; chances a loop and wheels into a shrubby copse, head down, hunting. Gone: brown into green.

25

In the fields a Yellow Wagtail is collecting horse hair from the paddock, her mate dozing on the fence rail. As she flies to build at her chosen nest site, he follows. Yellowhammers stay put, providing light.

Nearby, a female Wheatear stands on a clod, stock still. Beyond, a male flycatches and pounces on prey. Two new Lapwing chicks stride around in down: white napes fluffy, legs strong. Their parents watch and chase off any intruders daring to come too close.

A sitting Skylark sings from the field where a Linnet collects for a nest, and in the far corner another pair of Wheatears shine out from earth. Stock Doves strut, blue-grey in the brightening day. Whitethroats scratch a tune from the thorny hedges and bottle-blue Swallows twist by.

Another field: and another pair of Yellow Wagtails, disappearing into deep furrows and emerging again on ridges, restless.

In this calm a Pheasant's call, like a car crash, splits the air.

But something else is in the field, far off. Beyond a flattened Hare, ears folded back along his back, another movement directs the eye. A Whinchat, a stunning male, whose beauty outshines all the rest, perches mid-field and hunts as the Wheatears do. The day cracks a grin.

Over and behind, two Kestrels chase each other in a ritual of pursuit: flickering wings flash and shadow. Lime-rumped Greenfinches bounce away along the lane; the sun pushes a parting hand between the clouds.

MORNING HAD KEPT THAT PROMISE

DAWN. Liquid flutes from Blackbirds roll out across the early light, oscillating in the chill grey. Song Thrushes pulse their answers, still in hiding from shadowed shrubs. A Wren zips the softer sounds, stitching songs in a rapid crescendo. Rooks in black cry hoarsely from the distance, low cloud carrying their calls across a full moon sky.

The thin icicles of Robin song melting to honey in the pooling day, coloured by the cadence of the Coal Tit's two-note ditty. Daylight drops slowly, deftly, on Spring's frosts. A Chiffchaff has the final line: a simple coda to the chorus.

And the first bird above, scraping under the grey lid of morning: a Peregrine, low along the field edge, then rising to the steeple, where it perches in full view.

A scan of the land and, within seconds, he is away to accelerate at unseen prey – fast disappearing behind a nearby copse. But soon he is back on the church – on the leeward side and standing, gargoyle-like against the sky.

His brownish back and streaked breast mark him as a young bird, bobbing his dark-hooded head as he scans for prey. The local female Kestrel flies his way, below his perch, but she spots him and swerves away, her calls ringing back along the wind. A Heron flaps by.

Then the tiercel is off again – quicker this time and skimming the field towards the copse as before – then suddenly overhead going east now, and this time gone for good.

The sky, empty for a while, now becomes the stage for a displaying Sparrowhawk: a female flapping loosely and undulating in exaggerated bounds – in imitation of a butterfly, she makes for her nest site, a few short-winged flaps to rise in an arc, then on closed wings looping to repeat. She continues to the wood in this fashion and dives in – a needle into wool.

THE DAY HAD BEGUN

HUGE purple-flanked ragged-topped clouds: gigantic engines of wind and rain, scudding across the huge sky, showering icy slices of rain walls and aiming beams of sunlight to a first bright, then darkened, earth.

And amongst this drama, this potent and dynamic backdrop, come the Swifts. Swifts in dozens, Swifts in scores, Swifts now in hundreds from the shuddering heavens, scything and swerving against a steady earth, passing close enough now that their stiff-winged swerving audible. The closing weather forces them onward, surfers before the wave.

A deluge of stinging rain spikes blasts and rakes – white spears of hail fall in long, cold lines, and a squally wind buffets the ground. But it is brief, and before long the following sun breaks and the parted waves of the rough sky splits to brighter light.

Now, in the warmest, sunniest mid-most part of the afternoon, when even the thinnest, feather-like clouds have gone eastward, suddenly now Willow Warblers are singing: bubbling a descant from bursting bushes.

And the Coal Tits are building – carrying gobs of feathers to some hidden hole low in a tree trunk – alarming all the while at the chattering Magpies as they go.

Always, always, along the bright horizon, Buzzards are drifting: dark lines slowly drawn against the canvas. But, from due-south, a coalescing bunch of specks home in: resolving to hirundines, swerve in sunshine and grow: become brown-backed Sand Martins as they speed northward, and are gone.

A single Swallow's loops and curves are only distractions from its steady polar progress as she too passes. A beetle takes to the air. Buzzards mewl. Then, another Sand Martin, leisurely-paced, skims the wood and is overhead: brown-smudged breast and bright belly slipping silently by.

Across the field, from the copse by the steeple, rings a Nuthatch, clear as a bell on Sundays, unseen but peeling sound. Nearby, the quieter, subtle

29

sibilance of a Goldcrest's whisper washes across the brambles and soaks away.

Two Jays flop in with a "weir squaw, weir squaw" and extinguish their colours amongst new leaf, and a Kestrel wobbles on a sapling's pinnacle, soft brick in the afternoon light. And here a Great spotted Woodpecker props herself on her stiff tail against the tree and alarms, her crimson vent burning in the sun.

And, lastly a Bullfinch pair bounce over with soft whistles, as the Nuthatch continues to peel by the Jackdaw-thick church.

At the canal a dozen Tufted Duck wing their way eastwards – over a Great-crested Grebe – following the waterway to breeding grounds for the new season. Two Greenfinches fly their butterfly display-flights, singing intermittently on the round, above the blackthorn blossoms shining Turner-esque by the stream.

A Yaffle's call undulates in the spring air, ringing along the morning. Lapwings flap figures of eight above the puddly meadow, where frosts still sit at night, where Hares now hunch, low and soil-brown.

Linnets skip hedges topped with fighting Blackbirds, darker than shadows, jousting in streaming sunshine.

By the river a Treecreeper comes ever closer, calling an incessant susurrus as it shuffles, propped on its deeply cleft tail. The Yaffle calls again. A Great spotted Woodpecker, alarming, turns its head at some threat, at the top of an oak, but is soon displaced by four Jays, crests raised, fighting for territory. Their squawking raucous above the striding stone wall, where primroses still show pale and lovely in the shade.

At the end of the alders, at last, the Lesser spotted Woodpecker drums and calls, showing just for a second, red cap glowing like a blown ember, and flies back to stately beeches, already in bud and leaf. The Moorhen submerges herself in the shadow of her nest to hide: black into black.

Bullfinches on fluffy lemon-yellow willow flowers catch the throat with their beauty. A Chiffchaff sits restless, beside a Wren, and sings, and in the briefest interval between "chiff" and "chaff" a Yellowhammer calls from beyond the mill race.

And, by the bend, sits a Kingfisher, dagger head bobbing, blood orange and blue, watching. Then he flies to his mate, low in the willow, and they rest for a while, side by side, brilliant in shadow.

Spring progresses infinitesimally with the Buzzard, soaring high above, turning a great circle, slowly revolving with the earth.

Down past the Badgers' setts and out along the lanes, Swallows swoop over grassy meadows, Stock Doves poke into a hole into the oak, and a Crow's tail sticks out from a nest above them.

The Crow has begun to nest now: one of these will be used by the Hobby pair – they will wait patiently for the owners to vacate their home when the young finally fledge. Within their territory the Hobbies will watch for a suitable site – often reusing Crows' nests – a good fit for their own family – and usually high up for vantage and safety. The Crows begin in March, the Hobby won't lay until June. For now, the Crow sits on her eggs, still to hatch.

Out in the wheat, sun ahead and strengthening in a pale and clearing sky, young Rabbits hide under hedges, wary of Buzzards' attentions.

Then, distantly, a Yellow Wagtail's song reaches over. There: singing on dew-soaked grass, bright as a buttercup, olive-yellow above, tail half-spread – showing its white outer tail feathers. His calls are answered, and the female, along a tractor track, sits, looking over her shoulder. A Skylark, sitting in the next furrow, lifts to sing in the blue.

Down past the farm: a marshy meadow, pitted deeply by hooves, bright with celandines, anemones, marsh marigolds and cuckoo flowers.

Bumblebees, heavy now with spring, float by. A warm waft brings a wobble of Willow Warbler's song, batter-thick on the air. Across the stream, under the wood, bluebells blue the green. Their hyacinth scent like a weightless wave drifts down the almost-wind.

Blackthorns in frothy bloom hold promises of Brimstone.

A twig over the water: Kingfisher-splashed but bare. Buds swelling to breaking point, yet to explode in green. Spring holds summer in check. Cress and mint-choked ditches; Hares in pairs, black and white tails tucked in, black and white ears like masts with sails furled, pause to wash faces with dew-soaked paws.

A tiny feather-lined, lichen-covered cup sits in a safe hollow of a thorn-caged hedge, bristly briars bending round the thorn – the Chaffinch pair wary on their perch above. Beyond, Lapwings chase Crows in an endless and noisy battle.

A Buzzard beginning a display puts pigeons to ashes; he finishes with a looping flourish in an oak.

Back at the busting bramble patch, freshly green in new leaf, waiting to send sprays anew, the Long-tailed Tits are still lining nests started in late February. Feathers are brought in by both birds, the female placing proffered filaments after a furtive approach to the exquisite lichen and cobweb-covered bauble suspended in thorns, still visible, for now, through the buds.

This small sea of bramble undulates and grows in the reproductive season – a belly swelling, protectively pregnant with nests, awaiting summer's birth days. Deep within the once snow-compressed tangle of arcs of thorn, birds and mammals hide away to breed.

Early morning sees young, snub-nosed, short-eared Rabbits venture out to feed on spring greens, nervously hopping back to their bramble patch at the smallest whiff of danger. A Buzzard calls. A Jay responds.

Bullfinches arrive at the brambles and brighten the hedge with pinks and whites; then another pair are suddenly with them – intruders in their territory. Silently, gently, the intruders are approached. They retreat, feeding in the willows as they move off. Two minutes later they are gone – not a feather ruffled in this gentlest of disputes.

Throughout this a Chiffchaff sings and a female Blackcap arrives to listen to two rival males singing nearby. She will choose one for her mate. Blue Tits glide in and display, floating down on stiff wings, just like the Stock Doves above.

As the day brightens imperceptively slowly, a thin bright light shines on the western horizon.

Songsters fill the bee-flown day.

The next day starts blue and bright after a cold night and a scrape of frost.

The Little Owls are out sunning themselves in their oak, fluffed up and squat. Overhead a Golden Plover flock shines as they perform aerial manoeuvres – flashing gold and white as they swirl.

Along the canal two female Sparrowhawks are fighting over territory – one displaying by slow wing-flapping and stooping at the intruder – a younger bird. Several Swallows keep their distance as the raptors pass.

Two fluffed-up House Martins sail past like sooty-capped snowballs as a Buzzard comes in to land on top of his mate on the pylon.

The year's first cuckoo flowers stand brightly amongst the juncus as a Bullfinch pipes from frothing blackthorns.

Along the river a female Great spotted Woodpecker sits horizontally on a limb, her tail raised, and the male joins her in a brief mating, and departs. From a willow shrub a Kingfisher takes off and speeds across the meadow, aquamarine on emerald, cutting across the meander back to the water.

A Sand Martin fizz-buzzes past as a second Kingfisher flies off to re-land just out of sight. Noisy Nuthatches call from several trees and Treecreepers whisper.

Two Buzzards circling like synchronised swimmers, become eight as they ascend the thermals.

In a tiny bay, where new leaf touches the water, a Moorhens' nest is anchored. Liquid warbles from Willow Warblers hang in the air.

The dagger-board of a sickle moon strikes down from the keel of heaven, moving through the clouds as if they themselves are still, as it ploughs the sky, a surf of white breakers rolling over the blue.

Below, purposeful Swifts trawl the air and accelerate along a steep and sloping line until impossibly fast. He screams his song and meets his mate in mid-air – fitting together – four wings whirring: a single dragonfly vibrating. They separate and arc around the ridge.

Two Tawny Owls hoot across the slope from deep dark cover, bass notes briefly bomb the valley and a shell-shocked silence follows. Time restarts and the faded moon slips beyond the horizon.

Cumuli, at first towering, pale-edged, benign, begin to tower and crumple, crease and fold, darken with menace. Anode and cathode: earth and sky, an arc apart, begin to arc.

Metallic crashes, distant at first, draw ever closer. Zinc and lead and molten iron clash and crash, buckle and bend, releasing flashes, rumbles and drum.

And beneath the basso profundo, the treble of bird song. A Chiffchaff's metronomic countdown ticks the time between flash and thunder. A Song Thrush warns in repeats. Robins' thin scratches pierce the darkening day. Somewhere distant-ward a Pheasant yelps a hoarse alarm. Birds begin to take cover.

The smell of wetted earth drifts in from the approaching storm: rain imminent. Lightning cracks a sheet across the sooty sky, and birdsong pauses in the beats between. Darkened wheat stands: a million lightning rods urging discharge from an overburdened sky.

Rooks make for nests, as rain, fat blobs squashed on a parched land, begins to break, as Blackbirds hail the downpour in sweet liquid bubbling to the darkening dusk.

The next day, up the lanes, the gutters are full of stripped leaves from wind-torn trees – bunches of oak and ash and snapped snag branches. And today the wind is stronger than ever.

To the east from where the gale is coming, an ominous dark wall of cloud moves inexorably closer – yet, overhead, the sky is blue. Fragments of ripped cloud skim quickly away on the wind and vapour trails lie like banana strings on a duck egg-blue plate.

Bird sound is muted and muffled – in roars' respites a Blackcap warbles. Swallow are keeping low and skimming the wheat stalks, where whirlpools form and rush across the field. The wood top is a maelstrom of surf on rocks.

Rain closes in and summer is lost in a dark swirling sea of rain and wind. The world retreats, animals seek shelter and nesters sit, protecting young still too vulnerable to face such fierce elements. For the rest of another stormy May day, life seems suspended and hunters must wait.

A new day and a different world wakes to a calmer landscape. The storms have gone and life begins again after its enforced pause.

And there is a Hobby: about tree height and close. At normal speed: that is fairly swiftly, and rising gradually, and circling, gaining height in a deliberate manner. Above and ahead are Swifts – they try to outrace their predator for the heavens, keeping distance, and, if possible, height.

Turning until it is almost over the steeple and continuing to rise until just a speck in the blue, for a moment it turns back, as if returning. But then, something extraordinary: turning away, the falcon flies into a cloud and disappears. Gone. It has deliberately gone into hiding, high up, using the cloud as a cloak.

Back on earth, as if this phenomenon had never happened, the world carries on as normal.

The Little Owl is on his oak branch, staring yellow-eyed at the world, and the now empty sky. The Swifts too are invisible, so high up they are simply no longer there. The Owl's mate is on the cottage roof, actively hunting from this vantage into the corn field below, then returning to the gutter – perhaps they now have young of their own, and food demands have increased exponentially. As she hunts a varied mob of mobbing birds follow and alarm: Tree Sparrows, Yellowhammers and a single Whitethroat.

Then, events take an unexpected turn.

A chimney-perched Owl sees a movement to the right, and all eyes swivel that way. At some incredible speed, a Hobby, at three feet above the ground, whipping its wings in short, shallow beats, is going for some prey beyond the hedge. It is head-on, closing so fast as to stop time itself, one primary feather missing on the right wing, dark-capped head and now the yellow eyes visible, blotchy breast a blur in the speed of it, red vent burning above the corn as it vaults the hedge like rapids over the swell of a boulder, and disappears beyond, showing those long slate wings as it goes.

With its departure it's as if time slows, the normal world so pedestrian, as if in treacle, the heartbeat only comes once a minute.

Only then are the Swifts noticed – they have been following behind, tracking their nemesis, to keep track of their greatest foe. They circle and dive, as if in the knowledge that they are not the chosen prey, today.

As May progresses the Hobbies become ever more elusive, an instinct in them keeps them at bay. And, courting done, territories re-established, there is little to do until their season begins – when their nest will be chosen, mating takes place, eggs are laid and activity brings them to light again.

For now, endless searches have little to show. The falcons spend much of their time perching on some lookout, tucked beside a copse, deliberately unobtrusive; or, feeding high up beyond earthbound eyes, catching insects. Occasionally their choice of prey turns to birds, and a hunt brings them lower, and these irregular forays make them spectacularly visible – but all too infrequently. For hours every day they are simply invisible. Then, high summer will compensate many-fold.

Until then, brief glimpses have to suffice, and other sights and sounds of the season fill the void.

High up in the air a Kestrel is nailed against the sky, quivering into the wind, its tail splayed on a slope of air, peering patiently for prey. He waits for the vole to emerge and move along its run, seeing in ultraviolet the urine-marked trails of his potential victim. Seeing a movement, the Kestrel slides down his aerial pole, closing the gap on the strike, stopping to hang again, head motionless though his body moves in the breeze.

Lilacs press the nose, rounding the air with a smothering pillow of scent, and the hawthorn is covered in a blanket of blooms like snow newly fallen.

In the breeze a Buzzard lifts from the wood like a kite on the coast, straining against its tether, reaches the top of its arc, then turns and simply sails the long wind, over wheat which ripples a dark and shining wave towards the beech.

In sombre shadows a Blackbird's song reaches out into sunshine, where the jigsaw piece of a Comma probes the mayflowers for sweetness, proboscis busily bending in the search.

Swifts, too high to see, scream faintly over the frog-burp of a Moorhen's call, tripping from the pond, and a Blackcap blasts a couple of couplets sweetly from the briar.

Now the Long-tailed Tits are feeding their young in the bramble patch, where seven other species have also nested. They hover above the thorns as they wait to enter the feathery dome, beaks crammed with insects. Then a quick dive into the now-hidden nest and they emerge to fly away to collect again, in an endless provision for the whole day.

The Song Thrushes have almost fledged their first brood; but the Goldfinches are still finishing their nests with mosses and feathers. Whitethroats and Blackcaps are busy here too, occasionally singing between feeding the young.

A Dunnock ménage-a-trois comes and goes, a Chiffchaff flicks in now and again to a nest low against the ground, and, behind, in a young conifer a Goldcrest continues his song that hasn't stopped now for months.

Out in the fields, ploughing is in progress: potatoes are being planted. The Lapwings and Oystercatchers, wary of the Lesser Black-backed Gulls that join in the newly-turned earth's bonanza, have young to protect. Skylarks pick off insects too, taking them to their own hidden nests in the wheat fields beyond.

Tree Sparrows are taking feathers to their nests in a cottage's eaves; Linnets search for seeds. The Little Owl, on his usual perch, stretches a wing, then crouches as a Kestrel flies in to stride for worms on upturned soil. He fills his gape with these moist offerings and flies to the barn – his mate is on the telegraph pole with a limp vole, and from within the barn the clear calls of their young echo around the roof spaces.

The days lengthen, the world warms, evenings no longer bring a chill. Birdsong continues into the dusk. Songsters: Robin, Blackbird and Song Thrush, three or four of each, compete unseen in the failing light. For the Song Thrushes this is their seventeenth hour of almost uninterrupted song.

The Blackbirds fade away as the colour drains from the sky, a sharp silver moon low in the west, screams out light from a quiet heaven.

As a smoky wisp of gnats blows faintly in the lee of a horse chestnut, the first moths begin to fly. The "caw" of Rooks reaches from their roost in the wood, far off. Jackdaws join in. A single quack of a Mallard sounds out from the canal. The first star appears in the east as the Blackbirds 'chack-chack' to night shelters. A bat, possibly a Pipistrelle, flickers by.

The sun, quickly turning yellow from orange, rises in the north-east. Mist gradually thins and rises from the wheat into damp, motionless air. Already the bramble patch trembles with life. Blackcaps sing in competition, Long-tailed Tits are busy feeding young, Gold and Greenfinches are finishing nests, twittering and bickering.

Overhead, almost missed in this activity, a Peregrine powers to the south.

Down the lanes, a Leveret rounds a bend, running this way, then turns in a tangle of long legs and lollops away. Yellow Wagtails and Yellow-hammers show off their yellow tones, flanks to the sun. Skylarks rise from furrows, watching an airborne Kestrel above.

Young Oystercatchers and Lapwings on sturdy legs, strut, as parents keep watch from the field edges, taking noisily to the sky when danger threatens, their young crouching simultaneously, relying on camouflage and stillness.

Leaving behind the Blackcap and Willow Warbler songs battling in the rowan, between water and wood where Chaffinches spout songs from steel-blue bills, brightly, cockily handsome, the path leads out to lush meadows, ranunculus-studded – ten thousand suns nodding to the one above – where umbels froth and drooling cattle graze between stately sycamores.

A Treecreeper dashes from a trunk to snatch a passing fly, and resumes its stealth up the tree, carrying prey for young elsewhere. Stone walls, crevices crammed with foxgloves and ferns, hide a hunting Wren, and a Robin's nest.

Up then to a sculpted gateless gatepost: a gap-toothed grin, reveals what lies beyond: hay meadows high, thistles thrusting through clover and grass and sedge, where butterflies swim, jerk and dive to the surf of blooms.

Bracken rushes the walls – filling the fields to brim the tops – where Meadow Pipits sit. And, from the drowning wood, the suffocating sound of Blackbird swells out into the warm, meeting the sweetness of Skylarks' tongues falling from the hazy bright where Black-headed Gulls swoop on St. Mark's flies swarming in the thermals.

Up again where Linnets sing and Swallows swoosh. A Kestrel carries a dangling mouse towards the abandoned, half-tumbled farm.

But it's the Cuckoo's call that pulls – from wood to meadow, to hill, along the ale-brown beck trickling between the cleavage of the land, dropping in swirls and cataracts beneath oak and rowan, and still-bare ash.

Untickled trout in dappled pebbly pools, sway to the flow of moor-cool water. Above, young heather blushes on the breast of the hill – coloured like Burgundy in the bottle – and bilberry, fresh and green and rushing to ripen: too-young fruit just showing. Green Hairstreak Butterflies mate and lay, keeping low, even in the sun.

Now the bubble of Curlews' songs ripples down the summer's noon and, as if in plaintive answer, a Golden Plover calls from the distant tops.

Orca-coloured, dolphin-blunt hunters of aerial plankton; fin-winged, notch-tailed, plump and piebald: the House Martins have found a shoal of flies below the continental shelf of the hill side opposite.

Unlike the shark-like Swifts' dash, their slow swim takes them level by the wood – whose deep dark disappears them – except for their rumps, spotlight white – which dot the trees now.

Then, out again, against the sky, and suddenly blue and brown, sailing at leisure over waves of meadows. Float and line along the valley. A sudden sally, to net or hook; this small school is silent, slides away – as soft rain sullies silver skies grey.

As if stooping under a low ceiling, the valley's head is lost to the mist. The grey shroud stretches above, hiding the tops. Cold funnels up the vale – condensing on its rising – piling on the clouds.

Life has cooled. The cow-browsed oaks spread above meadows, thick with buttercups, drooping with recent rain. Swallow sweep between, dark in shadow.

A Chaffinch and a Willow Warbler half-sing in the gloom. A single Swift squeezes between the dropped sky and the rising slopes. Rooks, no darker than the inky insides of the woods, feed quietly among the trees.

A half-heard song of a maybe Whitethroat trips from the blossom-loaded hawthorn hedge, hanging wet tresses: a wedding dress in the rain.

Now a sudden Little Owl stands by the roadside, arms-reach close. Its head pivots. Speckles and bars on loose-shaken feathers are drying after the shower. It drops to a tumble of stones by the wall and runs on wet turf, stooping to snuffle at some small prey.

The soaking sky sheds yet more rain: wet to already wet. Only a distant Mistle Thrush continues to sing now. The curtain falls.

Out at dawn, and a croak amongst the Crows' caws: a Raven is circling the steeple – then it lands on its base. The resident Jackdaws set up a din of alarms. For some time, it sits, cronking into the morning, until, from way off east, another Raven – this one crop-full – approaches. It too, lands on the steeple. This second bird is the adult – and proceeds to feed the first – a juvenile. For a time, they sit side by side, then fly to the north-west.

As the day progresses the wind increases. Poplars are bent into bows by the blowing. They shake loose an incessant swell of sound that assaults the silence. A Holly Blue – a piece of powdery sky – jigs and skips around the olive leaves of the honeysuckle as a single dune of cloud scuds and slips away.

Afternoon becomes evening and the tilted moon rises like a jellyfish through water. An alarm sounds as a Sparrowhawk, already clutching prey, makes for her nest, and, in the after-calm an unseen Raven croaks a "cronk" somewhere downwind.

Two Cormorants head east, neck and neck.

Morning sun bounces off Yellow Wagtails, bright in the paddocks, where, first two, then three, become six, leverets – running and boxing amongst dewy grass – crystal droplets flying from paws as they chase – half-grown and springy with energy – dodging hooves of horses whose steamy breath hangs ghostly in the air.

In other fields parent Hares sit in furrows, dozing in low-slanted sun. Flies, like dust, kick up into the warming light.

Across the barley – now waist-high and besom-topped, nodding heavily and shining silver-green in the young day – to the sliding green river, where a drake Shoveler gets up and circles silently.

An Oystercatcher display-flies past – wings deliberately deeply swept and slow as it calls. Soon there are three – the mate and an intruder, and "kleeps" fill the clear sky. Yellowhammer and Skylarks sing: one briefly, one unending.

Along Linnety lanes to a field with a Grey Partridge pair – slowly picking amongst weeds at the hedge base. Whitethroats scratch a tune, in and out of cover.

By the canal a Lesser Whitethroat is in full song – flying between shrubs across his territory – once showing well in may blossoms. House Martins skim ranunculus-heavy meadows, Badger tracks running through. Swifts boomerang arcs above.

Once, just once, a Willow Tit calls, deep in shadowy shrubs and does not show, as usual.

Below, where the river crosses under the canal, a one-second neon blue flash; a call of a Kingfisher. And gone. Another bright rump – this one yellow and attached to a Green Woodpecker – a long flight bounding and then binding to an ash.

Young Rooks, now out of nests, squabble noisily for food from parents – a ruck of Rooks in a black ball by the river bank.

Suddenly a Broad-bodied Chaser takes off from the riverside brambles – young and golden – takes a few short flights and re-settles. The year's first dragonfly.

The afternoon in marshy meadows – thick with hawthorns in mounds of snowy blossom, drifts of campion. A stream is banked by buttercups.

By a pool a Large Red Damselfly shares a dock leaf with a Common Blue Damselfly – delicately dancing and landing. Bullfinches call from bushes as a Buzzard rises, grass trailing from talons holding just-caught prey.

Scrub sounds: a medley of warbles: Garden Warblers and a Lesser Whitethroat on the same patch, but neither shows. Instead butterflies delight the eye – Red Admiral, Holly Blue and Orange Tips.

A MOOD-ENHANCING, SOUL-WARMING, SMILE-INDUCING, DELICIOUS DAY

A BREEZELESS, sun-filled morning: air sparkling. Warmth and peace. Leverets, nearly full-grown, bask amongst ribbons of newly-sprouted corn shoots, bright on russet soil. Skylarks bring insects to hidden nests past Hares' ears poking from furrows. An Oystercatcher watches as a Buzzard circles over – lazily, effortlessly, gaining height – head cocked to keep an eye on the predator, its blood-red bill angled to earth.

Lapwings and gulls give chase, but the Buzzard is unmoved; simply drifting slowly away. A pair of Red-legged Partridges pecks in the corner of the paddock, where a young Pied Wagtail wags and walks by a puddle.

Down by the lazy river – barely an eddy showing – Whitethroats and Yellowhammers sing from fat nettlebeds, where all other song has ceased. Heavy barley heads hang in the heat, wafted by white butterflies. Heat builds with the climbing of the sun. Torpidity drops dreamily on the day.

The Little Owl oak, now fully clothed in young leaf, hides its hosts. A languid Heron laps droopily by.

A Yellow Wagtail, beak full, breaks from the wheat with a sweet call and slides down sun shafts to its nest. For a long, measureless moment the world lies back and luxuriates.

The spell is broken: a squabbling, squawking ragged gaggle of young Starlings flies in and begins to peck noisily in the corn field.

Up above, the blue, Hobby-less skies stretch across this painting, the canvass waiting on their presence.

But, the next day, with the weather's change, brings another picture entirely.

Swifts in the maelstroms and squalls, in sun and in showers, arcing and twisting: Swifts in their elements. Swifts in shoals – rising over the hedge like flying fishes, silver in the sunlight, silent and skimming sunlit wind-ridges over dandelion and daisy burning in the meadow; over horses – head down, teeth to the turf.

Swifts, brown then black; half silver, half dark, tilting and turning, rounding and returning, gleaning the ragged air.

Suddenly the wind drops; silence for one second, then: the small sounds of House Martins' gritty whispers, distant Yellowhammers' calls, a Whitethroat's throaty alarm, all pierced through by a bright Yellow Wagtail's note.

Then, as if taking advantage of the squall-stop, Swifts scream their songs, rise in the brightness, and are gone.

By a copse, forty House Martins in the lee, gleaning flies alongside swifter, stiffer, Swifts, while a Skylark bubbles a sweet song high in the cirrus-smear.

Swallows are picking short straws from the fields to build in the barn, and Chaffinches in wild cherry blossoms are cryptic and hidden.

A male Kestrel sits close by on a telegraph pole – then slides away – his colours: cinnamon, grey, black, highlighted in the slaty day. A Bullfinch dives into a hedge, flashing his white rump, over a pink belly.

An Orange-tip Butterfly defies the grey and skips to the verges where the first cow parsley dares to bud, as a Blackbird 'pinks' a flat-piano protest as the Little Owl flushes, broad-winged, to a further tree.

The sky now is barely able to hold itself aloft, as clouds thicken; it drags and drapes from east to west. Out against the distant hills, folds of sodden clouds crease and darken.

Cold and grey now, and blowing half a gale, the Little Owl is porcupine fish-like on its perch.

Swifts in the wind skim the trees and hurl themselves at flies, Swallows slide an inch above the grass.

Suddenly, a falcon, an apparition, is over the copse and getting close: it perches not two hundred yards away. A Peregrine: a juvenile male.

After a minute he's off downwind, rising in turns against the dark sky – then transforms into a hunter.

He streaks westward, gathering speed, finally vanishing in his distance.

His speed was impressive, but he's about to comprehensibly outdone.

Further paths onward and the Swifts have found food in the shelter of a copse: flies boil off downwind from the blowing leaves. The Swifts arc around the trees in manic, rapid circles, their movement a blur of brown. Then a Hobby is above them, sharp and shapely wings pinched and angled, closing in against the wind, changing height in a rolling traverse as it approaches.

With a sudden twist it dives at the base of a tree, loops around a big oak, so quickly it seems to be two, then swerves to follow the hedge-line and hugs the earth, inches from the ground. He flick-flacks, back this way, belly showing, along the hedge's edge, the wind now assisting his acceleration to tremendous speed; he swerves and passes – first left, then right – successive trees, without loss of velocity, before looping a third as if attached by a cord, and then just vanishes – too low and unpredictable.

The world closes its mouth.

Forged on the gale's anvil from quicksilver solidifying to steel; honed by lightning for meteoric speeds; fire-red exhaust powers his flight. He's a razor in the wind, a silent sabre unsheathed.

Somewhere above, an ever-hidden sun begins to set.

Blue sky and black clouds. Plenty of hirundines and Swifts – and even a late Wheatear atop a telegraph pole.

Suddenly the Hobbies are both here – rising in the unseasonably cold wind. And the wind is bringing them closer. A flock of House Martins and Swifts rise above them, fish before the shark, as they climb several hundred feet – circling quickly overhead.

Their relative size, now they are together, is easy to see. He, the smaller, leads the way. Then, from vast heights, he begins a rapid zigzag descent, flick-flacking a twisting dive on half-closed wings. She follows in less dramatic fashion, though keeping pace. There is a feeling of show, of prowess from the male, until they reach the treetops, where, not slowing down, they land at the back of the copse.

Later, one is visible in the crown of an oak: the female, looking this way. There she remains for many minutes, until flying again – joined in seconds by her mate. They disappear again, too soon.

This pair has survived their separate journeys to Africa, their winter hunting the woods of Angola, and the return across the equatorial rain forests and the vast Sahara, finding each other again in this corner of England to begin a new breeding season. Once again, this small green patch will be enhanced by these beautiful little falcons, and spectacular hunts will become more frequent as the summer matures.

Two hours pass, three: clouds roll on, the day tries to warm, but breezes wash away the sun's strength and cool is the order of the afternoon.

Crossing fields and wandering lanes and paths around the territory and, then from the eye's corner two familiar forms are approaching from the north, low. One lands out of sight, the other in plain view on a near sycamore. Then she flies to the tree adjacent, not ten yards away, twenty feet up, only a hedge between. She sits and preens, then changes perches to come even closer still: so close now the black claws are clearly visible on her yellow feet; the yellow cere and nostrils. Not only every feather – lovely brick-red undertail coverts and barred undertail – but the filaments of the feathers themselves.

She bobs her head, seeing some prey and judging distance, glassy eyes framed in yellow. These eyes far, far more acute than a human's, spot a speck and weigh its potential: its potential as her meal.

One of them makes a soft keening call: the call to hunt. That speck had been assessed as worthy of a hunt. They are off.

It is he who makes the first move, she follows. First, they fly to a more distant tree and perch again, but not for long. Flying a circle around the field – one calling loudly now – but before long the hunt is suspended and they land once again.

A minute. Two. Then they are both up and rising fast, running a parallel towards the western sky. Long wings power them on a diagonal – he just ahead and above. They begin to disappear into the vast chasms of the sky, just specks, then specks of specks. He disappears, but she, only just visible, is turning, now right to left as she begins to come back. For two minutes she gets closer, lower now – towards the trees.

Suddenly the object of her attention is obvious – it's another female! This is an intruder on her territory – and she dives towards her, as the trespasser swerves and begins to flee. Her mate hangs back, way above, watching the action as a top-speed dog-fight develops in the heavens.

As the intruder flees in a looping streak, the territory-holder dives and attacks again and again, virtually hitting her in mid-air, then they part and the attack is repeated. The male, way up, keeps station, his wings a blur in his effort.

The invader heads off east and the chase is off – but the pair are still in high spirits – and they follow this battle with an incredible show of flying prowess – reinforcing their pair-bond. Each tries to outdo the other with turns of speed, with dives and loops, for several minutes, until they streak down to the trees and land.

Within a minute, their blood still up, they are up again to stoop at a Buzzard, one of them screaming at it as they circle vertically at the large raptor, which doesn't budge.

Through the season they would be relentless in their harrying of Buzzards, which represent a very real threat to their unfledged young.

Finally, their efforts done, they settle to a tree, where they remain for much of the rest of the day.

Cold again the following morning. After some searching, the pair are calling distance-ward. They come in from the north – he carrying a small morsel – perhaps a large insect – and she is begging to him.

They land just out of sight, possibly mating. She follows her mate from tree to tree, getting closer the whole time. Finally, they settle. For a while, things are calm. Then, she is off at full tilt – low against the field – short wader-like calls, "klip, klip" reach back – she has seen an intruder.

It is a female, hence her response – she sees off her female rivals, he sees off his male interlopers.

The intruder is making off, rising and heading directly away. The male has followed – but after a few seconds and a few hundred yards, they both turn back, leaving the interloper to circle and rise, eventually going off south.

It is possible this other female is a daughter of the pair, returning to the territory of her birth and the land she knows best. During the season offspring of the pair will appear – but not always will they be treated with hostility.

The pair have been keeping an eye on a couple of occupied Crows' nests, and now, with the parents away, the female Hobby leads the way to one and they both sit right by it. Young Crows now look fully grown – and are visible above the nest rim of late. Then, the parents return and a scuffle between corvid and falcon sends the Hobbies back to perch nearby.

It appears they might have chosen a nest site.

The Little Owl is perching conspicuously as he scans the fields. Then, a Kestrel flies in and, within seconds, is diving at prey beyond the hedge. Starlings squawk in panic and alarm – they are with their young – but the falcon has already taken a House Sparrow. He takes his prize to a telegraph pole top, where he balances on his still-wriggling victim. With a bite he stills the sparrow and begins to eat.

The prey is despatched head-first: eyes and cheeks are torn away and swallowed greedily, then the remainder of the head is pulled off, and swallowed with some difficulty. Plucking some of the feathers as he goes, the Kestrel works his way down the bloody body, gulping gobs of bright flesh.

His appetite satisfied, he takes off and circles for height, carrying the half-sparrow with him to the barn and his family. He has made most of the journey when the Hobbies – led by the female – take off from across the field and head for him.

Quickly catching him up, the female dives at the Kestrel. He rolls to defend himself as she whips a tight arc around him, renewing her attack. Again, the Kestrel swerves and tilts, much the lesser flier, and the male Hobby buzzes him, too. The Kestrel carries on to deliver his prey to the barn as the Hobbies turn and head the five hundred metres back.

Half a sparrow seen from half a kilometre!

The female Hobby makes straight for the potential nest tree and perches – the male circling close, then away to an adjacent tree – a tree from which she can watch the Crows' progress, ready to take over once they vacate the nest. She calls softly, and the male flies in to join her in a mating.

She then takes off and begins to insect-catch in the scalloped sky, replete with scrapes of thin cirrus and little puffs of cumuli.

She stays within a few hundred yards of the nest tree as she circles, loops, roller-coasts, and snatches insects in an effortless display of hunting at ease. Each insect is caught in her talons – which she brings forward under her head at the last second, both feet together, though one makes the grab, and it is immediately transferred to her bill, as her head bends to meet the feet, her wings and tail adjusting in the balance, gliding along as she eats.

This goes on for a while, the peaceful, loose, gliding and sailing taking her to differing heights, sometimes a shallow dive, then back up, using thermals, and any slight breeze, without any working.

Then, she transforms into a sleeker, faster beast, and, taught now, turns on her power. She accelerates this way. Suddenly birds are alarming: not at her, but at a Sparrowhawk which she now buzzes at speed, easily overtaking the hawk, then she spirals up again to resume her insect-taking. Her lazy morsel hunt continues for some time, until, once more, she changes form, and becomes a true hunter.

A rapid looping series of dives takes her from sky to grass-tops twice, as she slices at Swallows skimming the fields, which send out alarms and scatter. But she comes away without prey, powering up strongly, and, again begins to fly at flies.

From the north the male makes a rapid approach – he homes in on his mate, wings blurring as he rises to her level, then, synchronised, they sweep the blue together, drifting away as one, gaining height, until, with a sudden tilt, she plummets earthward – he following.

In the far distance they are hunting co-operatively, co-ordinating swerves and dives. Suddenly they are gone – lost to low greenery and the shimmering heat of the afternoon – vanishing in a blaze of glory.

The morning warm and glass-clear, already stirring blurriness from the remains of the dew. Out along the lanes a Corn Bunting sings, claws wrapped around a telegraph wire, sitting in the sun. The last of these rare breeders here – always late to begin their season. His song rattles out along the hedges.

The female Hobby is on her distant perch tree, calling out across the meadow. He, for the main, remains impassive, but then, he too is calling quietly in answer. For an hour or more they stay sitting in that spot, occasionally preening, but otherwise immobile.

Far up, a Skylark's song drifts down, with a perfect mimic of a Marsh Tit intoned in its midst.

It is June. The egg-laying month has begun. The Hobbies wait patiently for their nest, their time to come.

The Buzzards continue to display – singles and pairs gather and circle in thermals, in easy air, marking territories and meeting neighbours, reinforcing boundaries only they can see. Their loops and dives, with upward stalls tipping them back towards the ground, as a mewl escapes them, fill the warm air for an hour or so – then they split up, each pair back to their own patch, from where the drift has taken them. There is no antagonism, merely a drawing of lines.

At the farm the House Martins are sailing back and forth, to and from nests under deep eaves. Some are nest-building – taking grey mud lumps on the top of their short bills from muddy edges of the pond – others are already feeding young. They are constantly in movement, white rumps glowing in the shadows, and glinting blue black-backs in the sun. Their gritty calls speck the air, peppering the sky, as if replacing the flies caught as they go.

As the day warms, the butterflies, at their season's start, emerge to brighten the verges and hedges, searching for food plants and mates, never still for long, seeking out sunny spots to warm small wings. Speckled Woods drop from the copse to the meadow, swirling in fights and mating dances; Green-veined Whites flap over dandelions and pause to sip, wings opening and closing in loveliness. A Large Skipper flicks by – ever restless and on the move, jinking away, almost impossible to follow.

One oak tree holds a small colony of Purple Hairstreaks; they spin around the top-most leaf cluster, tiny and inconspicuous unless on the move. Once perched they become almost invisible, crawling along twig and leaf – and only occasionally flashing tiny iridescences from the upper surfaces of their wings.

Down at the large pond the Swans have seven cygnets now – small and vulnerable, their parents keeping guard. And the Great-crested Grebes have young too – four young, floating by their parents, awkward and zebra-stiped.

Smaller movements quicken with the warming day – damselflies and dragonflies are skimming the water's surface, only days old in their newly-metamorphosed forms – but looking for mates. Azure and Blue-tailed Damselflies – tiny dots of neon gleaming – and Large Red Damselflies are patrolling daintily. A Four-spotted Chaser skims from perch to perch, fighting off any intruder, keeping his territory without ceasing. A Broad-bodied Chaser becomes the chased as it approaches too close, and skims across the pond away from its aggressor.

Out on the lilly pads the Red-eyed Damselflies sun themselves, sitting close against the glossy leaves – and making small forays for flies and rivals.

A Curlew calls as it passes high overhead.

The young Song Thrushes are out of the nest now – and hop by the water's edge, picking at morsels, gangly and awkward. In the depths of a tangle the Robin sits on her nest, rock-still and inconspicuous in the deep shadow-contrast above the dazzle of the water. Nearby the Bullfinch pair are still building in the briars, moving cautiously against their showing.

Young Coal Tits and Long-tailed Tits are moving through the willows, dangling from leaf clusters, whispering as they go.

Out along the river the Sand Martin colony – eighteen deep holes driven into the steep sandy bank – is at peak activity. Half of the holes are occupied and the parents come and go quickly – diving straight into the bank – or perching at the already-full entrances – where young have emerged into daylight now. Cows along the bank top munch impassively and drool in the ease of the lushness.

At least six Hares are running circles and sprint-lines across the meadow, competing and playing – full of energy. Strong, long legs take them, in seconds to the field's edge, where they spin and return, jumping over each other, mock-fighting, kicking up their hind quarters and prancing.

Suddenly, mid-day, a Tawny Owl calls from the wood.

On the old, half-rotten, cattle-worn fence post by the stile, evidence of the Barn Owl's presence is portrayed – long white droppings, like white paint spilt carelessly, run from top to bottom.

Back along the hedges and the Linnets are building their second nests of the season – small neat cups taking shape in the thorn. A Corn Bunting sings. His short rattle sharp and rasping against the soft day.

To the paddocks and arable – where the Lapwing chicks are now hatched and strutting, feathery jewels on sturdy pins. Two Hares stretch in the dust, head-top eyes half-closed, long ears heavy against their backs, dozing in the warmth of the afternoon.

Tortoiseshells flicker across the flower-heavy meadows and Swifts scream from high in a pale blue sky. The Swallows twitter around the barn and telegraph wires, dropping to drink from the canal in deft, brief, blue-backed dives along the water. Others following, dunk themselves to bathe – creamy breasts wetted in the quickest of washes – and rising to shake off the water and loop back to the farm to preen, still twittering.

Horse tails swish against the flies in the paddock, whose muzzle-worn fences, grey and thin, like whale bones drying in the sun. Onto one a Yellow Wagtail rises from its pickings beneath the hooves, and calls a sweet two-in-one note to the world.

Beyond, on his oak tree, eyes half-closed in the glare beyond its shady leaf, a Little Owl sits and waits for the opportunity to pounce. It won't be long – afternoon-warm beetles scurry quickly below his lookout.

Suddenly a Weasel breaks from the base of the hedge and runs across the lane; gone in a gingery flash. Then, out again, jumping above the grasses and flowers of the verge, diving into crevices and nooks, sniffing at Vole and Rabbit holes, fierce eye glinting, rearing up on hind legs, long creamy under-belly showing, whiskers twitching, then down again at a run, snaking half-seen in the undergrowth.

It runs in bounds across the lane again, spinning back on itself and around again, jerking in stop-starts, then makes for the far verge and dives in like a swimmer, and is gone, submerged in lush grasses and deep green pools of shadows.

Out towards the Hobby nest site all seems still. Warm wind wafts and bees hum. The sun begins to lower in the depth of the afternoon, but the heat continues to build.

A small movement near their oak attracts – some glint gives out from a sunlit spot: a Hobby, the female, is sunbathing on the ground. She is lying, wings spread, against the short turf, moving only a little to catch the full strength of the westerly sun. Her upper wings change colour as she turns them to the light – blue from brown and back to blue again as refractions change her hue.

She keeps her head up – alert in her prone position – watching for danger. She spreads her tail for balance as slight shifts in tilt keep her various surfaces turned to the sun.

Time stands still and the world closes around this little falcon. She fascinates and fixes the eye, her beauty and grounded incongruity amaze.

Then, with a feather-gathering twitch, she stands and rises from the field in a single movement, circles as she climbs, to her perch-tree beyond the old Crow's nest, and settles to preen and watch the cubic miles of her domain. A yellow foot stretches from under her as she deftly scratches her face, then, closing her claws, she puts the long reach of her leg back on the branch.

A loose feather separates from the sleek line of her cheek and floats away, rising, not falling, as it drifts into the distance.

Beyond, above the snaking, dark, tree-line of the river, a Grey Wagtail undulates, heading into the west in long curves – its sharp, far-carrying call reaching right the across the world, drawing a line under a sublime, sun-filled day.

The following day – and three Hobbies are circling and insect-catching together, right over the territory. There is no antagonism, no dispute, only shared skies. There are hirundines with them too – with no sign of panic, and for the falcons, no attempt to hunt them.

One Hobby then drifts away, across the territory's centre, unmolested by the resident pair, in some strange benign mood. They continue to eat on the wing, lazily and deftly picking insects from the sky as the sun shines on. This continues for some time, until, satisfied, the female heads down to her tree, and hides herself away amongst the far branches.

He slowly drifts away, keeping pace with the breeze-driven flies, gradually fading into the haze some miles distant.

The Kestrel pair are hunting close to the female now – and she makes no response. She seems serene in this calm day, allowing the incidents which usually agitate her.

The Grey Wagtail brings its long tail down to the dry ditch and bobs along, wagging its behind as is his habit. Then everything is put up by a tractor moving along the field's edge – and suddenly both Hobbies are together – he having returned unseen sometime in the passing hour. She circles and, before long is back on her favoured tree, but he has gone once more, somewhere above his patch.

A hazy day passes in warmth, and peace has settled in the dust of these dry days.

Birds continue to build, feed young, dustbathe and sing; and the Swifts only scream-sing half-heartedly. High in the hazy air, unknown specks cross the horizons and insects rise to invisibility.

In this heap of summer, the Hobbies wait and rest – their egg-laying time is near.

As tree shadows creep like puddling oil across the meadow, the westering settling sun plays on the falcon's back, as evening breezes roll the leaves of her bough.

For several days the weather strokes gently: balmy brightness lengthening towards the solstice as crops ripen, birds fledge and youngsters learn life skills. Second, or even third broods are out of nests and numbers multiply. This abundance peaks with the summer. This hill of life.

For the Hobby pair this is a crucial time – the final nest site choice must be made – egg-laying will begin. As this time approaches they are ever more discreet, and glimpses are hard won. She might already have laid the first of her eggs – she will lay two, three or even four. Until the clutch is almost complete she will not sit – incubation only starting as the penultimate egg is laid. But she will be very close – the Crows and Magpies will not hesitate to steal her eggs.

Huge galleons of cumuli sailing the blue this morning, spinnakers spread against the Swift-full breeze. Dozens of fast, insect-feeders swirling in the vortices, like fish shoals scooping the sprat.

And, there, high in the south, a cloud spits a Hobby to skim the heavens: he heads west, a dark boomerang against the bright.

Suddenly, increasing his speed with intent, in an effortless knifing of the air, he is on to a House Martin. With a swerve he arcs until vertical, head down, now blurring in speed. A jink, and he rockets skyward once more. But, in a blink, he heads down, and, still fast, very fast, looping for a second attempt, but his speed has put him to the distance and he disappears beyond a tree.

A THOUSAND FEET BELOW THE WORLD CARRIES ON

THEN, way up, hidden among the swarming flies and flocks of Swifts, a shape: Hobby, thousands of feet up, tiny in the vast void of the sky, against a towering cloud. Then, turning, the falcon enters the cloud and vanishes.

Ten minutes stretches in the breeze. Trees bend to renewed winds. Skies are full of swirling Swallows, Swifts and House Martins. Buzzards crimped in the rushing air. The scene is set.

Suddenly the Hobby pair are slicing low across the meadow and rising at terrific pace, wings ablur, using the westerlies to rocket east. For an hour they rise and fall, circling, first one way, then the other, always in sight above the centre of the territory. Once or twice a half-hearted attempt to out-manoeuvre a Swift – attempting to keep above their rising prey – takes them to new heights, but they never make a full-on attack, perhaps just assessing the fitness of the prey, as any predator does. Their time for Swift taking will come.

Meanwhile they are content to sail the gale at hundreds of metres, swerving and looping around each other, tearing at speed across the hemisphere of their world, in peerless perfect mastery.

Time floats away on the watching of it, with them in the wind.

Then reverie cracks in the splinter of a darting move: the male begins a dive – accelerating on whipping winds, gravity not enough, wings half-closed, now nearly vertical, flipping twice to swap direction, the earth rising, ever quicker, to meet him.

She follows, more directly, but just as fast – turning with him until twice treetop-height, then the pair level in a blurring line, streaking along the horizon, sun on them both, and, in a final arc to distant trees, they disappear.

The thought of rushing wind continues to blow for some time. Then the earth is back.

Warmth and sunshine and lazy days spent high in the sky – an idyll about to be violently broken.

Insects hum all around in the balm. The world settles in a summer's day.

Then, the sound of conflict: "tlip tlip tlip" . These calls signal an intruder.

Two shapes flash into a tree, then detach, as two falcons, talons locked, tumble to the ground.

After a minute, first one, then the other, are up – it's the female and a second, interloping female – and she won't leave.

Again, and again the female stoops at her rival – full-on attacks which have her rival roll to present talons in a flash. Then she gains height, working hard, to stoop once more – they lock again and fall screaming to the ground, where they sit locked, until a pair of Crows approach. They take to the air again and the dog-fight continues.

Twice more the intruder is forced away, each time choosing to return: making a deliberate attempt to take over the territory from its holder. But, tirelessly, she will not allow her rival to remain – pushing her from perches and attacking her fleeing form. Both now have some feathers dislodged from the fight.

The male keeping pace with the fight, does not get involved. The rival is a full adult, and appears slightly bulkier than the other. The fight continues as they fly towards last year's nest site – and talons lock again. They spin, joined, to the ground. This time a Buzzard takes notice – their din is unavoidable.

Up again: this time the intruder flies further away, disappearing low amongst the hedges and trees. The territory holder takes to the skies, soaring in a display of ownership. Her mate is nowhere to be seen.

This is a last-minute attempt to usurp the resident female from her territory, her mate and her nest. This un-mated bird is desperate to breed – she cannot unless she wrests all these assets from her rival. These last few days before egg-laying are her final chance, and, if she cannot win this battle her season has gone.

For the resident bird, the struggle to hang on to her mate and her territory is at least as essential. She will not give them up without a fight.

The next day sees grey days returning, sudden and unexpected after a week of continuous sunshine.

Greys in every hue hang from horizon to horizon: heavy smoky clouds barely heaving themselves above the trees, bank on bank of slates and pearls, ripple-edged and ragged, boiling coldly, but gradually brightening and lifting, parting only to reveal further layers of dank and dark, with just a hint of light from a sun in hiding.

But the world is re-awakening regardless: Swifts speck the sky, Skylarks ascend, tripping notes to trail in their sloping lift, tit flocks are noisy in the hedgerows, competing with Whitethroats. Young Yellow-hammers – streaky brown and yellow, lemon gapes down-turned as if in grimace to the weather – squeak from hawthorns, and elders in blown-out-umbrella flower fullness. Swallows swoop low and darkly against the land; a Blackbird fires noise at the Little Owl hidden in wet leaf, as Linnets and Goldfinches watch warily.

And, beyond, the cry of a Hobby: two are out from sheltered hiding to circle a copse still shaking rain, then in to land and there to mate, air steaming around their coupled pose. This brief encounter done, they join forces to put up a soggy Crow, driving it away from its own erstwhile nest. This done, they return to the ash.

A Kestrel, up to its hover, air-perched, attracts a swirl of House Martins – white rumps glowing against the grey. Swifts, screaming their songs and mating on the wing as they pass, overtake the martins and skim flies from rain-squeezed air.

Out west, a Sparrowhawk bobs at a ball of Starlings as it passes, trying to pick one from the tight knot, but their defence tactic holds and it misses. It continues to circle up towards the clouds. Two Herons, squawking, lap heavily past. Yellow Wagtails rise and fall into wheat where Lapwings hide. A single Gadwall flicks easterly at speed.

More calls from a Hobby fly across the field as they change positions, but they remain at some distance, backed by a horizon of charcoal clouds. The rain begins another spat, a failing sun extinguished again.

Ripples of wind across the clover-flecked meadow: specks of foam on a ruffled sea of grasses. Warmth pooling where hedges catch it, but otherwise fleeting in the north-easterly breeze. Bramble buds now are open along the hedge, where cow parsley has already gone to seed.

The breeze through the trees crescendos, then fades to leave the sound of a Hobby in the distance, a falcon returns to his mate on a snag branch, sheltering in the lee. For a while they sit close, she occasionally calling an invitation to mate, before getting up and flying to the nest.

He sits and preens, before launching an attack on something hidden behind the copse, circling back to her tree, calling as he approaches. Twice more small arcs vanish in the wind as he flies to the nest tree and is gone.

A Hare lopes by, pale in the sunshine just breaking, while, overhead, two Curlew skim the wind westward.

Out along the lanes the Skylarks' songs fall, soaking into the parched earth. A Yellow Wagtail on a wire calls to her mate. Two Great spotted Woodpeckers chatter alarms at the Little Owl, shuffling up the oak to its half-hidden, hunched form, their spikey calls piercing the shady canopy, red vents ablaze on the boughs. A young owl, perching by the nest hole, pops back into cover, but a sudden line of movement overhead snares the senses.

A Hobby slides silently on a diagonal, half-speed and steady, heading for a telegraph wire, where Swallows are perching: crotchets on the stave. They see the danger far too late. As the Swallows scatter, twisting down and away from the falcon, the Hobby picks a victim, swerves briefly, claws extended on stretched legs and takes its prey deftly, continuing its line as the Swallow makes its final wing-flap, tucked under its killer's body.

The falcon flies away, but detours suddenly, swerving right. It makes for a copse and calls ring clear across the morning, "klip, klip". A flicker of two birds low and fast, lost in shadows and distance.

In the dramatic pause Swallows swarm angrily around the treetops.

A moment passes: then, two Hobbies are rising quickly, one in pursuit of the other. The prey has gone, stashed or abandoned, and the two falcons lift into the blue. The pursued bird is using every ounce of its strength: wing tips meeting above its body as it powers up, its pursuer keeping pace. They rise ever higher, heading north.

The chase goes on until, eventually, their dots dwindle to dust and are simply gone – two miles distant and a mile high.

Back on earth Yellowhammers sing. A vole munches audibly under the hedge. Swallows start to settle. Bees hum.

Away from their usual spot the Hobbies are calling: the chase has concluded, the intruder banished.

Another bright and hazy morning: the Little Owls are active in their oak tree. Two youngsters, fluffy but full-grown, hiss softly to their parents as they clamber about, keeping close to the safety of the nest hole. The parents hunt and bring them food, sometimes perching right out in the early light. A small swarm of passerines flit about the tree in consternation of these four small predators – and the fuss attracts the Great spotted Woodpecker to add to the number.

Then, on one Swallow alarm, the morning becomes electric.

The female Hobby, palely grey-backed in the rising sun, lit beautifully in her pied and red, slanting gradually upward but still low, cruises towards the Swallows over the paddock. A quick arc amongst the prey and away again, to the next farm, where more Swallows are, as yet, unaware.

Accelerating now, as her prey start to swarm in panic, she makes a series of loops and figure-eights which take her from treetop to hedge-base and back again, as Swallows dart away and follow in rapid, flickering terror. But, by keeping her in their sights, they have the better of her, so now she begins to rise.

At a hundred feet she turns to the west and progresses that way at leisure for a full minute. In her sights is her next feeding point, and she begins to put on speed steadily: fifty, sixty, eighty mile per hour, and now she lets gravity add to her velocity as she dives in a steepening curve towards a House Martin colony and she disappears in dark trees' shadows.

Martins and Swallows swirl above the invisible falcon, as they keep their nemesis in sight below.

Half an hour later and she is gliding back towards the heart of her patch, empty-clawed, diving, on the way, at a Buzzard, already with a Crow harassing it, with prey for its own youngsters. She stoops on a dragonfly, jabbing out a foot at the last second to claw it from the air, taking her time to eat it on the wing. Two tiny wings drift down from her talons as she eats. A Little Owl yelps an alarm as she approaches.

In comes the male from nowhere up high, a blur of an arc to meet his mate, buzzing past her at top speed, then to roller-coaster away in a yo-yo of loops with wings ablur, calling to her. They keep this greeting up for a few minutes before settling in the nest tree to vanish.

Payne's Grey drops of clouds cram the sky, threatening, but not delivering rain; a warm breeze nodding the crops, over which the non-stop songs from Skylarks drizzle dryly.

Then, the Lapwings all take to the leaden sky with a knot of Starlings – and they circle up high and fast. There is a Peregrine about somewhere, hidden in the cloud. A Grey Partridge calls a warning and finches and wagtails bounce around the fields. The Little Owl alarms again, and Swallows bunch. For some time this panic wears to wariness, the predator presumably too distant, then things settle to their normal, easy alertness.

The corn is higher now, and the potatoes in flower – purple and white above the lush greens, heaped on ridges between deep furrows. Linnets and Tree Sparrows dash about, their young alongside them, while further broods are being incubated elsewhere. Whitethroats and wagtails: Yellows and Pieds, take food to their nests.

But the sky insists: Swifts and Swallows, the latter with their young, sweeping and looping all around, underneath a bright and cloudy sky.

Suddenly, off southward, the Swifts are organised and agitated, accelerating and swarming, bunching together. Above, jinking away, is a Hobby, paying them some attention, but keeping going until beyond the horizon.

Some ten minutes later a Swallow family nearby are alarmed and flying in parallel. There, way up above them, a Hobby streaks in from the north. Fast.

At a few hundred feet high, it closes its wings towards its body and begins a looping stoop, flicking its primaries to accelerate as it arcs ever steeper. Swifts are around it at first, trying to keep up, but the falcon outpaces them as it dives – dashing from the sky like bullet towards its prey.

Just as predator and prey are about to meet, they drop below the horizon, the kill unseen. A second later and the Hobby is sweeping back this way, flying directly overhead, some small bird tucked neatly under its tail. Too small for a Swift – a House Martin, perhaps has met its end.

A Stoat is running along the lane, head up and searching the hedge, looking and listening, hopping in bounds and pausing, alert. Its ginger-chestnut back and white undersides show alternately as it runs, then gets up on hind legs to peer fierce-eyed into gaps in the hawthorn, whiskers twitching, ears forward. It approaches ever closer, then, sensing danger, dives through the hedge, black tail-tip into the gap and is gone.

Warmth and time have turned the yellow dandelion heads to translucent balls of white – a cloud floating above the meadow. Above, early light pinks the parting clouds to reveal pale ceramic-blue skies. Hares gallop along the lanes and, in the corn shoots, four pairs of Lapwings combine forces to keep a Crow from one of their young – already well-grown and adult-looking.

A Moorhen tends to its chick in the pond as a Reed Bunting sings. Skylarks fill the heavens with sound. Greenfinches, lately arrived, begin to nest beside the Blackbirds in the hedge.

The Hobbies are flying together – a tractor has put them up from the perch tree – taking a long parabola low by the field and back to tree tops, where they sit for hours as the sun brings their colours to life.

Other birds are busy feeding all around: Kestrels are hovering, Buzzards circling, finches and sparrows always moving, picking, squabbling. But the little falcons are content to sit and watch.

Overnight rain has cleared eastwards and, now, the Little Owl hunts the hedges. Consternation follows him from tree to tree. Nervous alarms betray his hidden positions, then a Blackbird, mobbing him on the field where he has pounced, becomes potential prey – as the owl, only just bigger than the Blackbird, chases him to cover.

A perching Kestrel launches himself low across the newly-mown meadow and away in an arc towards the brighter west. Yellowhammers are singing from every horizon. Two dozen House Martins hawk above the barn in new light, and warmer, fly-specked air.

The day turns and the Hobbies remain, implacably placed on their tree.

The sun lowers against a brilliant bank of powder-slate-blue cumuli, setting off its magnesium flare, and sunlight shafts spit from a ragged tear as the west begins to turn orange-red.

As cool settles a single sight of a falcon, way off north, leaves its indelible mark on the day.

Along the hedge-line, where the sun is losing its battle to warm against a cool breeze, the Little Owl, active again, flies from his nest tree to the next oak, setting off a flurry of alarms from Whitethroats, Blackbirds, Blue Tits and Chaffinches. And Swallows loop around his perch, on the lookout for danger.

Puddles from a brief heavy shower stand muddily on the lane, thick with birds: Wood Pigeons, Grey Partridge, Mallard with five young chicks. A Hare stands, flanks to the early sun, still wet from the night.

Speeding in low from a bright eastern sky, trading height for velocity until just over the hedge, a male Peregrine, lit up against the field, whips his wings to torpedo across the grass tops. He has prey in sight.

Too slowly, far too slowly, a pair of Wood Pigeons realise the danger, take off vertically from their field and begin a heavy rise. But that is exactly the wrong tactic. In an arc which meets his target, the falcon hits a pigeon and a burst of feathers explodes in the breeze. In a second the Peregrine and prey are back on the field, but now hidden behind a hedge. Somewhere, out of sight, a Peregrine eats.

The wind picks up and Skylarks, lately silenced by the falcon, begin to sing again. A pair of Yellow Wagtails forage under horses' muzzles in the paddock, snatching flies disturbed by their feeding.

Three Oystercatchers, calling deafeningly, wing overhead, and Stock Doves display. But the Hobbies remain elusive.

A Kestrel takes a dangling vole to its nest in the barn. Young Crows sit in trees. Swifts fill the air, patrolling in the lower fly-rich layers of the cool day.

Then, there they are: sitting in their tree, the Hobbies – having just returned from a hunt. Almost straight away they are mating, the female lifting her skirts to reveal her crimson knickers, calling softly as she mates – he perching deftly on her dark back – lowering his tail around her raised one. Then he hops off to a perch above hers.

A minute or two, and they are airborne, he heading this way, his humbug body showing bright, flies directly overhead, then veers to rise into the blue. She, meanwhile, has sidled off below treetop level, and, following his higher route, rises more slowly. She then makes her way towards the nest tree, as he hurtles out of the heavens to buzz her like lightening, winnowing wings blurring, before rocketing back up, as she continues, swerving to the nest. He loops back and lands close by. Only seconds pass before they are both up, wheeling around the tree, then up into the sky, and away. The hunt is on.

Both rise, circling and powering up, Swifts bunching and rising now, above the pair. The male falcon tries to gain advantage, but his prey are always ahead, twisting in the wind to keep above. They all rise until the Swifts are invisible, he merely a speck, as he turns south.

Suddenly, he drops like a meteor towards the horizon, where he is lost to the pale distance. She too has slipped into the infinite and the sky is empty.

Still and silvery – mists slowly thinning – Crows sipping dewdrops from grasses, Skylarks invisibly singing, dripping notes from low clouds. A Hare gallops away, spray flying from hind paws.

And the Hobby pair sit, and sit.

The Little Owl is busy again, trying various vantage points – from oak to fence posts, fence lines and hedge tops, where the may blossom, now fertilised, is already turning. He stops and swivels his head as a Kestrel arcs above.

Sparrows and finches flit. Whitethroats sing. Lapwings and Oyster-catchers stride the fields. A Buzzard lifts sky-ward, trying to find purchase in the unsupporting air, flapping in the damp, attracting detractors and squeezing an alarm call from the owl: twice a quick "peeoo, peeoo" pulses through the mist.

And still the Hobbies sit and wait.

Passing Starling families and low Swifts do not tempt them; Swallows brushing the grasses below them elicit no response. Instead, though the female begs briefly, her low keening piercing the dank, their only movement is to preen.

Down along the canal to the river. Cut fields and crops growing. Lush life thickening with the season. Reed Buntings bob along the hogweed top, calling. A Sedge Warbler sings from nettles, thick amongst the brambles of the bank. A Little Grebe dives quickly below the slow, greenish soupy surface of the water, re-emerging upstream, hiding by the steep muddy cliff, where Sand Martins have their colony: a pepper pot of holes on the bank.

Herons hunch and Moorhens flick white tails, nervous along the river sides. A Cormorant lifts heavily and turns to the east.

Overhead, a Sparrowhawk is carrying prey back to her nest, her flap-flap-glide taking her, arrow-straight, towards her young. Long-tailed Tit families are feeding in the alders, moving restlessly along the ox-bow lake.

Through the wood, where bluebells still flower – still giving a heady scent to the day. Ahead, now, the copse near to the Hobbies' nest site is visible – and he can be seen, on the near edge, busy with something.

He is eating: his prey is a Blue Tit, which he is devouring hungrily. After a few minutes he takes the remains, two small legs still attached, to the nest tree. He disappears within the green canopy, then a minute later, he is out to the copse again, and begins to preen. Then, her approach unseen, she is with him too. They sit beside each other for a while, then she goes back to the nest: perhaps she has begun incubating at last.

AN ANXIOUS SEASON
STARTS AGAIN

NOW the quiet time really begins. For the next month the female will remain on the nest, except for short spells, when the male takes over guarding the eggs and keeping them warm – but only she has a brood patch to properly incubate them.

He keeps her fed, in the main, though she might catch for herself in the short spells she sends away from her brood. And both are at their most discreet during this time – he slipping in with prey – which she will eat very close to the nest – and back out to perch close by, or away to hunt himself.

The summer solstice stalls the days – dusks morph to dawns with hardly a pause between; hunting times are at their longest; life multiplies, grows, burgeons, thickens.

For a few species, like the Hobby, this is merely the beginning of their season. They are laying eggs, or incubating for the first time, and the last arrivals are still courting...

A Quail cracks a triplet of whips from the wheat: "wet my lips", in sixes: his triple beat pulses across the hot, ripening crop: some demented sonic automaton firing song from hiding, spitting air in short, sharp shockwaves which echo, echo, echo across the summer's dust. "Find a mate, find a mate", his chorus a calamity of unrequited phrases from a field too far – another of his kind unlikely to be within earshot. But he continues to sing intermittently during the long daylight hours, almost never showing from his hiding amongst the crops.

Nearby, two Tortoiseshells sit on a single bramble leaf, courting. Brambles, once flattened by winter snows, now fill the brim-full gap between wood and field, bursting in flower. The butterflies flicker – he shivers and shuffles towards his mate, their antennae like silver-topped ebony canes held above the bright, variegated rug of their wings.

A Comma and a Red Admiral flash and float in the gentle air, both out-doing the courting pair in colour and pattern.

Deep June dreams the long days and balmy warmth wafts gently along the paths and lanes, hardly stirring the settled dust of summer. Young animals play in the ease of the season, growing and strengthening for leaner times to come. For now, butterflies and blooms blow and glide along the sunshine, over nodding meadows, across slow streams, through scented woods and out to hazy horizons basking on the bed of a drowsy earth.

Then, with a sharp shout of alarm, a speck grows from the distance and becomes a Peregrine. A missile of danger approaches.

Out in the open, a woodpecker is caught between woods, high in the sky, away from the safety of the trees.

The persistent powering primaries of the Peregrine produce a bee-line in pursuit of the black-and-white, stop-start-stop wings of the wood-pecker, bound to undulate, but, dropping with a final bound to a bough, it binds to bark beyond the raptor's reach.

Puddles persist from overnight rains: sunrise, and the shadows run long – skimming shrubs as the climbing sun over-reaches ridges to spill into these small valleys of the plain.

The bright canvas of sky stretches its cirrus-scraped self above the glass-clear air; air still cold even in this peak of the summer.

A Yellowhammer pair perches on bush tops. Linnets take beakfulls of fresh straw to a new nest. A Jay, cinnamon against the dark lane, hops buoyantly, then flies, showing its blues and whites.

The first butterflies, now sun-warmed, begin to flit along verges, now overblown: dock and nettle are already seeding, willow herbs are in flower; a dozen different grasses high amongst budding thistles. Hover-flies and bees hum and buzz.

Somewhere in a wooded crease, two Nuthatches sing in turn, and the needle of a Grey Wagtail's call spikes across the sky.

Skylarks' alarms follow the Kestrels – a juvenile, lately out from the barn nest – and accompanying adult above the high hay. Cleavers, their quick climb now done, lie thickly along the walls, resting in the sun.

Now the stony pips of a Linnet trips from its songpost, like a pebble skipping down steep rocks. A French Partridge calls nervously below, half-hidden in tall vegetation, its speckly necklace like old black lace, as it strides jerkily, head raised, legs bent.

Whitethroats churr from blackberries and emerge to hop along the walls. The first Skylark now lifts into the blue to warm the still-cool air. Young Rooks, now independent, still awkward, glean spillings from the cut hay; barley, beginning to bend its head, nods in the field beyond.

Swifts slice over the long skies and over the woods where, the plumptious song of a Blackcap, as rich and moist as a fruit cake, sweetens the day.

A Jackdaw's shadow scurries along the tussocks, in and out of ditches, like a black fox. The metal petals of Goldfinches' calls, like foil confetti glinting in the sun, shower down to the hay field, now showing green again through its own straw.

A KESTREL GLIDES TO A POST
AND SETTLES

SWALLOWS skim the meadow, low over the grass, while Swifts jink and scythe above, amongst cauliflower cumuli billowing in the blue. House Martins glide between, pied and plump: each species in its niche.

The warm, rich smell of hay thickens in the heat; the languid afternoon barely stirring. Four flute notes of a Blackbird float from the hedge where the dog rose rises through the hawthorn. A Yellowhammer cock, disturbed by a descending Lapwing, flies from the stubble to sit on a wire.

Fat Wood Pigeons doze in the shady ash.

Then, there it is: the Hobby. Along the ridge where it can see the sweep of the land, it glides with a slow flick of his long rapier wings, heading west. Too quickly gone below the horizon, it leaves behind far emptier skies.

June turns with the newly-growing hay, towards July. A solstice-stalled sun has already begun to track back to the equator, barely discernible in its slowness. But, this Northern Hemisphere has much left to do, and summer's hill has still to climb.

A Hare gallops across the forest of stalks and of the newly-cut field, the mewl of a Buzzard rising from the wood beyond. Skylarks sing in a fresh sky and Swallows sit on wires like crotchets on the stave, a Starling a single minim. A skim of cirrus is brushed carelessly across the blue.

By the ditch yellow flag flowers now stand tall, and a Reed Bunting sings its four-note ditty.

One field is thick with Lapwings, still wary of the Crows that eye their young, as they search for invertebrate victims. On a mound where meadowsweet spill, a Mole lies twisted, as if surprised by the suddenness of its own death: its shovel feet paused in their digging.

Tortoiseshells fight in the nettle patch and Small Skippers sun themselves on clover. A pair of Bullfinches, tubby and gorgeous, undulate to the beeches.

High up, the Swifts are mobbing a Sparrowhawk as it flaps and glides, searching for a thermal.

But, from the cut meadow's edge, still lush with grass and weed, the whip of the Quail's "wet my lips" lashes out into the morning, and all the world stops to listen.

In the west the clouds begin to bank, and bruise to purple.

Before the rain a Sparrowhawk circles up, flapping and gliding with prey now, carrying it towards her nest.

Then the rain comes like arrows in an unending volley – slanting in from the west on a blowing. In the meadow a hundred Starlings crawl across the grass, heads down and probing, as one. From time to time those at the back fly to the front for the advantage, temporary leaders of the crowd, before this rolling herd made them followers again. In this flat, slinky fashion, the herd progresses.

Inches above them, a dozen or more Swallows, tails depressed and spread to slow their flight to nearly nothing, showing their silver-white tail-spots, pick insects disturbed by the Starlings below. They fly windward, against a stall, then swirl to the back edge of the Starling swarm to trawl again.

These two movements become one: Starlings rising briefly, Swallows dipping and swirling; a repeated pattern, which, from a distance, seems a single, loose, rolling ball across the rain-strafed grass, in which the Starlings swim, and Swallows, Petrel-like, pick.

Once or twice, false alarms sound – sending Starlings up to flash in synchronised twists, before falling back to the field, leaving unsettled Swallows to re-group and follow as the Starlings begin pushing through the sward once more.

Just as rapidly as it had begun, the rain ceases, and its last hisses fall to the now soaked soil. A blink, and brightness returns, and the sun peeps blindingly around the cloud's edges. Steam begins to snake above the field, and birds shake the water from feathers, in a quick pause in their feeding. Small rainbow-sparks flash from arcing droplets, to die in the instant of their birth.

Gulls begin drifting in to catch insects rising in the new warmth, and Buzzards display. A Kestrel catches a bumblebee on the wing, then lets it go again – the bumblebee carries on its way. The falcon catches two more insects and eats them as it glides.

The blanket grey cloud layer slowly clots and clumps, its coagulation leaving little patches of pale turquoise where the hopeful sky begins to peep onto this little valley, its sides dotted with shrubs.

Blackthorn and bramble, bracken and oak, ash and willow, thistle and gorse; and the scramble of honeysuckle sweetly clinging: this scrubby slope lush and full. The fern and nettle and nodding foxgloves are waist high above vetches, sedges, grasses and dozens of flowers blinking bright.

Ringlets, disguising themselves amongst Meadow Browns, their subtle beauty apparent close up: silver circles and wing-edges showing.

Birds in profusion: everywhere movement, everywhere sound: calls, songs, half-songs, tiny brushings of leaf, and the murmur of wings.

Willow Warblers are all around, "whoo-weets" and bubbly bursts of part song, the lemony flick of wings and tails, young and adults, in trees and shrubs, on flowers and in wood piles; chasing juvenile Long-tailed Tits.

Blackcap families and single Blackcaps 'chack' away, Whitethroats churring alarms and singing, moving amongst the thistles and up into elders. Young speckly Robins perching perkily, wait to be fed. Dunnock juveniles and Blackbirds dot the low shadows.

A white rump of a Jay floats across a glade – a slow-motion snowball white in shade. From the ox-bow the Little Grebe's call rises up like corrugated tin. A Chiffchaff sings. A Yellowhammer flies up from a drinking puddle, where fat black slugs slither slowly in the still-wet grasses.

Goldfinches sing – the electric buzz sparking across the gap between the bushes. Linnets and Bullfinches, sotto voce, bob above the wood.

From the copse a commotion begins: Magpies chattering and Jays squawking, Blackbirds persistently 'pink, pink, pinking' in alarm. A Red-legged Partridge splutters from the broom-covered slope between, Wood Pigeons clatter from the trees. A Fox suddenly shows, and slinks quietly away. The noise subsides.

In a single willow the Blue, Great, Coal and Long-tailed Tits', Willow Warblers' and Blackcaps' movements almost cover the stealth of a Lesser Whitethroat, busily picking at flies, its bandit mask against the bright of its throat.

And, behind, a Garden Warbler bends the outer leaves of a beech – plain and lovey in muted colours. A young Great spotted Woodpecker begins to smash into a rotten branch, its scarlet crown a shock on its pied body. It picks a fat white grub from the hollow it has made and manoeu-vres it inside the chisel of its bill, and swallows. It shuffles around the small dead branch, blue-grey legs clinging strongly, its zebra-striped undertail showing.

Bees begin to fill the foxgloves as the morning warms – disappearing entirely into the blooms and struggling backwards out again. A House Mouse creeps back into the cover of a mossy wall. A Goldcrest runs the gap between two trees, its thin call joining them like a silken thread.

Out on the brambly bank a Chaffinch sings, and Rooks sail across a brightening sky – black on blue.

Somewhere, up in the cubic miles of summer air, a Hobby, beyond visibility, slices the void, on the hunt. Now he will be providing for his mate. Now his tireless stamina will be tested. For him, the next three months will mean almost-unstopping hunting, his efforts increasing exponentially as the eggs hatch and his family grows.

For now, he has the air to himself, and she will sit tight, infinitely patient, waiting on his occasional returns. For him the freedom of the skies. For her the self-imposed open prison of her oak.

DARK CREEPS IN SLOWLY FROM THE EAST AND SOUTH

THESE longest days and warm nights bring out the bats. Before dark the Noctules begin to patrol, above the trees and across the fields – occasionally diving suddenly on some insect below, then rising again to feed in some other quarter.

Pipistrelles, seemingly silent, yet emitting a constant stream of sound, emerging just before the final glimmer of light, are hunting moths and mosquitoes, swirling around eaves and hedges, then disappearing in the blackness.

Over the pond the Daubenton's Bats skim close against the water, picking off insects just out of (and sometimes still on) the surface. And, by the wood the Long-eared Bats glean prey from around, and on the leaves of the trees.

Within the copse the Tawny Owl young, now out of their nest hole, begin to beg from the parents.

Badgers begin their nocturnal forays amongst the flowers of the wood, out along the ditches and into the meadows. Hedgehogs snuffle along the lanes, snuffling at snails, biting at beetles.

Toads, grown, and out of their ponds, walk the fields and hunt.

And high above, asleep on the wing, Swifts still turn in the black of the night.

Dawn comes early. The Fox, now with young, remains at large, sniffing its way through the woods and farms, still hunting. Near the pond a Buzzard sits astride a plump Moorhen, feeding. In the background a Grasshopper Warbler is singing: reeling out a constant stream of song, the sound of fishing line on a running fish.

Lesser Black-backed Gulls are dropping in from the sky, towards the fields where the plough provides new pickings.

Along the quiet early morning of the canal, a Common Tern, bill-down, flies steadily eastwards, dipping at times, to the surface of the water, to snap up a rising fly.

The meadows now hold common spotted orchids – small drifts in marshy hollows dot the grasses and juncus.

Then, heading for the pylon, a Peregrine, carrying a Blackbird, glides in to perch on the iron-work to feed. Soon, accompanied by the bobbing of his dark-hooded head, black feathers begin to drift down to the river. He continues to feed for some time.

Oblivious, below his pylon, young Goldfinches and their parents balance on fluffed-up thistle heads and pull them apart, sending the down of seed remains to join the feathers falling from above.

Four Curlew, calling their evocative bubble of sound, head high over-head.

Sunlight breaks above the trees and the warm morning warms further. A Brimstone, pale and beautiful, flaps by in dapple. A Kingfisher flies past, flashing in and out of sun and shadows, electric and stunning. As if in answer, the power lines' crackle crescendos as it goes.

Now the dragonflies begin to patrol. Over the reedy ditch, yellow flags glowing brightly, a Brown Hawker skims back and forth, turning quickly, pursuing prey, rising and falling as it hunts.

An Emperor Dragonfly, on his territory over the canal, as much in trespass-watch as hunt, in blue and green, shoots across the water to willow herb and willow, then, in a half-instant, returns to the open water, hovering now and then, dashing at flies and Common Blue Damselflies.

Above the waterside herbage Banded Demoiselle males display their grandeur, glowing blue-black and flashing their broad dark-blue wing patches. The females sit by the waterside, watching. Occasional pairs fly in tandem towards shallow water to lay their eggs.

A Broad-bodied Chaser, plump and plumbeous, glides past in curving, level flight. Above, briefly, the colourful form of a Southern Hawker zigzags amongst the overhanging branches of the trees. Sun glints off the water and blinds.

Back along the lanes and the small pond holds a Tufted Duck – nervous and wary. Reed Buntings and their young move away, along bull-rushes and reeds.

At the copse young Bullfinches feed on green buds and as a Cuckoo calls, just once. Overhead, a Curlew and a Common Tern cross paths at different heights, the tern following the canal, eastwards.

The Little Owl chicks are out from their nest tree and are hissing to their parents from the telegraph poles – always hungry. The adults fly back and forth from fields to the young, carrying beetles and worms, and the family progresses along the lane, further and further from home.

The paddock has filled with wagtails – Pied and Yellow – both with young, some feeding themselves on the fly-full gullies and field edges, some still begging from the adults.

Two fields along and the hay has been cut, lying in dark green untidy rows, the yellow grass between recovering from the shear. In the middle a Skylarks' nest with young has had the mechanical mower and tractor pass right over it – cutting within an inch of the soil – but the shallow cup shows four huddled young still alive and well, but now very exposed without the sheltering sward.

As the days pass the weather stays warm and dry, the grass re-growing in the field – and the Skylark chicks survive their close shave. On the drying hay rows a family of Reed Buntings picks at insects and seed.

On the top of a nearby poplar, a Nuthatch rings out in clear peels across the canal and beyond, toward the Hobby nest, where the female falcon is sitting.

Between the two, young House Martins are learning their hunting skills – families gliding down towards the cut hay to pick at rising flies – constantly sweeping and circling low against the field, calling softly with gritty notes. Occasionally an alarm sounds and, briefly they all lift in a spiral, then fall back to feeding above the meadow. The young meet their parents regularly to take food from them – a quick aerial head-to-head – and back again to catching.

The young Lapwings are almost full-grown now, some are able to fly, and the families range further afield, making use of the mix of arable and pasture, moving from meadow to the rolling potato fields, and striding amongst the cut hayfields. The Lesser Black-backed Gulls still watch them – but these survivors are now largely out of reach of their danger.

Now the House Martins alarm again – and this time the alarm is for real. This time they rise and bunch in a corkscrew – gaining height as quickly as they are able. Within seconds they are three or four times tree-height: and now the reason for their panic becomes apparent.

Head-on and closing rapidly the male Hobby is on a bee-line towards the Martins. At first, he is above them, but his falling slant now has taken him below the rising prey – which have turned away to try to keep distance between them.

Until then he has been gliding fast, wings just slightly bent towards him. Now he whips his long primaries and his acceleration is very apparent. He begins to rise, gradually at first, towards the fleeing Martins, still picking up speed – ever faster and faster.

Now, predator and prey are level, and the falcon is closing, when the ball of bunched Martins swerves towards the earth. He follows.

In a zigzag dive, as he picks a victim, he closes in. Now within a few feet of separation the Martin flock split, and each group twists away in different directions. The Hobby arcs around at one and, diving on it as it makes a desperate flick left, he suddenly stabs a long leg out and grabs his prey.

His speed now turns him back towards the sky, and he makes for the nest tree, slowing to merely rapid – his prey almost invisible, tucked under his tail.

As he approaches the nest, cries ring out across the field, rising in intensity, and now the female is streaking towards him. They greet in rising, symmetrical arcs and he brings the prey forward and releases it. The female stalls in her catching and lets herself fall, twisting back towards her tree, now carrying the Martin under her. Calls continue – both falcons crying out in the frisson of the hunt.

She glides to the adjacent tree and disappears within. He turns, circles once or twice, then heads off to hunt again.

It is July – and now his hunting will become ever more frequent.

Now the sun brings beauty: Ringlets are flying amongst the Meadow Browns – both constantly on the move over the meadows, along the verges, in the dapple of the copses, where Speckled Woods spiral-fight and Small Skippers flicker around thistle and clover, vetches and stitchworts.

Brown Hawkers skim past, never still on the hunt, amber wings glinting. A Southern Hawker approaches, curious, stares and turns away. By the canal a rare Black-tailed Skimmer perches on the stone by the water, flattening his powder-blue self against the warmth. On the ivy above, overhanging the arch of the bridge, two Holly Blues find each other and settle to mate, their silvery underwings a silky sheen: two tiny triangles joined.

In the wet meadow – awash with yellow flowers – Large White Butterflies are sailing a bright sea – a hundred white yachts from horizon to horizon. At the brambly edge a Red Admiral is opening and closing its wings – alternately showing off and camouflaging.

Along the stream an Emperor Dragonfly is hovering and darting at prey. Below, where the tiny levees reach the water edge, thirteen Grey Partridge – full-grown young – crouch against the dusty bank. The adults nervously creep in cover nearby – almost invisible.

To the river – and on the hogweed tops a Stonechat is perching, handsome and globular, on his small lookout for insect prey. And, as he sits, a Mediterranean Gull wings by, bright, almost translucent in the sunshine, following the river on some voyage. Both of these birds are only very occasional visitors to these parts.

Banded Demoiselles flicker beautifully on the riversides – just above the lush vegetation, now at its tallest – at times the banks are thick with their whirring wings. Suddenly a Kingfisher swerves around the meander, an arc of neon, and gone.

Ragged robin and purple loostrife are still flowering – and above them a Common Darter zigzags and hovers – before settling – turning its wings to sun-ward – before taking off again.

Back along the wood-edged field there are sixteen Mistle Thrushes hopping through the limp grass – several broods from one or two families. And, on an overhanging ash branch, a Spotted Flycatcher is upright, inconspicuous amongst the grey twigs. From time to time it sallies out into the meadow to snatch an insect, returning to its perch in a long loop.

Beyond, the pylon holds two Peregrines: a juvenile and an adult. They sit on separate spars, both looking eastward. Their attention is on a third bird – an adult male – which glides in slowly to join them. Nothing passes between them, and the three falcons sit, watching the world from the high vantage of this incongruously huge structure, bestride this little valley.

On the little pond by the copse, the Moorhens now have ten chicks – two broods joining in a loose black raft, drifting and spinning across the weedy water. Blue-tailed Damselflies, dainty, tiny, exquisite, dot the edges with sparks of electric blue.

A Redshank suddenly gets up from the sedges, and rises, calling, towards the lowering sun, legs on fire in the light.

As the day closes, eight Hares gallop together towards the north-western sunset.

Impatient young Tawny Owls begin to call now – these short nights reducing the nocturnal hunting, but their parents remain silent until full darkness hides them away. The first of the bats flickers out into the gathering gloom and colour begins to fade from the land and sky.

Night along the lanes: moonlight and stars.

The Tawny Owls are all active now – and young and adults are both calling – their various sounds slipping out across the darkness, throwing voices and moving on silently to confuse the ear and the night-blind eye.

Suddenly a scream shatters the sky, repeating and growing as it nears – a Hobby is flying overhead – its cries are incredibly loud. But, despite the darkness it is moving at high speed, proclaiming his territory to the night. In seconds he has gone into the dark distance and the night is silent again.

Just then, in the faint moonlit glimmer, a Barn Owl slips silently from the barn nearby, circles just once, and heads off across the canal. This ghostly apparition ends the day.

Mid-morning along the canal, and House Martins are alarming and all flying east. A female Sparrowhawk is speeding the same way and the Martins are following, mobbing her, keeping several yards to the rear of her tail.

Now she starts a long, shallow dive – gradually increasing speed as she drops to tree-top height. The Martins accelerate too, staying with her at an increasing distance, as she appears to have some other prey in her sight.

Then, she rises suddenly, in a loop, turning vertically and then over on her back, upside down now and still she arcs. Now the Martins are under her, and she completes her circle and is on them, amongst them. Her manoeuvre has completely out-foxed them and she strikes out and takes one as she levels out again.

The others scatter in panic and confusion as the hawk turns and carries her prey towards her nest in the wood.

At the pond and high summer shines on a myriad of insect life. The Great-crested Grebe young are now fully grown. Broad-bodied Chasers and Four-spotted Chasers patrol and fight over the water's edge and the tall vegetation surrounding it. A dozen Brown Hawkers sail over the surface, out between drooping willow branches and over the field adjacent, swerving to hunt as they go.

Out in the centre, with the Mallards and their young, sits a Mandarin Duck – a fine drake in all his exotic splendour. Sedge Warblers sing from the rushes where Common Blue and Blue-tailed Damselflies float gently and perch on yellow flag tops in the sun.

A Reed Bunting family is searching amongst the rushes and willows, and two Lesser Whitethroats, lower down amongst the heap of brambles, creep into cover.

Then, dropping in from the deep blue sky, a group of Black-headed Gulls lands on the water – two adults and their juveniles just out from some distant breeding colony. Meadow Pipits stride amongst the short grass of the field, as clouds of Meadow Browns, three species of Whites, and Small Skippers dance delightfully in the noon-day sun.

Back out by the arching bridge of the canal and a Common Sandpiper is bobbing along the towpath, its breeding season over, it is moving now towards wintering grounds, stopping off to feed, incongruently on this small strip of habitat. Its raised rear yo-yos up and down as it picks at the stone, always moving, always alert. Suddenly, it is off, skimming over the water, arched wings almost touching the smooth green surface, then, lifts off into the sunshine and is gone.

Beyond and along, the canal curves, and opposite, the tumble-down, glassless greenhouses lie amongst high nettles and brambles, reclaiming once-used land. And from the deep vegetation a Grasshopper Warbler sings – sitting vertically on a dead stem, low amongst the green. The season is late, and this singer might go unanswered.

Then a Common Hawker is in the air – for him the season is only beginning – dashing low and always turning, and typically it is too soon gone – into a copse to hunt.

And in the wood, the trees are busy. Nuthatches on the trunks, head-down, hammering at wedged nuts in bark crevices, and above, Treecreepers on the undersides of thin branches creep and probe. Young Coal Tits and families of Long-tailed Tits share leafy hunting spaces and warblers flit and flutter with them.

Overhead, three Siskins, calling brightly, shining yellows and greens in the afternoon sun, drop down to the scots pines where the Sparrowhawk has built. The young hawks will, undoubtedly, be in the nest still.

To the Hobby nest tree, and an Emperor Dragonfly crosses the path, steadfastly northward, head-height, arrow straight. Young Yellow Wagtails are in the lane, parents nervous on hedgetops with beakfulls of insects, tails bobbing.

The male falcon is on his perch tree, and two Magpies approach, ever curious and pugnacious. They sit close by him, and hop from branch to branch, goading him, long tails cocking and calls rattling like shaken spears.

For some time, he sits passively, hardly moving except to swivel his moustachioed head, then he takes off, calling, circles his tree, Magpies in pursuit. All three disappear, but their calls continue for a while.

Along the hedges, gaudy butterflies: Red Admirals and Painted Ladies, Tortoiseshells and Peacocks, spin, flicker, float and glide, and Green-veined Whites perch on dandelion flowers, slowly opening and closing their wings. Out in the meadow, Meadow Browns and Gatekeepers: never more than a foot from the grasses, flutter in the warmth of this late afternoon of the summer.

In the near-still air hangs a Kestrel, working hard at keeping her station above the field, near vertical in her hovering, tail spread and translucent against the sun, chestnut-capped head hunched between her shoulders, long wings raised and spread as they row steadily.

Then, all feathers closed against her, head-down, she drops to the ground, her yellow legs at the last brought down in a thump at the Vole she has been waiting on. Her head dips quickly, delivering death deftly to her prey, and then she lifts into the air with her meal.

Simultaneously to her, a dozen others rise with her – darting away as she makes for the telegraph pole to eat: Meadow Pipits and Skylarks, Yellowhammers and Tree Sparrows, until now hidden, swirl upwards briefly, then drop back to their own gleanings.

A bank of cloud out west blots out the falling sun and dusk begins too early. The remainder of the sky still pale blue, as it has been for days: but the incoming tide of storm clouds seem to foretell of a change to come.

Then, before the daylight has ended, a bat is silhouetted against the sky. It is in pursuit of a dragonfly, and twists and turns as it follows. It is a Serotine. A bat rarely seen well – and even rarer in daylight. Too soon it has gone to the distance and the day fades in glory.

Tawny Owls hoot in the early night, and the air begins to stir fitfully. The sky darkens from the west and a thick, threatening canopy of cloud begins to bend from the horizon. A distantly-faint flash of lightning lights the black to sulphur briefly, and the night closes in.

The night brings storms, lightning closing and thunderclaps quickening, and squalls of heavy showers batter the earth. The aftermath is strong gusty winds and wall-to-wall grey – clouds hanging and blowing throughout the day.

The temperature has dropped and butterflies are in hiding. The ponds rough-topped and dark. The ducks and Moorhens are hidden away, and even the Swans are sheltering amongst the vegetated edges, rain running like quicksilver down their backs.

The damselflies have gone and even the birds cannot be found. Trees bend in the wind and leaves fly from them, littering the lanes and choking the ditches.

In the paddock horses huddle, but the wagtails have gone. Each field appears deserted, save for a few Lapwings and gulls, hunkered down, heads to the wind.

Slicing through, a Peregrine, low and with the wind, passes the barn, direct and unaffected by the buffeting, but not a single bird rises to his dark menace.

At the Hobby nest site, there is nothing to see except for a couple of young Crows, hanging onto the trees as they shake and roll, clinging on, horizontal in the wind. Beyond, in the copse, an old oak has cracked, and a huge branch hangs from the new wound, bright yellow wood showing through the brown bark, and leans at an angle against the ground, its leaves still alive and, as yet, still green.

For a few days the weather remains grey, though the wind eases and fewer showers fall. The world has paused, half-drowned, more by wind than rain, and has been stripped, it seems, of life. The river runs dark, full-banked and grey-green, eddies swirling along the meanders, debris floating: branches, soggy and waterlogged, swim by like otters, heads up and wary. Weeds strand themselves on bankside branches, dipping now beneath the running surface.

The pasture has been churned and puddle-pitted where cattle hooves sank down, darkening to mud where grass once stood, and ditches, lately nearly dried, are full and darkly brown.

Swifts, if seen at all, fly low against the land – the only flies kept down by the cold. Swallows shelter in the barns – their twittering echoing out to soak away into the grey.

Then a brightness begins to return, with half a day of stronger winds, then white breaks from greys, greys lighten and, at long last, blue blinks from the chasms of cloud, and even the showers have lost their force. This evening, before darkness falls, a Song Thrush is singing again.

And, with the gathering night, well over a hundred Rooks, a conglomeration of several local rookeries, young and adults, fly in to a communal roost – dark scraps falling to a dark horizon.

This morning the day starts cool, and rain clouds, though white-topped, still remain. They slide gradually eastwards, slowly replaced by blue. The sun, now on its southerly swing, breaks from the edges of the retreating storms, and life, it seems, starts again.

Benign cumuli begin to build, drawing dampness from the wetted land, fed by the sun-warmed earth, and fill the sky with huge white masses, crowding close and billowing, towering, spreading at their tops to cover the sky.

And the warmth turns to humid heat, and steam begins to rise, puddles start to shrink; and summer, from days in hiding, throws open the door, dons its wellies and steps out again.

Now the hedges and fields, woods and ponds, flicker and float with life. Leaves strewn along the lanes start to dry and curl, puddles retreat, and even the river has already returned, though fuller, to its former self.

Insects now, are on the wing again, birds dot the sky. As if a spring tide has finally ebbed, the land shakes off the retreating sea and begins to bask on the drying beach.

Swifts and House Martins now fly, high amongst the galleons of clouds, which sail slowly across the dome of the sky. A buttery Brimstone bats large yellow wings along the still-muddy lane's edges, and Blackbirds peck at drowned morsels in the gutters.

Birdsong, returned to the world, sounds out along the hedges: Goldfinch and Linnet, Whitethroat and Willow Warbler; and Great Tits hop on hawthorn tops, holding caterpillars which droop from their beaks, before flying to the oak on the corner, where a nest in the bole holds several hungry young. They alarm suddenly, and dive for cover as a blur of Little Owl loops from tree to tree, as low and as quiet as a shadow.

And, out at the Hobbies' tree there too appears to be a change along with the weather.

Way up the male Hobby is circling slowly, drifting with the slight air flow, rising on the currents and, now, merely a speck.

Down here, at the nest tree, some small movements give away the female on the nest. She seems restless, shuffling and re-arranging herself, always mostly hidden within the foliage. The nest and its contents seem to have survived the storms, and, now there are signs that the eggs have hatched.

For a long while calm and quiet settle on the day. A few Rooks strut, legs wide, in the meadow, moving slowly with the herd of cows, whose broad muzzles chop and pull at the grass with audible bites, drool and dew mixing, huge pink, veiny udders swaying heavily. The sun catches purple sheens from the Rooks as they turn to probe the pale conical horn of their bills into the turf, dodging the wet mounds of glistening cow pats, each with their crowd of orange dung flies.

Suddenly, the Pied Wagtails, which have been feeding in the yard by the barn, all rise in panic and swirl; Swallows take off from the rooves, gutters and wires and join the spiralling bunch, as they give off their Hobby-specific alarm – "wee-wheet".

Coming in from the sky, the male Hobby is sliding a line directly towards his nest. A Swift's wing pokes from beneath his tail coverts, and even now he bends his head and deftly snips this flailing appendage, and it falls like a sycamore seed – spinning slowly down as he continues.

At the same time as the panic started, the female has already spotted her mate – recognises his success in the hunt, and gets off the nest and begins to scream – her "kee-kee-kees" carrying across sky and field as she accelerates towards him. Still at some distance, he steepens his drop and careens in mock-evasion as she approaches. He swerves away as they close, and she follows, her cries a crescendo which stuff the sky with sound.

Within a few seconds, they meet, way above the trees, and their talons join, his with the prey, and he swaps the prize to her. She swivels and, heading away, glides down to the riverside, inspecting her meal – head and feet meeting beneath her – and swerves to land out of sight in the top branches of the broken oak.

Meanwhile, her mate has disappeared – perhaps to the nest to stand guard while she eats.

It is ten minutes before the Swallows, having risen and fled to invisibility, begin to return cautiously to their barn. The Pied Wagtails have already resumed their picking amongst the straw-strewn barnyard.

It is the most part of an hour before the female falcon appears from her feeding, and now she makes straight for her nest, she is carrying a small morsel, almost entirely hidden in her talons. With an arrow-straight, arrow-fast glide she stabs herself into the tree and vanishes. A slight shadow-shift betrays a movement, and the male falcon slips from the back of the tree and is fifty yards off before his form can be seen, the rapid ripple of his rapier wings taking him away to hunt again.

Around this sacred spot others continue their own lives.

Swallows are feeding second broods in the same nests in the barns, their older young still occasionally trying to beg as the parents return with food, and are ignored. The Tree Sparrows, out from tree holes and the eaves of the cottage, keep a watchful eye on the activities of the Little Owl family which share their oak and rooftop, and the comings and goings of the Kestrels who still frequent their barn and adjacent paddocks.

From the canal an adult Heron chases a young bird from its feeding zone along the towpath, the cries of the fleeing youngster echoing under the bridge as it rises on huge bowed wings, legs daggling, and makes for an unclaimed stretch further east. Their menace has put up a Grey Wagtail – which bounds long undulations, lands to bob its long tail on the brickwork of the bridge, then descends again to the water's edge, sulphury undertail lit up from the sparkle.

In the brambles which spill over the canal's bank, a Blackcap is feeding, while, directly underneath, a Moorhen bobs, nervously flicking it tail. The fallow field beyond holds a colony of Small Skippers, and Large Skippers mix with them on the flowers and grasses, alternately sunning themselves and jinking in jerky flight, tiny jewels flitting between the copse and the water, where the vetches scramble amongst the grasses.

Tall thistles poke purple heads above the sward and bumblebees, honey bees and hover flies crowd their dense blooms, probing the composite flowers with short probosces.

Under the trees a crowd of balsam flowers attract more bumblebees – and in their nectar-gathering have been covered in pale-yellow pollen – which has turned their stripes to a single custardy colour.

New molehills track across the meadow, the mounds indicating the underground passages of a mammal rarely seen. They stand in varying states of wet and dry, according to age, turning from black to grey-brown in the sunshine, crumbly crumb cracking as they tumble, infinitesimally slowly back to the earth.

On the pond the Reed Buntings are agitated, flying from bullrushes to willows, looking at the water's edge. Their attention is on a small head which is poking from the surface, slowly moving, a fork-tongue flicking: Grass Snake. The snake swims slowly, almost entirely submerged, right across the centre of the pond, and begins to slither out amongst the reeds and sedges on the far side, its long green body camouflaged, and quickly vanishes into the vegetation.

The heat builds: even the early morning shows promise, with a slight sunrise-breeze already warm.

As the sun begins to peep over the trees the Kestrels and their two youngsters are out, in and around the paddock. Three Oystercatchers keep a wary eye on their movements, though they have nothing to fear. The falcons are gradually making their way down the lane, using the trees and telegraph poles as alternate perches, keeping Linnets on the move, alarming the hedgerow nesters and verge-side feeders, but the only prey items taken are beetles and worms; the juveniles watching and begging from the parents.

Young Magpies spy them and approach to investigate, aggravating the falcons and chattering in staccato phrases. After a while they lose interest and move on to be noisesome elsewhere.

In the picked potato field, untidy with fallen stems, like seaweed washed randomly on the strand, stand a few large gulls: Herring and Great Black-backed, huge amongst the Black-headed Gulls, all head-on to the slight breeze. Beyond them a family of Stock Doves trots and pick at the nearly-bare earth, grey against the brown, keeping away.

Across the canal the fields are thick with butterflies now; the sun well up. A dozen different species flutter over the flower-studded meadows: whites, browns and gaudy Peacocks, Tortoiseshells and Red Admirals. The Small Skippers flicker fast between them, and a Common Blue or two show briefly, before melting away.

Beyond, towards the wood, a Sparrowhawk carries prey towards her nest, still occupied in the pine. Purple Hairstreaks pepper the nearest oak, crawling along the leaves far bigger than themselves, tasting the foliage and searching for mates.

Brown Hawkers and an Emperor Dragonfly patrol the glades, endlessly on the hunt. Above them, through the shrubs and trees come forty Long-tailed Tits – several families already joined up, now the breeding season, for them, has finished – their thin calls spin like spiderwebs filling the wood with silky sound.

Out in the farmland the harvest continues. Most of the wheat has been cut, swathes of stubble stretch, golden pale, like a felled forest, stripped trunks yellow in the sun. Banks of, as yet, untouched stalks stand above the cut: exposed edges naked and pallid.

Rooks waddle and squabble amongst the stalks, picking off insects and other invertebrates uncovered by the shave. Tractor tracks – flattened stalks squashed against the damp earth – hold Yellow Wagtails, which run along these runnels on a similar quest.

A Green Woodpecker's call laughs out from the tree-line and draws the attention back towards the Hobby nest.

Above, two male Hobbies are hunting together.

Though one is obviously an intruder to the territory they appear to be co-operating, and tolerating each other. One, a first-year bird showing paler under-tail coverts, is probably one of last-year's young – now one year old and back in its natal ground.

They have some House Martins in their sights and start to hunt in earnest.

The Martins are circling above the falcons, trying to keep the predators under them, trying to keep the advantage. Both predators and prey rise, the falcons' efforts obvious – long wings in deep and rapid beats, almost meeting tips above and below their bodies, blur-fast – as they spiral upward, tirelessly trying to gain on the prey.

They split up – one turning westwards, the other continuing east with the Martins. The Martins, seeing this, begin to split their group, but quickly come back together. This manoeuvre has slowed their escape and the nearer falcon closes, accelerating under them, corralling the flock to the west, where the other falcon has flown. Still they all rise, now hundreds of feet up, the Martins mere specks, the Hobby shrinking into the distant heights.

Suddenly the second falcon streaks in from just above the prey, and they are caught between the two Hobbies. The flock divides and individuals scatter across the sky. One, the lowest – perhaps the slowest – however, has been picked out, and the upper Hobby dives towards it, forcing it down.

Now both Hobbies are above their intended prey.

In turns, they sweep arcs so rapid, that even from a distance the eye can barely follow, and the Martin uses every ounce of speed and jinks away, its size giving it the advantage in its dodge.

But, this is what the falcons have counted on, practised for, honed their skill to achieve. Their momentum from their greater size and weight, gives them speed advantage, and each hunting curve, each slicing arc, brings them inexorably closer.

They differ each arc and direction of attack, the Martin trying to keep both in sight as it flees, using gravity to speed towards the earth, twisting away from each approach, but the attacks are so quick in succession, and relentless in the hunt that, the exhausted bird makes its one and final error, and is taken from the sky at a speed so fast that a blink would miss it four times over.

After several dazed minutes, the world closes its mouth.

The Hobby, with prey, now glides towards the nest tree, closes its wings for a second, then shaking them loose again, stoops towards its mate. She has got up on his approach and is closing in on him rapidly. As she nears, a few feet below him, she rolls onto her back, the House Martin drops from his talons, is taken by hers in absolutely accurate, soundless co-ordination, and as they pass, she rolls back upright, simultaneously turning his way, and both make for their nest.

The other male, much higher, now flies above the pair, yawing and winnowing his wings, zigzagging in show, right over the nest tree. The pair ignore him and land nearby. Now the male goes to the nest, and his mate eats.

The following day is noticeably hotter. The air barely moves. Dust from the continuing harvesting drifts in a yellow haze, and strips of straw eddy in hot air currents, rising to the tree-tops and beyond.

A Corn Bunting sings. Young Buzzards are on the wing in easy thermals, revolving tightly, keeping to their territories. Along the hedge young Wrens peer and peep from dusty weeds, faint churrings tripping across the corn stalks.

In the meadow twenty Mistle Thrushes move in hops and stops, upright on the pause, then delving to prod the ground.

By the canal convolvulus buds begin to open and a Hummingbird Hawk Moth hovers over them. Bird-like and bird-bright it stills itself, mid-air, as it probes the blooms with its long proboscis.

Brown Hawkers skim over, and, on the raggedy ragworts the Cinnabar Moths are gathering: gaudy and gorgeous, cerise and shiny, they push the hoverflies from the yellow flowers, and are, in turn, moved on by the bees.

In the heat a Green Woodpecker calls again.

Stock Doves are still displaying – gliding on up-swept, stiff wings, down to oak trees where they have their nest holes. Sand Martins swim with the Swallows in the blue heat, wobbling in the haze as if through rippled glass. A Kingfisher, incongruously, flies across the fields, a bright, tight, fast, just-curving line, dagger bill guiding, towards the distant river.

But at the Hobbies' tree there is a cry, which steadily grows.

The female is off her nest, and is calling. She circles the tree and, in figures-of-eight, sweeps around, never moving away. Then, another Hobby – also a female – approaches. As she comes in she calls an unusual 'trrrr, trrr, trrr' and flies at the other falcon.

They meet mid-air and the intruder rolls, presenting her talons towards the other, which keeps up her loud and high-pitched 'keee, keee, keees'. They disappear behind the trees and the commotion dies, neither becoming visible again this day, though the nest owner must have sneaked back to it in typical fashion.

Below, in the fields and hedges, several birds are feeding young, still in the nest. Whitethroats and Song Thrushes – surely now on a third brood – bring in food to hidden cups in hawthorns. Yellow Wagtails still fly from feeding in the stubble to further fields with beak-fulls of grubs, and the House Martins and Swallows carry insects to eaves and barns.

Rooks and Crows, Lapwings and Oystercatchers, Mallards and Moorhens, all have independent young, while the Little Owls' and Kestrels' offspring still demand to be fed, as their own hunting skills improve.

Out on the pylons a Peregrine progresses from one high lookout to the next, powering above the power lines which arc their upside-down arcs across the farmland, fizzing with energy.

The barley is being cut now, and soon all the standing crops will be gone, stubble standing in their place, the dry, hot weather ideal. Combine harvesters, in parallel with the following tractor, spew a steady stream of seed heads into the trailer, as the chaff belches from beneath the gigantic machines. Black-headed gulls and Rooks and Jackdaws follow closely, waiting for exposed invertebrates and small mammals. A Buzzard joins them, broad wings spread above the field, and it pounces now as a Vole dashes for cover. Hares gallop away as the machines approach, searching for new hiding places in the raw wounds of the land.

Along the river, in quieter, shady spots, the afternoon heat has brought out the butterflies and dragonflies. A Dark-green Fritillary, on rapid wings, darts past quickly, its beauty gone too fast. Emerald Damselflies float above the bank's vegetated greenery and Banded Demoiselles flicker in pools of light. Somewhere, across the river, a Grasshopper Warbler sings.

On a wide pool, by a fallen tree, the water stills to almost-stop, and, there, a Tufted Duck with her young are swimming. The mother dives, teaching her chicks, disappearing under the dark surface, emerging upstream a minute later.

Back along the footpath, as the sun begins its dip, fifteen Crossbills come over, calling. The *'jip jip jips'* give them away, and in the dazzle of the bright sky, just one shows the scarlet of his adulthood.

Along the lane a rowan, now laden with bright berries, holds a Mistle Thrush. It has already taken up its guard on this abundant store – and will defend it from all-comers in the weeks to come.

Above, a Hobby and a Sparrowhawk are sparring against a sunset, circling each other and lashing out with long-reaching legs. They rise high, their arcs and swerves keeping each other close. Suddenly the hawk closes its wings and drops towards the earth, accelerating in free-fall until at terminal velocity, a dark blur against the evening sky.

But the falcon, twisting head-down, powers towards it on whipping wings and easily catches it up long before the hawk has reached the tree-tops. Such is the speed of this phenomenal falcon.

They both disappear into the darkening foliage, and the day ends appropriately on the spectacular.

The warm morning starts to heat as soon as the sun shows, stabbing through the copse in orange gobs of molten iron, changing to yellow-white heat as it tops the trees.

There is a commotion from the part-cut barley field, two-thirds done, one third still standing like a fence around the cut stubble. A Fox is jumping, and fifteen Grey Partridges are scurrying around in the bare scar of the cut-edges. Eleven of the partridge are half-grown young – and the Fox runs brief sprints at them, as they run, half-flying on half wings, trying to keep it at arm's length. Pied Wagtails skip above this hunt, watching in curious alarm at the life-and-death contest.

Predator and prey move away, the outcome uncertain, but in the days to come this covey of young gradually shrinks: eleven, to eight, to seven: such is the mortality rate of these birds.

The Little Owl family are out and about along the lane-side perches, the usual consternation of the hedgerow nesters following their leap-frogging movements from tree to pole to fence.

A Little Egret laps by overhead, like a limp owl in the blinding sky. Twenty Yellow Wagtails shine in the pasture, where the cow herd chew on glossy grass. Wall butterflies have hatched and are on the wing, brightening the shrubs by the canal, where a Whitethroat sings a sub-song in the brambles – subdued, mimetic notes barely emerging from the thorns. A juvenile Sedge Warbler, bright in fresh plumage, keeps, mostly, in deep cover, emerging occasionally, carrying a green grub.

Beyond, across the humpback bridge and into the molehill-flecked, flower-filled meadow, small movements insist: first one, then, a second Stoat emerges from the grass. They are chasing and fighting, lightening quickly in attack and riposte, tumbling in a ball, kicking with short legs, separating and sprinting together in a single chestnut undulation towards the ditch before the wood. The black tips of two stubby tails disappear into the nettles and they are gone, as if they were never there.

A Chiffchaff alarms at their passing, her nest low down by the ditch, and she waits, bill-full, until she is certain the Stoats have gone, then dives quickly to cover and delivers her meal, emerging moments later carrying a faecal sack.

A Migrant Hawker is skimming past, below the trees' overhang, head tilted slightly down, its rear just raised beyond the horizontal, its blues and blacks blurring on the turns.

The afternoon wheezes, breathless in the heat.

From the heat-shimmering field, and the forest of cut stalks, a female Kestrel rises with a mouse. She takes it to the corner where the Little Owls nest, then away to the barn's brick gable, where she stashes her catch, caching it away for another day.

But, from the Hobby nest a rising continuum of cries stabs through the heat.

The female is on the nest, but restless: up on the edge where she is just visible, moving in agitation and calling for her mate. For some time she keeps this up, then, patience gone, she flies from the tree and her helpless young.

Now she is calling again, flying a circuit around the nest tree's vicinity, searching the empty skies.

Finally, she lifts higher and rises up amongst the insects. In deft dives and quick swerves, she catches three butterflies – two Large Whites and a Tortoiseshell – eating each on the wing, and then upwards and on to snatch flying ants which are beginning to pepper the hot sky.

Her hunger somewhat satisfied, she returns to the nest, still calling for her mate.

Out to the west there is a wall of black: a huge bank of cloud blotting out the horizon, its top beginning to mushroom as it grows; and approaches.

A first fitful stirring of the air – and the sun goes in, extinguished by the cumulo-nimbus out west, now rearing over the sky, anvil-topped: a gigantic aircraft carrier in dark steel. Now, flying ants are swarming in thousands and thousands, rising with the heat. And with them come the birds.

At first just dozens, perhaps scores of Swifts, begin to circle the ant swarms, looping lazily, taking easy prey. Several Swallows and House Martins join in and keen-eyed Black-headed Gulls fly up to join the feast. Now, Swifts in hundreds and Jackdaws, too, are crowding the air, rising against the darkening sky. The Gulls blink brightly against the bruise, but the Swifts become difficult to discern – black on blackness, no light to light them.

A type of coolness begins to coalesce, and the once-still, heat-stalled air begins to stir, drawn in to the storm cloud, which now covers half the sky. The birds have depleted the ant stocks to unprofitability, and they disperse: a once cohesive flock now scattered to the sky.

A shiver of cool air begins to blow fitfully across the overheated land, like a summer fever, and evening makes an early entrance on an electric stage.

Soon the Swifts are dropping from the blackness, slanting in ahead of the storm, heading away from roiling air and updrafts too strong to battle. Dozens dash past – heading east – still swerving to feed as they flee, long wings scything the ever-faster moving air which tries to suck them back towards the black wave of cloud which is about to crest and crash to earth.

Owls begin to 'kee-wick' and the bats begin to emerge, sensing, perhaps, that their night's hunting might well be foreshortened. The sky is still plentiful as they spiral, taking the last of the flying ants, now returning to lay eggs back on earth.

Suddenly, as night and storm collide, a Hobby is amongst the bats, and, in the near darkness, he out-spirals one and takes it from the gloom.

Lightening cracks and lights the sky, blue-black to silver, and the thunder, when it comes, is quick and deafening. Another bolt crashes down, and a third; then the first, fat, blobs of rain begin to splash the dusty ground.

Before long the once well-spaced drops crowd, become a deluge, and the trees start to rock in the storm. Streams of water cascade down the lane and the rain bounces high from the barn.

Everything has gone to shelter, and on a wind-torn tree-top nest a Hobby hunkers down, protecting her chicks from their first storm.

The thunderstorm has long-since cleared the sky by morning, and a fresher air drifts along the canal. A young Heron ambles along the towpath ahead and Pied Wagtails cross the water with food. At the far bank, covered in umbellifers, a party of juvenile Long-tailed Tits hisses into view. Chiffchaffs and Willow Warbler young flit amongst them, picking at umbels. A Blackcap keeps to the oak shrub behind. Snails, like bent humbugs, cling calmly unstung to nettle stems.

At the lane side a limply-dead Polecat lies, as if still forever taking the corner, watched by a covey of young Grey Partridge under the hedge, wary of this dark-masked predator, even in death. Through the hedge-gap are corn and barley crops, separated by set-aside, bright with poppies and ox-eye daisies, nodding in the warming morning.

Two brief calls of high and unseen House Martins fall like grit from the sky, and, sure as their promise, a Hobby drives the spirit to sprint before it, splits the before and after, and in a thin slice of silence, is gone.

Three young Buzzards sit in the beeches of the copse, mewling for food from absent parents. One, a female, is noticeably bigger than the others.

Barbed wires provide perches for dozens of young Swallows, which launch themselves at parents for aerial feeding. Yellowhammers sit and sing, with its crests cocked. A Song Thrush slots an Oystercatcher into its repercussive repertoire, fooling the ear for just one second.

Beyond the buzzing power lines, a speck circles: Hobby. Spiralling an upward corkscrew, buoyant as a cork, drifting this way. Suddenly it shuts to a dart and drops, arrowhead down and out of sight.

Meadow Browns begin to flit, and a Brown Hawker, warmed by the early sun, begins its patrol along the hedge, towards the Hobbies' nest.

And, at the nest site, nothing. For an hour, nothing moves, nothing shows. Crows come past and leave again. Another hour: perhaps a movement on the nest – perhaps a change of position by the female, shuffling above her chicks.

Cumulus clouds drift and grow as they go, eastwards on an air-conveyor, renewed from the west, unending and relentlessly similar. Their shadows race across the wheat, where blue-backed Swallows skim. Swifts swish, in and out of light, low and fast, like tilting coat-hangers. Just-out-of-the-nest young Song Thrushes, vulnerable and short-tailed, downy antennae blowing softly around their ears, flutter feebly, trying to vault the fence. One pale-bellied Sand Martin swims past them, gliding like a miniscule manta, over the hedge and down to the grass tops beyond.

Gulls and Cormorants, tacking into the breeze, head west. Then, the alarm of Swallows.

Out towards the river's green shady ribbon, a Hobby is heading this way. He comes in just over the willows and oaks, a dark arrow widening. As he swerves behind the nest tree the sitting female sees him, launches herself out with loud caterwauling screams, and together, they circle, as she takes something, something that glistens brightly red, from his outstretched claws.

Two Crows approach at the commotion and move toward their nest, but the male falcon makes for them both, dives at them with ferocious speed and intent, driving them away. So fast is his reaction that both Crows are met, despite their differing paths, and nearly raked by his drawn talons.

As they go, he turns to join his mate. She is hidden somewhere in the adjacent oak, feeding, and preparing the food.

Five minutes later she slips quietly to the nest, and her small movements can just be discerned through the oak-leaf clusters. The male takes off again, turning into the sky, reaching with his long-fingered wings, shoulders pumping, rapid in his ascent. In the far, far distance, he can see Swifts, up against the cumuli tops, and he heads that way.

Two minutes later he is two miles away, and two thousand feet high. He keeps on going, until the distance takes him, simply vanishing him in his shrinking.

The afternoon's clouds continue to drift. The last of the year's young Lapwings still stride the fields – most have moved on now. Young Black-headed Gulls join them and House Sparrows dust bathe. A Southern Hawker approaches, takes a look, and moves on. The Little Owls doze in their tree, moving less than once an hour, otherwise they are as the lichen-covered branches themselves. Occasional Red Admirals flutter into the oak, tasting sticky greenfly secretions, which gloss the leaves.

Suddenly, along the hedge, a series of Blackbird alarms sounds, like a small bouncing bomb. A Fox is trotting by the thorns – a big, bushy-tailed male, bright eyes alert, sniffing the air as he goes. Rabbits, ahead of him, thump the ground and sprint to their foot-worn holes under the shrub trunks, white tails disappearing quickly into the dark. The Fox makes a sudden leap – an arc with all fours under him – and pounces into the flowers. His head goes down and re-appears with a Vole, its brief squeal silenced as the predator bites. The Fox continues his hunt – carrying his prey as he goes, heading for the next field as he darts through the hedge. His progress is occasionally marked by rising birds: Yellow Wagtails and Skylarks from the fields, Tree Sparrows and Linnets from the hedges.

As the sun begins to dip towards the horizon, and blinds of orange-red fill the western sky, two Ravens come in from the east, getting nearer and ever nearer, until they roll in from a darkening dusk, to land together on the very top of the sycamore, immediately adjacent to the Hobby nest tree.

As darkness thickens these two coal-black forms settle for the night, watching the Rooks going to roost, calling their *caws* and disappearing into the ashes of the ended day.

And the next morning they are still there: two young Ravens, backs to the rising sun; the Hobby ignoring them, on her nest. Then a Buzzard flies by.

With screams of protest the male Hobby, out from a nearby tree, flies at the Buzzard, and the Ravens take off in pursuit, quickly gaining on the Buzzard, cronking as they go. The Buzzard continues onwards, with tilting wings as the Hobby drives at him, twisting around his bulky form, until he is at a distance from the nest tree. The Ravens continue to chase, and the three disappear to the west.

But the morning's drama isn't over. Before her mate has returned, the female Hobby is off her nest and is making for a Sparrowhawk which is passing her tree. She flies at the now accelerating hawk, which dives into the copse nearby. She and her mate join in the air above and she returns to the nest, but not before flying at her mate, begging calls ringing clearly in the morning sky, urging him off to hunt. And he does.

As he accelerates away northwards, rising as he disappears, calm falls from the clear sky. Lesser life continues around the tree.

For an hour, as the heat builds and butterflies begin to fill the meadows; white and brown flickering forms as far as the eye can see – the world is quiet. Only a small "tick" from a Robin on the hedge, and the sometimes call of a Crow, the only sounds. Swallows and Swifts are in the sky, and, up high, a Kestrel hovers, and Buzzards circle. Hawker dragonflies are patrolling now: Migrant Hawkers and Emperors, above the hedges, along the canal's linear line, passing silently.

Then, the alarm from a Chiffchaff: 'whooeet', loud and clear; swallows suddenly diving out of the sky at full speed, and the Hobby gets off her nest. She arcs around the tree, making for the south, where, still at some distance, her mate is sailing in, leisurely gliding, holding something under him.

As he approaches, he bends to pluck at his prey, wings straight out, tail spreading and closing, legs coming forward under him. He is still quite high, but the glide brings him lower. His mate, her calls piercing the quiet of the morning, races to him, as he continues to eat on the wing. She closes in on him, but at the last, he twists away and dives, making for a copse. She follows as they disappear into the trees, her cries still peeling through the branches.

After a few minutes she has the food, and now makes directly for her nest and the waiting young.

He has taken off too, and rises insect-catching as he goes, making do with smaller morsels to satisfy his hunger. Soon he is up amongst the Swifts and Martins, which rise with him, bunching in defence, and they drift away until all have gone.

At the nest her movements can just be discerned: her head pulling at the prey and bending to dish out tiny morsels to invisible offspring. This continues for ten minutes more, then she settles down and only the nest's bulk can be seen.

By the river Ringlets are mating, restless in their searches in the shade and sunspots of bankside trees, flapping low amongst the grasses and flowers, searching for mates, investigating other butterflies – Meadow Browns, Gatekeepers and Tortoiseshells rising to chase them off in tiny spiralling flights, before re-settling to sunbathe. A Brimstone flutters by: ghostly pale and lovely, out across the nettles and the canopy of gunneras, now head-high huge, as a Kingfisher calls nearby.

The water flows slow and low, green cream sliding by its banks, in summer's low ebb. Banded Demoiselles above, dance and skip, seeking sunlight to show off their blue-bruised beauty, abdomens shining. A white tail of a Moorhen slips from the stage of the water's surface, and into the curtain of water weeds – which close around it, swishing back and forth under their own momentum.

Sedge Warblers slide on upright stems and delve into their creases, catching emergent insects, only just climbing into to their new world. Somewhere below, hidden in the lushness of the thick vegetation, a Vole is chewing a stem, tiny crunches spitting out into the church-quiet calm of the river. The sudden peeling of a Nuthatch, ringing out from an oak's top, breaks the reverie as a dark form arrows overhead.

It is a Peregrine. Wood Pigeons, until now quietly feeding on summer buds, clatter from the willows, wings smacking against the branches as they try to make their escape, swerving in uncoordinated panic as the falcon, ignoring them all, continues down river.

The peace is splintered, and alarms ring in a chain at the Peregrine's progress, Jackdaws rising in noisy protests, Crows cawing and Blackbirds, diving for cover. The world spins and is emptied. Only insects continue, unaffected by the passing predator. In the ensuing calm, a Tawny Owl hoots in the middle of the day.

Along the footpath a Green Woodpecker, feeding on the ground, gets up and, calling its laughing yaffle, lands upright on an oak, its red crest contrasting its oak-green back, as it turns its chisel-headed face to watch the ground, strong toes digging into the rutted bark. Then, turning its body downward, it takes off and flies away in audible undulations, yellow rump glowing in the sunshine, long-fingered wings in whirrs and pauses taking it away into the shade.

The remaining crops are being harvested: combine and accompanying tractor march across the stubble, scything the standing crops as dust spews into the air, two red giants almost incongruous in their own landscape. A few gulls follow, but late July's pickings are few.

At the barn, the Swallows sit, dozing on fences and eaves, preening between short sleeps, occasionally alert for danger. Sparrows dust-bathe. Pied Wagtails strut and fly at flies on the straw-strewn cobbles of the yard, desiccating cow-pats dulling as they dry.

And, out at the Hobby site, the male falcon is perching in full sunshine, belly feathers fluffed out in the warm air, swivelling his head, resting but ever on the hunt. Swallows pass under him, seemingly unaware. Blackbirds hop under the hedge.

Suddenly, spying a movement, he drops from his tree-top and, instantly at speed, he is along the hedge, turning a tight circle, and then makes a sudden jink, punching out a long leg, and makes a stab at something trying to escape from the thorn.

He has caught a young Blue Tit, and, as he rises back to the sycamore, it lies limp in his talons. He lands and reaches down, quickly eating, tearing at the small bird. After just a few small mouthfuls he is off to the nest tree, needling into the branches, delivering the remains of his catch to his mate, who – presumably dozing – has been unaware of his successful catch.

As she begins to feed he slips away and is off into his sky to start another hunt.

Now three, then four, Magpies are in the nest tree. They have seen the Hobbies' nest and, tails jerking in alarm or excitement, they chatter and goad each other to approach. Gradually they close around the sitting falcon, swapping perches and getting bolder.

Then she is up from the nest, and the Magpies scatter, she goes for one, but the others stay close to her nest. She swings back quickly, diving at a second and a third, driving them away from her brood, and the first makes a return, as two fly to the next tree. The falcon spins on her axis and accelerates at the Magpie closest to her nest, and forces it away to the next tree. All four are in the sycamore adjacent to the nest tree, but they begin to hop towards it along the canopy. The Hobby goes back towards her nest, but two Magpies follow, flying across the short gap.

The falcon turns, and, as she starts to pass the lead Magpie, she suddenly rolls underneath it. The birds pass – Magpie and Hobby inches apart – but as they separate it is clear that the falcon has dealt a death blow.

The Hobby continues, turning back to her nest, and, as she does so, the Magpie begins to fall, already dead, to the ground, arcing a neat parabola as if in surprise at the swiftness of its death, never flapping again as it plummets earthward.

As she passed, the falcon had raked a talon along the Magpie's belly, with enough accuracy and force, to kill her tormentor instantly.

With one of them dead, the other Magpies hurry from the scene, the Hobby simply settling back to her nest.

The afternoon continues, quietly, as if in shock. The summer sun bends its way westward and shadows begin to creep across the fields, joining woods to woods, hedge to hedge; a dark rug pulled silently eastward until only pools of sunlight splash against the barns and hedgerow trees, gradually colouring as the sun sinks. The arch of the canal's bridge begins to darken now, the warm bricks still radiating heat back into the evening, as the first of the Pipistrelles twists silently out from the cottage's eaves, flickering darkly as it starts to feed.

The morning brings with it a grey wash that seems to have been brushed across the entire world by a careless hand. Cooler air sinks from the sky. The horizon is undefined, dark on dark: a wall of gloomy slate. A breeze stirs the water of the canal, grey-green and dulled after days of dazzle. Neither a butterfly, nor a dragonfly can be seen.

Out in the paddock, the horses stand, slowly chewing at hay from rope nets by the wall. No Wagtails flicker under their hooves, no insects rise from their moving. Crows sit in the lane-side trees, watching nothing passing below, and even the hedges seem empty. The Little Owls are hidden, and the Swallows line the wires, bunched side-by-side, conserving energy in the fly-less day.

Slowly at first, then more quickly, the rain starts to drizzle from the grey. Dusty lanes glisten, wooden posts darken. Leaves begin to drip. The morning continues wet, but the sky starts to break, coagulating from a continuum to differentiated greys, and eventually brightness shows.

As midday passes, clouds begin to show edges, those edges then separate, until, at last, the sky takes on colour and mercury turns to silver, silver to blue.

As if on cue, as if waiting for this beginning, a Hobby is up high, and he is hunting.

A few score of Swifts circle and rise; they are already high and, for good reason, are gaining more height as fast as they can. The Hobby is under them, but not far off, as he powers up and up, trying to get above them for his advantage. He makes a sudden extra spurt of speed, even though it appears he can go no faster, and the Swifts split into three groups as he nears.

Now, he turns to reach for one of the bunches, and they swerve away, still out of his reach, the others fleeing in the other direction, now safe.

A dozen now in his sights, this little falcon squeezes yet more effort, wings flexing with the strain of his power, twisting this way and that, trying to confuse, as he picks out an individual which has lagged behind the others by just a foot or two. But still his prey eludes him, still rising: flying for its life. Predator and prey close and part, close and part, as the hunt continues, now just the two of them streaking across the towering clouds.

Tiring now, the Swift turns earthwards as the Hobby closes in again, and now the falcon is above him. The Swift makes some distance, but the falcon has allowed him this, his strategy based on experience and practice. He follows in parallel, keeping his victim under him, allowing a gap between them, a gap judged for his next move.

Now, he dives: an arc takes him from horizontal to vertical as he goes for the Swift. His prey heads downward, trying to keep him at distance, but the gap shrinks as the falcon accelerates. Now both are head down and earth-bound, the Hobby gaining.

The Swift begins to twist as he drops, flying at his fastest and jinking as it goes. But the falcon follows at even greater speeds, as both halve the distance between heaven and earth. As the two almost touch, the Swift suddenly swerves upwards – and the falcon, heavier and with more momentum, though he follows, cannot keep it in touch.

Though his arc is wider, and they separate, his speed is greater, and, now he too is heading upwards, and he closes quickly on the Swift. Sensing his approach, the prey once more turns to the earth, rushing up towards them, the Hobby again gaining and still accelerating, as they drive towards the near horizon: tree tops now in sight. But the Swift cannot land, there is no refuge there. So, it begins a desperate loop back heavenward.

The Hobby, close on his tail, follows. And now an incredible phenomenon unfolds.

The Swift, rising, still in its turn, is flying at its hardest, wings blurring as it arcs upward. But the following falcon, at his full speed, now starts his arc – but he is no longer flapping his long wings. The Hobby, with greater heft, now tightens his arc progressively, judging time and distance to perfection, he too is rising – and accelerating. Without another wingbeat, the centrifugal force of his parabola accelerates his speed still further, and, in an instant, he is upon his slowing prey, and springs out his long reach to take the Swift from the air.

And so ends this matchless hunt, unequalled in nature, this incredible falcon, honed in the wind, has achieved the incredible. Tomorrow he might well do the same.

The hunt has brought him near to his nest, and now he simply turns and flies towards his tree, the Swift tucked under him, almost out of sight – but his mate has seen it.

She is off the nest and flies to meet him, calling to him as she goes. She flies lower than he, and, as they near, he drops the Swift, which tumbles towards her. She reaches out and takes it from the air, as her mate passes over. They both now make for the sycamore where she lands to deal with the Swift.

Unaffected by his recent chasing, the male Hobby turns once more for the vast expanse of the sky, to start again.

Down on earth the land warms, puddles shrinking in the lanes and barnyards, wisps of water vapour rising back up to the sky.

The canal reflects the billowing cumulus and shines again, and Common Blue Damselflies lift off from a patch of water lily leaves, making tiny flights out into the meadow, where the flowers spread their petals to the sun: whites and yellows and tiny specks of blue, the glint of water catching the light in miniscule rainbows from a thousand remaining raindrops. Big black slugs, shiny-wet, slide back slowly to cover from the drying sun.

Spider webs shine in thousands across the meadow, each aligned roughly to the small and intermittent breeze, lifting into the air and taking their makers with them, sailing on long threads away to new homes downwind. Butterflies skitter from flower to flower, from food plant to food plant, laying eggs on the underside of leaves, abdomens heaving and angled wings opening and closing, low down where ants scurry and beetles crawl.

Above, hovering and darting, Common Darters zigzag over the meadow, resting on the tallest plants, pointing their red abdomens at the sun, transparent and veiny wings stretched and glistening, legs angled forward under their big-eyed heads, sometimes chewing some tiny fly.

The House Martins are up high. Many young have tripled, quadrupled their numbers, and a loose shoal swims by, picking plankton from the sky. The Swifts have returned, and angle by like boomerangs arcing, hunting the spaces between towering clouds.

A crowd of Rooks strut in the stubble, delving into softened earth for beetles, pecking at spilt seeds.

But, in the paddock a strange scene.

A Sparrowhawk sits, an adult male, powder blue back and orange breast, wild yellow eye staring. Opposite, just a horse's length away, a Magpie stands, staring back at him. Now the Magpie takes off and flies over the Hawk's back, only a foot above him, and, as it does, the Hawk swivels to face the Magpie, which has landed on the opposite side.

Then, again the Magpie flies over the Sparrowhawk, again the Hawk turns to keep his head facing his tormentor, as the Magpie lands where it had started from before. This manoeuvre is repeated, and twice more. Each time, the Magpie and Hawk are the same distances apart and still facing each other.

Now, a Stock Dove, seeing this strange behaviour, flies down, and in its curiosity, sits in the paddock, and now the three of them form a triangle.

The Magpie repeats its leapfrog move, positions changed again. But, now the Sparrowhawk has had enough of the Magpies' attention, and turns his attention to the Dove. For a moment the Hawk and Dove watch each other, the latter in some state of trance, not understanding the danger.

Without warning the Hawk flies straight at the mesmerised Dove, which, at the last moment, realises the mortal threat, and takes flight. The Dove has only made a short distance, barely leaving the ground, as the Sparrowhawk reaches it, grabs its back and forces it back to the ground. But the prey is as big as he is, and he doesn't have a real hold, tumbling from the Dove as it tries to rise again.

This time the Stock Dove makes better ground, but the predator's greater acceleration closes the distance quickly, and the Sparrowhawk, swerving sideways, grabs the Dove from below, finding a softer target, and his claws sink and bind.

Both fall back to the paddock's bare earth, the Dove flapping one wing, trying to fly. But the Hawk has it now and climbs on his prey, wings out to steady. Holding it down, his wings a canopy, mantling his prey, he begins to pluck.

Soft grey feathers float from the Stock Dove as the hawk plucks it, baring a patch of flesh on the Dove's back, then he starts to eat. For half an hour the Sparrowhawk feeds. The Dove's movements become weaker and less frequent. In that time the entire back of the Dove is stripped down to bone, as the Hawk fills his now-bulging crop.

From time to time he rests, looking around himself for danger, out there in the open, then continues to feed, noticeably bulkier now as feathers surround the scene. Wet blood glistens.

Eventually sated, the Sparrowhawk finally takes off, rising heavily away. The half-eaten Dove, after all this time, gives a deep, sigh-like pant. It is still alive.

As if in some silent reverence, the sun disappears behind a small black cloud, and, for a moment, a small shadow hangs over the scene.

Dawn: a thin pewter mist hangs between the dew-wetted grass and the browse-line, separating the fields from the trees. Below, as if in reflection, tiny silvery spent spiders' filaments lie along the meadow, damped and grounded after their flight.

Before the sun reaches the brightening horizon, all the land is grey. Grey-green grasses and grey-green leaves, merely pencil-sketched, waiting for their colour-washes.

A hunched Heron, wings a thick blue-grey dressing gown, keeps warm by the pond, waiting for sunrise. It seems to slumber, statuesque, but suddenly uncoils its snake-like neck and stabs at the water by its long yellow toes. As it brings the spear of its bill back up, a Frog, its rear webbed foot scrabbling at the Heron's right eye, is brought from the water. Blinking, the Heron jerks its head and the Frog disappears down its throat, a small bulge ripples down the Heron's neck as it goes.

The Heron goes back to its deceptive doze, from stretch to hunch, white thighs disappearing under its wings once more.

Out on the water, the Great-crested Grebe family stir the surface, as the first of the sun's rays catch their chestnut head feathers, crowning them with light.

A Common Sandpiper skims across the pond, curving to a muddy shore, calls whistling shrilly in the still cool of the morning, wings bowed and flickering as they almost touch the surface. Two Sand Martins dip into the water, bathing on the wing, and continue out to the south, perhaps already heading back towards Africa.

Water lily flowers, night-shut, now start to open, pale and lovely in the early low light. Below, a large Pike disturbs their stems, sliding stealthily into their shadows, then stills, now in ambush. Small ripples bob the Pond Skaters, keeping tiny territories on the surface, toes denting the tension in tiny dimples. A Carp rises and gulps the air, then turns its mirror-faceted sides back to the deep.

Reed Buntings begin to call, late to rise from night-roosts, climbing water-side stems, handsome black-and-white heads in the sun.

Across on the other bank, a Kingfisher is under the willow's over-hang, red belly glowing, reflected in the pond. Even now it dives the small distance into the water, re-emerging in a half-second, a tiny Minnow showing silver against the dark of its bill. With a rapid and deft flick, the Kingfisher turns the fish head-down and swallows. With two bobs of its big head it settles again to watch. A small drop drips from its red legs, back to the pond. A Moorhen swims underneath it, reaches the reeds, and pushes into the green.

Overhead, a Cormorant circles the pond, head dipping in search, huge, pterodactyl-like and incongruous. After two circuits it decides against landing and makes off over the trees, white thigh patch a landing light against its black.

Along the canal now the sun's reflection follows its course, blinking in and out of shadows, blinding as it re-emerges, low against the land. In the shadow of the bridge a young Grey Wagtail bobs its tail, confectioner's custard-coloured belly pale below the grey of its back.

Swallows drink on the wing, angling to the water, slowing as they touch just the lower mandible to the surface for a second, then rise, the gems of sapphire-blue backs into the sun. A Rat scurries along the towpath and dashes down a chink between the bricks.

Perch rise stealthily, filling the canal with ripples, never breaching the surface, shadows in the murk. A Heron stands sentinel on a narrowboat, feet on the tiller, watching.

On the paddock the corpse of the Stock Dove has gone, scavenged overnight. Only a few pearly feathers stir in the almost-still air. The Little

Owl, seemingly half-asleep, squints into the sun, balled up on its oak branch, warming itself.

Out at the Hobbies' nest tree nothing stirs. No movement can be seen. A Chaffinch sings from the sycamore, perky and loud. A Song Thrush, under the hedge, stretches upright, listening, tilts its head, jerks to horizontal, takes a small step, then stabs at the earth. Some small invertebrate is despatched, and the Song Thrush moves on. A Blackbird emerges from the shadow and chases the Thrush off, which flies to the hedge-top and down to the next field.

By the copse beyond, two Grey Partridge sit in shallow dust hollow, loose feathers fluffed, like two deflated footballs abandoned and faded.

Yellowhammers flicker into the cover of the hedge, white-edged tails poking from the leaves. Overhead, a family of Bullfinches, soft piping calls falling from them, head to the river, plump and plummy: a bowl of bright fruit.

A Green Woodpecker yaffles in the distance, Rooks call alarms. A Peregrine, in from the north, glides to the pylon and lands on the side-spar. It perches there for some time, head moving as it watches for prey, then takes off, powering away towards the sun. As it goes Wood Pigeons rise in a wave of clattering flocks, from fields and trees, in panic and terror. But the falcon continues, speeding now as it melts into the sun.

Almost unnoticed, the butterflies have filled the fields. Suddenly it is warm. Wasps chew the fence posts by the lane, removing tiny strips of wood audibly, moving slowly as they munch. After a few minutes they each fly to their nests, the fence depleted in tiny increments, showing the pale scars of the Wasps' activity.

Under the nettles a bulky Red-tailed Bumblebee returns to her hole, manoeuvring like a loaded helicopter, trying for precision but making misses before finally landing by the entrance, and crawling in to the darkness.

Basking Greenbottles shine, glinting like dark emeralds in the dust. Hoverflies stand in the air, then dart at rivals encroaching on their airspace. A Lesser Whitethroat calls from the hedge, where green budding blackberry fruits cluster tightly on prickly stems, arching through the thorns.

Then, two Swallows' alarms, Hobby-specific, high up in the clear sky.

Out from the glare of the noon-day sun, several House Martins appear, rapidly heading north. From the paddock a rising, panicking swirl of Wagtails, as House Sparrows head for cover. Seconds tick away like minutes. Then, a dark form materialises and in comes the Hobby, driving down from high, sprinting at the Martins.

They have fifty yards or more on him, streaming away, silent and hotfoot. Then, the female falcon, having slipped unnoticed from her nest, and having risen above the prey in anticipation, makes an arcing fall at them, completely catching them unawares as they run from the male.

She just misses one as she dives – the Martin swerving in desperation at the last moment, inches from her passing, and now she arcs upwards, whipping her wings to even greater velocity. Her mate, has continued on his direct flight, and now the Martin, having made its detour, is slower and nearer. Though the falcon is blurrily fast, he now puts on an incredible extra burst, and is upon the Martin in a flash. But again, at the last, it jinks away, just as he reaches out with both feet.

From out of the sky, now, the female Hobby, having turned, dives upon the hapless bird and she takes it from the air in a rapid loop that defies the eye.

The chase has brought her directly over the nest tree, and now she sails past it and lands in the adjacent sycamore, spiralling into its crown, prey under her. Her mate circles a victory display over her, flickering his wings in a shallow whir, then turns eastwards to start hunting again.

The cleared sky begins to fill again: wary Swallows rising toward cloud-high Swifts, sweeping back from the horizons. Calm falls from the battered air.

For endless minutes the falcon remains in the sycamore, then she slips quietly back to her nest, landing on its edge just visible in the leaf-gap. Now, for the first time, two small, white-downed heads rise from the nest to beg from her. Tenderly she begins to tear tiny morsels for her chicks, dishing out the flesh, bone and feathers to each in turn, and perhaps, to another, hidden in the cup of her nest.

This meal goes on for half an hour or so, until she takes the scraggy remnants away to finish them for herself. After a quick wing-stretch and preen, she launches into the blue, lifting easily on small thermals, flexing her wings to catch the updrafts, allowing herself to drift, then commences to fly-catch. Far above her, unconcerned Swifts scythe the skies on a similar mission.

This afternoon her catch-rate is roughly an insect or two per minute. Almost all she takes with outstretched talons, following a quick dart, dive or upward drive to take her to the prey. Occasionally she makes a long deliberate hunt at a particularly worthy morsel, sometimes spying the tiny dot from considerable distance: maybe a small dragonfly or flying ant. Rarely, and always in a direct line, she takes the prey directly into her open mouth, Swift-like, perhaps just the slower, smaller and more easily caught insects.

Though she is far off – in height as well as distance – she always has her nest in sight. Though a mile or more away she can return in well under a minute. In the afternoon's heat the sky is white rather than blue, and a dazzling haze obscures her form as she rises.

Two Magpies approach her nest. Always curious and opportunistic, they examine it and its contents. But, perhaps instinctively knowing that her young are large enough and feisty enough, she does not return to drive them off. Instead, after a long time up hunting, she suddenly re-appears, visible again in her proximity, and glides slowly back to her nest.

Below, in the brambles, a Red Admiral and a Painted Lady fight in the afternoon heat, leaving a Comma to bask in peace. Wasps, in search of aphids, and meatier meals, scurry over leaf and stem, always on the move.

The woods are quiet, late summer has halted the birdsong, heat and easy living has quietened even the young animals, the season leans back against the hill of plenty and, for once, it rests. Migrants are already on the move, their season done.

But, for the Hobbies, now the most frenetic and demanding time is upon them.

Overnight rain had dampened the world, and now the sky shows the threat of more. To the west a wall of rain in a slate sheet is falling, and the dark clouds tower. Intermittent rainbows arch between the rainclouds, growing and shrinking, brightening and fading, as the sky blows in.

In the stubble fields a crowd of Great Black-backed Gulls: post-breeding birds on their journey to wintering grounds. A few Herring Gulls sit among them, grey backs amongst the black. The Black-headed Gulls crouch with them, and all face the incoming weather out west.

Yellow Wagtails are still feeding chicks and, on the canal, the Moorhen has yet more chicks. They bob about on an undulating surface, too buoyant, scurrying to the parent bird whenever food is proffered, otherwise picking morsels for themselves.

In the hedge the Whitethroat too is still at her nest – the tiny cup hidden low and deep, with four almost-grown young.

The bluster is keeping the insects hidden, and even now a shower of rain falls from a closing sky. The temperature drops correspondingly as the short deluge descends. Swifts fly in front of the rain, low, brown against the charcoal sky. Young Swifts are with the adults now, in fresh and just-paler plumage, only visible in their close proximity.

The Swallows skim the fields, swimming across the surface of the land, ankle-high, black-eye blue in the darkened day, tilting at insects only just airborne.

The Yellow Dung Flies are back on the softened cow-pats, mating and laying, dabbing at the rain-moistened surfaces. In the paddock a Little Owl whirs above the wetted dust, catching worms as it pounces. The horses huddle, hinds to the rain, manes ragged and dripping.

In the shelter of their oak, two young Little Owls wait impatiently for returning parents. From time to time they hiss a begging call shrilly, out towards the paddock. All around them leaves drip, but now the weather breaks: the shower heads off eastward and the sun shoulders in between the crowding clouds.

Suddenly, from the Hobby site, screaming cries ring out.

The female falcon is off her nest and, with loud 'kee-kee-kees' is attacking a Buzzard which has approached far too close for her tolerance. The Buzzard is already lumbering heavily away as she twists around, talons out and making contact, forcing the Buzzard to roll and present its own claws to her, but she is lightening quick, and each time she is away and back upon the Buzzard before it turns upright again. With an audible smack, her primaries hit the Buzzard's as she passes, still screaming at the retreating bird.

After a few hundred yards the Buzzard dives for the trees by the river, and she, satisfied at the distance she has driven it to, turns back to her nest. When she arrives, the male is in the sycamore, newly arrived, and now, her spirit still high, she screams at him as she nears. He has a large prey item, partially dismembered, soggy brown and bright with blood. He has already eaten, and now, as she lands by his side, he allows her to take it from him, and she goes to the next tree to deal with it, disappearing beneath the canopy.

He sits in the brief sunshine, cleaning his claws, bringing each yellow foot to his bill and picking small feathers glued to him with gore. This done he sets to preening, reaching down to his damp breast feathers and teasing the filaments. Next, he reaches round to his tail, which he swivels sideways towards his head, and zips the tatty edges back to streamlined neat ness with deft pulls.

For several minutes he sits, newly primped, plumped up again, dazzlingly handsome in the sunshine, turning his black-moustachioed head to each horizon, large dark eyes searching, always searching.

She has slipped unseen back to the nest. The young have been fed. Now she flies out to join her mate on his tree top. She sits by him and begins a low keening call, her bill closed as the sound escapes. He sits, seemingly insouciant, but he understands.

Now she takes to the air, still calling, circles above him, beseeching. She turns to the north and away, and he flies up and follows. As the sun is covered once again, they ascend towards the giants of the clouds, twinkling in and out of light, until the dark sky swallows them.

On the nest a single white reptilian head peers out over the rim, watching them go.

Back at the paddock a Kestrel is driving Crows away from two young. The juvenile Kestrels are sitting on the horse-thinned wood of the fences, watching the wet ground for easy catches: beetles and worms. The Crows, more curious than threatening, don't want to go, and the adult Kestrel tries to drive them away, her cries much like the Hobbies' – but half an octave lower in pitch.

Above, on the wires, Swallows are gathered – pegs on a clothes line – and among them, a few smaller Sand Martins dot the line – full stops between the commas. As the showers come and go, groups take off to feed, returning to the wires, their numbers rising and falling the whole time. Many are young birds; buffy throats of the shorter-tailed Swallow young, and diffuse sandy throats and breasts of the Sand Martins show amongst the adult plumages.

Now they all scatter as the Kestrel lands on the nearest pole, but they don't fly in panic: she is no real threat to them. Before long they begin to accumulate on the wires again. Below them, Linnets are searching, balancing on flower heads now turned to seed, and dropping to the verge to pick the already-fallen fruits of the flowers. They are seemingly unaware of the Kestrel only yards away, but now, as the falcon takes off, they rise as one, bunching in a twittering flock, and skip away, down the lane to safer verges.

At the corner, under the hedge, a Rabbit and a Grey Partridge share a dry patch, sheltering from showers. Neither move– both are hunched, dozing. Bumblebees buzz past them. A Dunnock emerges from the hawthorn's skirts and drops to pick around them, restlessly flicking and hopping as they remain, their breathing their only movements.

Overhead a chevron of seven Cormorants, heading east along the canal's course, tilt, stiff-winged, as a gust of wind slaps them. The Great Black-backed Gulls are still present – sitting in the picked potato field, huge and dark. One or two stand, heads hunched, murderous and bulky beaks towards the weather. In the field's corner, almost overlooked, a rare visitor has just moved to betray its presence, now stock-still again. It is a Ringed Plover, attracted by the puddly soil, on its way elsewhere – between breeding and wintering grounds. Well camouflaged, despite its brightly pied head, when it stands still it disappears. Now it moves again, and suddenly there are two others visible. They all make quick darting strides at the puddle's edge, picking daintily at flies.

These temporary visitors show the season on the turn: full tide summer beginning to ebb, leaving its bounty on the beach.

For another two hours, it seems, the Hobbies remain away, hunting the shower-laden wetness of the sky. If she is still away, this is the first lengthy foray for the female, and might signal a shift in her behaviour. From now on she will increasingly leave the nest and help her mate in the hunt.

But, at the nest, her back is visible: she is standing on the rim. Once more her arrival has gone unnoticed. Perhaps, he too is close, or he is still amongst the heights: in either case, invisible.

Now, amongst the dark clouds, a dark speck, growing quickly. Between the speck and the field a Kestrel is hovering, unmoving head to the wind as it keeps station, steadily beating his wings, body angled, black-banded grey tail half-spread.

The speck has become a Peregrine, and it has the Kestrel in its sights.

At forty-five degrees the Peregrine, at over a hundred miles an hour is just seconds from the still-stationary Kestrel. The gap closes rapidly, and only now the Kestrel sees its attacker, and breaks from hover to plummet towards the earth, trying vainly to keep the distance. Another second and the Peregrine, wings almost closed as it stoops, is at striking distance, when the Kestrel makes a last-moment jink to the left, turning upward as it does so, and the Peregrine, tilting to face it, lashes out a single foot, but the Kestrel escapes unharmed.

But the larger falcon hasn't given up, and now loops upward, its speed rocketing it towards to fleeing Kestrel, closing in again.

Even with the height advantage, the Kestrel cannot out-fly the Peregrine, which is making ground quickly, lashing long wings as it rises. The gap becomes almost nothing again and the Peregrine seems certain to make the kill, but again the Kestrel's last moment flick, its advantage only in its lesser momentum, takes it away to the Peregrine's side, just as both sets of talons are deployed.

The Kestrel now turns again and dives towards the ground, as the Peregrine turns a greater arc, trying to follow, the advantage lost. But its greater weight and strength accelerate it towards its intended prey again. It stoops a shallow stoop at the Kestrel, but is no longer at full speed, and the Kestrel, this time, evades capture more easily, rising with all the speed it has, making off as the Peregrine gives up the hunt and flies away, picking up speed again, across the river and into the dark horizon.

Simultaneous to this spectacle, all the birds in the vicinity have risen, including all the gulls. Clouds of corvids dot the sky, wheeling against the clouds: black dots on purple-greys, and Wood Pigeons flee in every direction. The Ringed Plovers have gone, towering up rapidly, along with a few Lapwings. Even a small flock of duck have risen from the river, and now begin to turn, flashing against the sky.

For many minutes the panic continues, then calm starts to fall, bringing the birds back from the heavens. The gulls drift back to the potato field, angled wings allowing descent, and the Rooks and Jackdaws helter-skelter back to the woods, the Jackdaws calling as they come.

The Swallows and Sand Martins begin to land on the wires once more, twittering and flicking wings before they really settle, fear draining from them after some time.

A rumble of thunder rolls across the meadow as a new shower falls, and, at that moment a Mole, out from its underground home, scurries quickly across the meadow, over the little rise, and into the copse. A Hare, in shock or astonishment, leaps around to watch it go, on four spring-stiff legs, ears up and wild eyes staring.

The rain closes in again, and somewhere out west the quenched sun starts to set. As evening begins, and thunder drums again, the sky slowly takes on a burnt orange hue, with the perhaps promise of a brighter day to come.

As a short stab of lightning sparks out west a Tawny Owl glides silently, obliquely across the lane, broad-headed and bowed wings; a dark, short-tailed shadow into the darker night.

Dawn: the aftermath of a rainy night, the lanes and paths shine wetly, leaf-drip intermittent from the trees, and a late Hedgehog meanders, little legs scurrying quickly by the verge, wet nose quivering on the pauses, then through a tiny trodden track under hedge – back to bed.

A Migrant Hawker is already up, patrolling the hedgerow at head height, tilted forward, searching for the early flies, and Honey Bees, too, are on the verge-side flowers, cramming the most from the summer's day, bright yellow pollen sacks already filling.

The Little Owls are along the lane-side perches – two adults and two young – wings whirring as they pass from post to post, tree to tree, as Pied Wagtails descend to the wetted paddocks, calling their "chissicks" as they drop in on bounding lines, from their communal roost.

The sun breaks the horizon: a dark yellow yolk split and spilt, pouring out along the meadows, running its yellow-orange richness across the world.

Linnets arrive, spiralling down to the field-edges and hedges, bell-like notes brightening the brightening day. The gulls have gone – all except one – which stands alone mid-field. Stock Doves strut by, pecking at the bare earth, as a dozen Grey Partridge rise to skim the undulating ground, away to the far hedge, running as they land, looking over shoulders, then slowing to a walk.

A Yellow Wagtail calls at the sun, reflective glory shining. And now the Swallows are up to join the House Martins already out on their forays, still feeding young at the farm house. And finally, the House Sparrows, always late to rise, begin to chirp brightly – their easy day begun.

Suddenly in the stubble, a commotion.

A Kestrel from his pole top perch, which had been watching a small group of feeding Starlings below, has made a sudden dive and, before they all had chance to rise, has pinned one to the ground. The other Starlings, in a tight flock, wheel away, calling alarms too-lately given, as the victim struggles under the Kestrel's yellow feet.

The falcon stares around him for a few seconds, checking for danger, then drops his head to the Starling's neck and, with a single snip, silences his prey forever. He takes it back to his pole top and sits, as if in contemplation, the Starling lying limply under his feet. Two Magpies approach, ever opportunistic, but the Kestrel flies off with his prize, leaving them to other mischiefs.

Two Voles, hidden in the verge, are fighting: their high-pitched tiny screams needling out through the hedge. A Willow Warbler pauses, then continues to move along the thorny foliage, grabbing insects from under leaves, occasionally flying out in a stabbing arc, to snatch a passing fly. Young Blue Tits are following, and this little yellow flock slips in and out of dappled gaps as they pass along the hedge. A bigger Blackcap pokes its head from the leaves, briefly, then disappears again.

Above the meadow the Magpies have found a Buzzard, which departs as they fly at its tail, tormenting the bigger bird which calls in annoyance, looking over its shoulder at as it goes to ground in an oak.

The meadow is a sea of clover heads now: small white clusters of flowers reaching above the rain-flattened grasses. Bumbles and Honey Bees, hoverflies and butterflies wander this nectar forest and plunder.

Three Hares lie amongst the sward, almost invisible if not for the antennae of their ears poking, pied amongst the greenery.

And so, the path leads inexorably on, always to the Hobby nest.

The female is visible – and she is moving around the nest, on its edge, and two small white heads are below her, showing from time to time in tantalising glimpses through the oak leaves. Bluebottles dance around them and occasionally one makes a snap at the attendant insects.

The female, her dark shadow flickering through the oak, flies from the nest, but disappears behind the tree. For half an hour she is gone, but then returns to land in the sycamore, watching the western sky, bright cirrus scraping the blue.

Another hour of patient waiting, she upright in the shadow of the sycamore's canopy, before her mate makes his return. As Swallows scatter in alarm she is off, on an oblique and inclined line to the south west.

She flies steadily, until more than half a mile distant, when the male finally becomes a speck. He is still a mile away, but she had seen him at twice that – and that he was carrying something. For a few more seconds they close until they meet, some hundreds of feet up, and she arcs at him, he reluctant in the handover. For a while, as both approach, he still has some prey, and swerves and speeds away from her beseeching flight. Now she is insistent, her loud calls ringing clearly across the meadow, and with a last twist from her, he rises and hangs his legs, prey below him now, and she rises with him to take it as he drops it at last. A dark shape passes between them, and now she makes straight for the sycamore, gliding in on a shallow slant, and disappears within.

The male Hobby flies over his nest tree, and continues out above it, heading north east now, suddenly dropping below the trees and out of sight.

She is quickly back to the nest, and, standing on the rim, begins to dole out torn morsels from the prey. Small feathers drift around her as she pulls at the carcass, dipping her head to each chick in turn, two heads rising to her offerings. But, from time to time, her head dips out of sight and it appears that she is feeding a third, smaller chick in the cup of the nest. This meal continues for twenty minutes, then she takes some bony remains away to the sycamore and finishes the bird herself.

Without her presence the visible fragment of the nest appears empty now: the chicks have hunkered down within and nothing can be seen. Only the tiny movements of Bluebottles around the nest betray any presence.

She now circles up from her tree perch, turning on a tiny thermal nearby which takes her up effortlessly, with merely a flexing of long wings. The sun catches the gloss of her upper wing as she turns, blue-brown and brown-blue alternating in the angles of the shine.

Up and up, for hundreds of feet, gradually drifting towards the river, away, getting smaller now.

Then, a Sparrowhawk is under her, heading steadily west, and she breaks from her spiral to dive at the hawk, which is speeding away. She catches up without even flapping her wings and corkscrews around it in mock-fight. Then, as the hawk heads away, she resumes her rise towards the flies in the sky.

For many minutes she is high up, hawking insects in a characteristic glide and snatch, drive and pounce; legs extending forwards to capture and on to meet her dipped bill, wings straight. She drifts away, following the insects, into the ice-white of the distance.

Down below there is a quick movement of House Martins. Scores are fleeing fast and low across the fields, small gritty alarms sounding as they pass, white rumps bright against the green.

They disappear to the south west, and the lower layers of the sky are empty now. A minute passes. Then, there is the male Hobby, two or three hundred feet up, flying fast in steady progress to the north east.

Caught in surprise, and too low to take to the heights, the Martins have taken the only other evasive action available – they have risked flying under the falcon in the opposite direction, and their stratagem has worked. Seeing their approaching nemesis, and with too much of a height disadvantage to flee ahead on the rise, they have risked passing under the Hobby.

The falcon continues, over the river and suddenly accelerating, dipping beyond the boa constrictor of the trees along the water course.

The smell of hay fills the heated air: the whole world straw. Ants scurry over summer-cracked soil. Beetles, gloss black-backs and knobbed legs scuttling, hurry through the forest of stubble, seeking crevices to secrete their vulnerable selves. Centipedes are hunting, the spiky train of their articulations bending their curves around obstacles, disappearing in and out of cracks, short antennae quivering.

Clouds begin to accrete in the heat haze, creamy cauliflower heads rising, boiling, ever-changing. They are crowding the sky now: shadows darkening under their overhangs, ponds of their shadows creeping over the warm straw, damping the dazzle.

Small groups of Swifts are sailing the upper sky, specks against the cliffs of cumuli, on strengthening updrafts, plotting a steady course to the next swarm, watching further flocks which have already found feeding grounds. Groups join, until all are in a single flock, hundreds strong, wheeling around as they deplete the shoal to unproductivity. Then, all scatter to search again.

Across the river a shrubby bank basks in the afternoon heat, its lush flanks dipping towards a marshy meadow. Ox-eye daisies and hogweeds in whites, red poppies bending, thrusting thistles, brambles and cleavers scrambling for supremacy, blousy white convolvulus trumpets blowing over purple vetches, grasses and clovers: the riot silently deafening. And, amongst this tangle, clouds of butterflies and bees, flies and beetles, busy collecting from these summer flowers. Meadow Browns and three kinds of Whites, Small Skippers and Gatekeepers, Tortoiseshells, Red Admirals flitting and fighting, displacing and being displaced on favoured blooms by big Buff-tailed Bumblebees, Hoverflies and Honeybees pushing at the edges. A Garden Warbler watches from the scrub, moving to snap at insects, keeping low and always half-hidden.

On Rabbit-worn turf, where ants swarm, a Green Woodpecker is sitting, angled on its stiff tail, lime rump glowing in the sunshine. It digs and licks at ant larvae, unearthed from underground nests, disturbing the colony, its occupants exposed, desperately scuttling away with their tiny pearls of eggs, across the sandy hump of their ruined home.

Amongst the dry Rabbit droppings sit Common Darters, wings glinting as they twitch – watching passing prey – then suddenly needling into the air to capture gnats which rise from the boggy ground adjacent.

A huge Badgers' sett shows new workings – massive mounds of new soil spilling downslope towards the river's floodplain. Dozens of large holes along the long slope have sinuous paths snaking away amongst spent bluebells and campions, under bramble patches and through the woods.

At the sunny end of the slope, under spreading beeches, the redundant, older end of the sett has new occupants: four Fox cubs are resting in the shady hollows. Two Jays, above them, make strange rattling calls and peer down from the tree, cinnamon in the green.

Seven Oystercatchers fly along the river, bowed wings carrying the carrots of their orange bills. Below, the giant form of a Swan dips its entire neck below the green moving water, then upends its body to reach the deepest weeds, white tail pointing skyward, emerging to swim upstream, rounding the meander against the slowest current by the balsam-covered and shaded bank.

Two Peregrines cross the river, towards the pylons, their favoured perch. Out there, past the Stock Dove-occupied Barn Owl box, the mole-hills scattered across the cow-trodden meadow, they sit, one far above the other, on the central spars of the steel giant.

Suddenly, one flies – beating long primaries as it drops towards a flock of corvids beyond a copse. As it passes the trees it swerves downwards and right, towards the flock which only now begins to rise in panic.

Rooks and Jackdaws scatter, then try to re-group, but the Peregrine is among them and binds onto a Jackdaw, the two lose height as the falcon grapples with its prey, finding purchase while still flying. Then, righting itself just feet from the ground, the Peregrine rises heavily with the prey, which still flaps forlornly for the sky. The second Peregrine follows its sibling as it turns back to the pylon with its victim, landing nearby to watch as the other begins to pluck the bulky, already dead, Jackdaw.

For forty minutes the falcon feeds, then is off, carrying some scraggy remains, bulging crop heavy, as the other follows in its wake, their deadly forms fading into the late afternoon haze. Under the pylon, in a watery ditch, a Moorhen slides back out from cover, still nervous, and starts to feed again. A Nuthatch, as if giving the all clear, sings out from the beeches beyond, and a Great spotted Woodpecker dares to cross the gap from there and the copse, undulating in long curves as it flaps and rests, flaps and rests. As for the corvids: they have gone.

Following a different path as the warm day lingers on into late evening, looping around the Hobbies' territory out east...

Air, treacly and still, sticky warm and honeyed from the heat of the day, stalls in the evening. The setting sun still fiery low against the burnished and brassy land, languishing in the afterglow of the summer's furnace.

Back across fields where hay lies pungent in the heat, lying thick and growing pale in the meadow, the cut and fallow contrasting as shadows stretch and fill. A Hare on hind legs, long ears like wooden boats aloft, watches warily on the rise.

Butterflies have given way to moths, and the legs of the copse, out west, show beneath its see-through skirt: revealed by the low peeping sun now resting in the nook of the ridge. The sneeze of a Snipe wheezes as it towers from the ditch, zigzagging the meadow and looping a long return. A group of young Curlews drops in to roost where Rooks hunch in bunches, their gleaning done for the day. Stock Doves fly to night perches, Swallows, like pieces of shadows, still skim the pale sky, slipping over fields and woods and into the ash of the day. A Kestrel's silhouette passes along the ridge.

White flowers begin to glow in the twilight. A Grey Partridge calls from a ditch, and the low mournful moan of a Tawny Owl heralds the night.

Bats zip by in near darkness – fast and jagged over hedges and into dark fields.

And, last, before the last light leaks away and ink fills the hollows, the stubby shape of a Little Owl shows above the wall and takes the remains of the day as it blurs into the night.

The nights slowly lengthen, stealing light from days too hot to burn too long. The next day starts warm and sultry, even before the sun's heat, like a trumpet's blast, slides over the heat shield of the horizon. Cirrus in metallic colours: coppers and rusts, oranges and violet, begin to bleach to dazzling white.

Swallow sleep on wires, Martins wallow past after heat-fazed flies. A Common Darter zigzags by. By the lane, where Gatekeepers flap, a Comma flicks to a nettle amongst the bramble. Its antennae, velvet caramel dipped in cream, the rounded jags of its underwings showing the silver C marking of its name.

From the dazzling fields, the copse, dark and green, just-damp with dew, is an oasis, drawing the thirsty eye. The world is taking shallow breaths in the heat. The sun begins to fill the shadows in the hollows of the meadows, and even the crouching Hares stand, stretch, and seek shade under hedges. Rooks, purple-sheened in the low light, peck and waddle, wide-legged bandy, gleaning now before the heat builds.

But, as the morning progresses, at first faint stirrings, then gentle wafts of air, sweep the staleness from the corners of the fields. The first clouds begin to bubble, gently drifting north. With them a Raven, high and circling, calls a *'crarr, rarr, rarr'* as it thermals away. Grey Partridges, from a ranunculi-bright meadow, answer.

Then, from slumber, swallows alarm, at once alert.

A falcon, in from the sun, and pale in the blinding light, is suddenly centre stage. All eyes are on it. As it approaches, the Swallows are up and heading for the sky, their *'wee-wheets'* falling behind them as they accelerate away, twisting in desperation as the Hobby closes. The falcon dives suddenly, a flash of light bouncing off it as it tilts, speeding and dropping until it skims the field, a Swallow just ahead.

The Swallow loops over the hedge, and the Hobby follows, almost touching the thorn as it surfs – then drops below its line at a hundred miles an hour. Predator and prey are lost to sight, but the reaction of others betrays its course. Swallows and Martins circle above a copse now, where the Hobby has landed.

At the nest site everything is quiet. Nothing is visible. Heat shimmers and cumuli gather: a Paul Henry-worthy landscape painted on the land; the breezes begin to stir.

High up, Swifts swirl and four Herons head west, flapping heavily.

Then, a Hobby chick's head shows above the parapet of its nest, as cries ring out. Now the female falcon is returning to the tree, carrying a Swallow, limp and blue. As she lands two more heads emerge to show above the nest rim, and for the first time three young can be counted – two now showing new brownish feathers through the white down of their heads. The third, smaller chick seems less developed than its siblings, but each, in turn, receive small pieces of prey from their mother.

Before the meal has finished, the male returns; he is carrying a House Sparrow, looking large in his slender talons. He sits in the sycamore and feeds himself for a while, picking pieces from the Sparrow and swallowing. But soon, his mate flies to him silently, sits close by for a while, watching, then she goes to him, and takes the Sparrow's remains away to eat.

Back at the nest the young have hunkered back down and are invisible again.

For an hour or more there is tranquillity. A soft intermittent breeze buffets gently on the back-turned, sun-warmed world.

Across the field, by the long grass-edge, hovers a young Kestrel. Two months old and independent already, it has the mastery of its elements.

As the breeze taps and presses it deftly adjusts: wings and tail flexing, fanning, to keep it on station, above the vole run.

Now it shifts height, and, as if perching on a lower shelf, stands on the air as if it were solid. Wings rowing and adjusting on every beat, it responds to each nuance of air, its body rising and dropping, yet its head nailed to the sky beyond – absolutely immobile.

Dark cinnamon flecks of its back, flicker against the green land as it watches, peering intently down at potential prey. Its pale head with grey moustaches bends against the working rest of itself and tilts groundward in its quest.

Suddenly it drops to five feet above the field for a second, hovering just above the hedge. Now its wings flex higher and forward, dark-banded tail adjusting to the lesser air, then it pounces in a blur of wings and talons.

Before the Vole is eaten three Crows spy the falcon and flap towards it. The Kestrel launches away and curves to a sycamore to hide its meal.

Above, Swifts scythe, slicing, swerving, jinking and curving: magic boomerangs. Time stands still. They come close, lower, the *'Fft-fft-fft-ft-ft'* of their wing-slap fills the ears as they pass – intent on flies.

And now, over fifty Lapwings get up and circle, alarming, and scores of Black-headed Gulls spin above a skimming Sparrowhawk, which, having hugged the hedge, cuts the corner across the field to land in an ash – the threat extinguished.

The Lapwings move on to the river, where a single Redshank joins the flock, distant yet distinct.

A Sand Martin slips, fish-like, by.

Linnets' songs and Yellow Wagtails' calls continue into the hot and soft-wind day, where Buzzards ride the billowing clouds on broad out-stretched air-gathered arms, and House Martins wobble in near-stall speeds as they gather the fruits of the sky, white bellies bright in the blue.

Up high a Hobby is making an insistent line across the sky, the eye unable, once caught, to let go: a fish on the hook. A Swift, oblivious, flies in the opposite direction some hundreds of feet below, and, as their lines begin to close, the Hobby dives at lightning speed in looping, tightening arc, closing in on the Swift, which is, only now, taking evasive action. The two almost meet – the falcon a blur, even at this distance, but a jink from the Swift takes the Hobby past it. So fast is the falcon now, that, in a split second, they are far apart, the Swift way above, and the Hobby, without slowing, swerves for a Swallow. It misses again.

For several minutes the Hobby circles and makes half-hearted attempts at prey, then suddenly closes its wings and makes straight for a copse in front. He sits and preens, bending to pick individual belly feathers in his bill, lifting each to re-zip the filaments.

Suddenly, with many House Martins' alarms, he's off. Then, the female streaks in from the other side of the copse and lands nearby, calling the whole way, beseeching him to hunt. He, by now, is high up again, heading east, fast. He is lost to the distance as she watches him go.

For an indeterminate while the world continues around the falcon as she sits, searching the skies.

Then, she's up, out from the trees and towering rapidly in a remarkable show of power and speed, accelerating continuously as she rises, twisting steeply until several hundred feet up.

Then, right overhead, she sees her mate. He has a Swift in his sights and is diving at it – missing twice as he loops vertically, roller-coaster like, the Swift's direct line just jinking slightly at each attack. But every pass takes the falcon a little nearer to the Swift, and now he is at the top of another loop and starting to fall back towards his prey, upside down at the apex, turning as he dives, wings flicking ablur all the time.

With a final twist the Swift tries to keep out of reach, but this time the Hobby's speed and agility have won, and he takes the Swift from the air, continuing his loop to a horizontal glide, prey still trying to flap, under his belly.

The female, having followed him across the sky, now catches up and the pair performs an aerial pass. She takes the Swift and closes her wings, dropping closer and closer, until three feet above the field, then a swerve takes her to her nest tree. As she lands the male is already there – out-pacing her with a direct approach.

As she starts to eat, he takes to the air once more, to head off for another hunt.

Nearby a Goldfinch makes a three-note alarm call. Out to the north a pale, Buzzard-like form is approaching, but even more pale and long-armed. Still a mile away, but getting ever closer, it resolves to an Osprey. Quite low at first, then over the next field, it circles and gains height on a small thermal, lifting heavily and showing its pale belly, dark carpal patches contrasting on long, long-fingered wings as it turns. A female Sparrowhawk joins it in the thermal, tiny in comparison, turning tighter circles just above the Osprey, which now heads west, following the canal towards the setting sun.

Back at the nest there is alarming from the female. She is attacking a Buzzard – looping around it and stooping at it as it sits doggedly on top of the nest tree, and, as she turns to make another attack, suddenly her mate dives almost vertically at the Buzzard, and the pair manage to dislodge it from their oak, driving it away to the riverside trees as dusk falls on the spectacular day.

Along the canal, a young Heron, flying low above the towpath, suddenly flops into the water, stabs at a fish ahead of it, then rises, carrying the catch and continues away. A Grey Wagtail flies away as the Heron nears, under the humpback bridge and around the curve, as the Heron rises over the brickwork and follows.

A Kingfisher sits on the edge of a narrowboat, brighter than the bright paintwork, staring down at the still water. Minnows in the murky shadow are just visible. The Kingfisher bobs its head, judging its moment, then launches – turning back in towards the hull and dives in. A fish is lifted from the water and the Kingfisher skims the surface with its prey, blue lightening flashing in the morning.

Out in the flowery meadow by the wood, Swallows and Martins are low against the land, sifting insects from the air, turning at the field's wooded edge to return, out from the shadows into the new light, never at more than knee height. Suddenly from the south, a Peregrine comes tanking in at speed, on a slant towards the meadow. All the birds rise up, ahead of the falcon – Wood Pigeons clattering and gulls spiralling, the hirundines heading off in haste as the Peregrine slices through.

With the falcon on their tails the hirundines flee towards the farm, and as they disappear behind the barns, the Peregrine makes a kill – emerging, on a rise, with something in its talons. It heads away to find a place to eat its catch.

The world seems cleared of the larger birds, scattered before the big falcon: a tornado's path, a swathe of devastation. Yet, the smaller birds soon return: Sparrows in the paddock, under the legs of hot horses trying to keep to the shade, tails swishing at flies; Linnets along the lane, from verge to hedge to field; Goldfinches on the wires, Yellow Wagtails in the stubble – now greening with new weedy growth; Pied Wagtails in the barnyard and on the rooves; even the Swallows have come back – and resume their own hunts.

At the field's fallow corner, a clump of willows, briars and brambles by the lane, and fringed with reeds at the ditch, a family of Long-tailed Tits and three young Bullfinches are feeding quietly. A Chiffchaff flicks around the finches, flicking and fast around their plump plodding. Small notes erupt from the tangles: bubbles from a bathysphere. Bumbles buzz: stripy, fuzzy, furry – and always busy. Above, a Buzzard, in lazy circles, thermals: rising without effort into the depths of the sky.

Morning turns to afternoon. In the fields Skylarks and Yellowhammers creep slowly, at a half-crouch as they search for insects and seeds, backs barely showing above the weeds, hardly moving a yard in a minute. For a long time they progress in this manner through stubble and weed, almost invisible in their stealth. Suddenly a knot of Starlings, alarms yelping from them, pass low overhead. As they do, the larks and buntings squat, hugging the ground, hoping camouflage will hide them from an, as yet, unseen attack.

The Starlings swish past, audible wingbeats hissing collectively from the tight ball of their flock, now rising to vault the hedge: horses at the jump. As they descend to the next field, in full flight, a Hobby is almost on them, following them at every twist and turn, flowing over the hedge like water at the weir. The Skylarks stay absolutely still, the falcon passing over them, intent on pursuit, Starlings in its sights. The slightly broader wings and heavier body mean this falcon is the female.

Half-way across the next field the Hobby puts on a sudden spurt, easily catching up to the hindmost Starling, stretches her legs in front of her and simultaneously pulling up as she grabs the prey, then rising rapidly with the Starling in her talons, slowing as she does so, bending to snip the neck of the Starling as she levels out, then tucks it under her tail and turns to the pylon. As she reaches the lower girders to land, some two hundred yards away, only now do the buntings and larks stand up to watch the falcon.

Feathers drift from the pylon as the Hobby plucks, then a set of primaries spirals down like a large sycamore seed, to the field below. The falcon, horizontal on the spar, continues to remove much of the flight feathers from her prey, eating as she does so, then takes off for her nest across the field with the now more streamlined remains. Before she gets to the nest, two Crows are investigating the feathers below the pylon, but there is nothing edible for them.

She flies straight in to the nest in a direct line, just a few feet from the field, rising at the last to reach it as she slows on a final upward glide, deftly slipping between the branches on half-closed wings.

As the shadows lengthen like an incoming tide three Hobby chicks are being fed. And the evening's hunting is not yet ended.

115

Colours bleed from the dying day and the sky takes on lividity, darkening gradually, bruising to purple and then black. Dusk: and bats begin to flicker from patient days in dark slumber to fly the night, as stars begin to pierce the dark skin of the skies.

Out across the big field which holds the pylon, a dark shape is hunting: a Hobby, almost invisible in the gloom, is after bats. In the near-dark it is cloaked from showing, and pursues the bats directly, not needing to have a height advantage, not needing surprise.

Predator and prey quickly disappear into the night – the falcon obviously completely competent in the darkness, its prey vulnerable to this prowess.

Out below the pylon in the following morning's cool, the sun not yet risen, the sky is an undifferentiated grey, and the air stirs, strange after the stillness of the last few days.

In the weedy stubble several remains of prey strew the field under the pylon. Bats' wings have fallen – and lie like scraps of torn umbrellas after a storm. There are at least two species of bats' remnants: one much smaller than the other – possibly a Noctule, and at least two Pipistrelles have been dismembered in the spars above, where the Hobby has chosen to feed in the night. The presence, too, of a few feathers, show this to be a perch regularly frequented by the falcons.

The sky, instead of brightening, grows ever blacker – and the sun's rise is hidden, as if the night will not give way to the day. To the west the grey curtain is now a black wall: solid and threatening. The air moves in fitful gusts: uncooked cold dumplings of wind hit wetly.

Now the distant faint flashes of lightening begin and the sound of thunder reaches across the land from out west, rolling in like cannon balls, as yet falling short.

Across the stubble, Crows and Rooks, backs contrasting with the pallid landscape, are feeding, side by side. Smaller birds seem to be in hiding already, finding shelter while they can. The wind picks up: stronger gusts stir the trees, which begin to bend and sway, as if trying to rid themselves of the blow, spilling air from branches beginning to twist in the breeze.

The towering curtain of cloud closes. Lightning strikes irregularly, catching the world out every time, and the accompanying thunder quickens its response. Several Hares are lined up in the field and now race each other to the shelter of the woods by the river, and, as if they have timed it perfectly, now, without one warning drop, the rain buckets down: sting-

116

ing spears in a deluge are thrown from the roaring sky, silver against the black, and a squall bends their flight to spiral-crash to the earth.

For hours and hours the wind gusts and rains continue, darkness fills the world. Trees bend and creek and the air through their leaves only add to the din of the storm. It has grown cold. The stubble lies half-submerged now, and still the rain falls. In the lane the gutters have joined at the middle, and run like streams to choked drains, brown water carrying soil, leaves floating soggily.

Well into the afternoon, and the deluge begins to break, and the sky cracks to reveal lesser greys between the charcoals. Showers become intermittent and the wind begins to drop. Plants lie flattened, flowers sodden and drowned.

At the Hobby nest, nothing: no movement, no indication of activity. All around, the world seems to have been swept of life. Water drips from every surface, runs in runnels, channels and newly-formed rivulets; pouring and puddling. The lane, in places, is a foot under water, and more still flows from the fields. Ditches are over-full, spilling out into the meadows, grasses swimming.

Another hour in and, finally the last shower ceases. Gradually birds come out of hiding.

Swallows start to swoop: keeping low and searching for food. Wagtails flicker on dry islands in the paddock and fields, picking drowned insects from the puddles. The Little Owl emerges from its oak-hole and blinks at the evening, and the half-submerged world beneath. A Heron strides along the meadow's edge, looking for victims of drowning. A bedraggled Kestrel shakes its soaked feathers on the pole top, and preens. A few Swifts slice through the tatters of the day, joining the Swallows low against the watery land.

The still-hidden sun begins to set, and darkness dons its black cloak again, and bows to the footlights of the lightning now way out east.

AUGUST, BROUGHT IN WITH THE FLOOD

TRACTOR tracks and verges, field hollows and furrows remain under water today, but the sky shows some promise, though clouds still cover much of the sky, and rainbows' arches come and go. One field shows an immense pond-like puddle, and dozens of gulls swim and wade through the water.

Common Gulls and Black-headed Gulls pick at the dirtied surface and Lesser Black-backs dip beaks to the mud below. Drowned invertebrates seem in plentiful supply. At the edge of this pool, a single Dunlin, still wearing handsome summer-plumage, runs at insects aplenty, black belly beneath rusty upperparts.

And, in the paddock a Stonechat, bold and beautiful, perches on the thistle tops and fence wires, flying down in short forays to insects below, then landing on its vantage posts again.

A Buzzard is walking at the edge, near the canal's embankment, picking off worms and drowned insects, wetted breast and belly clotted and clumped.

On the wires above, three types of hirundines are lined along their lengths: House Martins outnumbering the Swallows, and four Sand Martins: pale dots amongst the blue-black backs.

Greenfinches are singing in a light breeze. Their quiet, wheezy screams fizzing out from the lane's trees. Water gurgles at every turn, flowing from field and road. Spiders scurry along rain-squashed plants, driven from hiding by the water's rise.

A Kestrel hovers up high as a rainbow frames it, sunlight glinting brightly as it hangs against a black cloud. Two Hares race each other across the meadow, water flying from their feet as they go.

At the Hobby nest site, the female is obvious atop the sycamore, sitting facing the sun. Her feet shine against the branch. The storm has opened the small gap a little wider and about a third of the nest is visible. A movement – a brown and white head moving – shows life within. At least one chick survives.

The day begins to warm, insects rise; bees blunder over collapsed clover in the meadow, coaxing nectar from wet flower clusters, teasing petals apart and diving between, legs working. Butterflies open their wings to the sun, maximizing warmth, turning on leaf and bloom. A Willow Warbler sings.

In an instant the Hobby is off. She heads away, towards the river, and disappears over the trees there. Ten minutes later and she is on her way back, and not alone. Another falcon is in front, heading for the nest tree, but as he closes, his immature plumage gives him away: this is not her mate, but an intruder. And he is carrying prey, possibly a House Sparrow.

As they near, her soft *'krrr krrr krrrs'* can be heard, and now she accelerates to catch up with the young bird, probably her own offspring from the previous year, and dives at him, just as he reaches the oak.

Now she flies for him, as if in attack, but he seems ready for this and rolls as she reaches him, giving up his prey to her, talon to talons, directly. She takes the bird and, her cries intensifying, she drives at him, forcing a retreat. He is reluctant to go, and circles as she screams, staying close to her nest.

But she won't allow his presence and persistently attacks, until, eventually he gives up and flies away, back towards the river. She does not follow; instead, once the intruder is only a few seconds distant, she circles the oak and lands on the nest, to feed her chicks with the meal provided by their own brother.

The Sparrow is dished out, and two Hobby chicks' heads rise to greet each proffered mouthful, but she attends to a third chick out of sight. Then, as she moves around the nest rim, a third head peeps above its parapet – three chicks are visible for the first time. They are, by now, about two weeks old: half way to fledging. Two of the chicks are obviously more advanced than the other, each showing dark feathers through the white down on their heads, unlike the youngest. But the female makes sure it is getting a share of each meal.

One or two showers fall during the rest of the day, but sun and warmth return.

During the afternoon, while the female is away, her mate goes to the nest with tiny prey items – perhaps dragonflies or other insects – and feeds the young himself. Each time he slips in and out of the tree, coming and going in seconds. Each time he is back up to hunt, never seeming to stop, disappearing behind the trees, or rising away to the sky. Hours pass before the female returns.

By late afternoon the sun shines from an almost cloudless sky. The world perks up: flower heads standing tall again, puddles beginning to shrink. The gulls have gone from the flooded field, and so has the Dunlin. A Reed Bunting calls from the ditch-side herbage and the Swallows rise to track the rising insect swarms. Buzzards circle: from horizon to horizon a dozen or so dot the clear air – spaced above territories, without intrusion on the next.

At the edge of a copse, a Roe Deer stands, silhouetted against the yellow-green field. For a minute it remains, just flicking its tail, then trots back to the trees and is gone, hidden away for the next month or more, so seldom it is seen.

By the ditch, new Badgers' footprints show in still-wet mud, their tracks showing nocturnal ramblings between briar patches and wooded paths. A Yellowhammer gets up from the waters' edge, bill still dripping from its drinking.

The tits are beginning to flock together now, and in the wood, approaching sounds from thirty or more small voices push through the leaves. Small movements high up are all there is to be seen, but calls from Blue, Great, Coal and Long-tailed Tits are joined by Treecreepers' whispers and Nuthatches' louder proclamations. Sharp sounds of tapping on trunks, and bills hammering nuts, drop from the trees like husks to the ground. The flock moves on and the sounds fade away like water through sand. A Jay's retreating rump flashes white as it disappears through the wood.

To the pool. The water's surface is alive with movement: Emerald, Common Blue and Blue-tailed Damselflies float over the surface, many in paired couplets, as they mate. Above them Brown Hawkers and two squabbling Emperor Dragonflies vying for this territory, only big enough for one, their wings clattering dryly as they clash and part. At the pool's edge a female Emperor is ovipositing – her abdomen dipping beneath the lily leaves to plant her eggs, her wings still whirring, keeping on station.

Whirligig Beetles, bronzy backs like tiny gems shining, swim in crazy spirals and Pond Skaters stand sedately above them. Gnats swarm around the bulrushes, whose ripe brown heads are ready to burst, as a Common Darter dashes to snatch at one of the flies, then zigzags away. The jewels and gems of the pond glint and sparkle, and the neon lights of damselflies shine.

In the reeds and rushes, a Reed Warbler peeps at young Whitethroats and Willow Warblers flitting above in alders and willows. The water moves to fishes' swishes: long deep ripples above dark shadows: Carp, mirror sides reflecting as they turn, and in the sheltered, safe harbour of the shallows, a Smooth Newt basks in the underwater sunlight. Red-sided Minnows slip and chase, showing at the surface and submerging to green depths.

Spiders' webs stretch from reed to willow, dotted with midges: too many to eat. A Meadow Brown crashes into one, its wing just sticking, then extricates itself as it hangs, flapping furiously, falling free and away.

By the lane-side trees a Spotted Flycatcher sits quietly and sallies out to snatch a fly.

Wall Browns and a Common Blue Butterfly flicker over the verge, and Speckled Woods spiral in a dance-fight. A Large Skipper sits on a thistle top, probing a proboscis between the flowers.

Suddenly, two small commotions happen at once. Along the lane the tiny high-pitched squeal from a Common Shrew needles from grasses on the verge, and a Field Vole runs across the road in panic. A Weasel crosses in pursuit, bounding in sinuous hops to the opposite verge, stopping once to survey the surrounds, sniffing the air, then continues to cover.

But, above, the Goldfinches, in a line on the wire, have realised too late that a Hobby has closed onto them. The falcon slows from a stoop too fast, and twists around the wires as the finches, only then, take off – undecided on what evasive action to take, so near is the Hobby. Several flee directly away, some swirl down and back around, and one young bird, still clinging with one foot, dangles upside down from the wire.

The Hobby arcs around and heads back to the wire, and now the last Goldfinch lets go and flies away, falcon in pursuit, but gets away by landing in a bush. The Hobby rises and circles back to the other finches, accelerating quickly to catch up, low over the hedge, and as it goes, a fool-hardy Swallow mobs the falcon, swerving in so close that the Hobby's wing tip smacks it audibly three times. The Swallow swerves away as the falcon disappears after other prey.

Above, House Martins, from a safe height, follow the falcon's flight.

The world settles back down as the sun, rounding west to north, reddens against the horizon. In the evening warmth a Small Copper dazzles beautifully as it takes in the last rays on an ivy flower.

Rooks and Jackdaws begin to go to roost; at first ones and twos, then more and more as the sun sets, continuing to head to the north and the communal dormitory for the night. Even as the bats begin to patrol, the Rooks still fly the now-dark sky.

Along the canal, a hunched Heron is asleep, or simulates such, as a Pipistrelle passes it to drink from the water's surface on the wing, dipping delicately and rising once more to listen for its own echo bouncing from flies, homing in as it finds one in the dark, and, at the last, twists around to take it, then continuing on the hunt. A Toad hops along the towpath in a belly flop, then twice more into cover.

At the last telegraph post a Tawny Owl sits, as thick as the pole itself – like a stubby extension. But, it is too close for the Little Owl's liking and the smaller owl flies at the larger, and chases it away along the now dark lane, wings whirring as it keeps on the Tawny's tail.

Venus shines brightly from a navy-blue sky as the last light fades away.

On the pylon this morning, three young Ravens sit in drizzle, dropping in grey sheets from a bright sky. Skylarks come in to the big stubble field and disappear on landing. From the hedge a dozen Yellowhammers fly down to join them, vanishing in similar fashion.

At the base of the copse, movements draw the eye: two young Sparrowhawks are being chased, and, in turn, give chase to a Magpie. All are on the ground, or just in small shrubs under the trees, and their positions swap around as the chase goes on. From their relative size, the Sparrowhawks are male and female, both in the brown feathers of youth. The Magpie seems intent on staying with them, and they cannot drive it away: at each sally the Magpie simply returns to perch close by them, hopping closer until another parry is launched. This continues for half an hour – until the Sparrowhawks disappear into the trees.

The sky, silvered by the falling rain, seems empty. Across the field, the Hobby pair is at the top of a line of trees and taking insects directly from the leaves, skimming across the surfaces or landing in the topmost twigs to take prey items while sitting. Now, the female, holding onto a small leaf cluster hangs upside down as she plucks something from a leaf.

Suddenly, this unusual behaviour is interrupted, as a large bird of prey appears over the tree line, only yards away. It is a Red Kite. Gliding in on bowed, long-fingered wings, its pale forked tail twisting in the steer, its tri-coloured loveliness low over the green treetops, it continues south as the Hobbies take to the air. They seem unconcerned as it passes, circling just above it, watching it go on its way.

The sun breaks out with an arc of half-rainbow, punctuated in blue. A Yellowhammer sings.

The Ravens take off from their pylon and cross the field, straight to the Hobbies' nest tree and land. To add to this group, a Heron, from behind them, comes in to land beside them.

The Hobbies attack. But the Heron is already off, launching steadily from its lofty perch to glide to the ditch by the lane. The Hobbies ignore it and dive at the Ravens, screaming as they stoop and loop back to dive again. The Ravens seem unafraid, but the frenzy and persistence of the falcons pushes two, then the third, from the tree. The Hobbies follow – falling on the Ravens in rapid, twisting flights as they move away, along the power lines to the next pylon.

The falcons return to their nest tree, the female now calling softly to her mate, beseeching him to hunt. She takes off and skims the hedge, deftly taking a Migrant Hawker in flight, returning as she eats it, to chivvy the male again, circling as she rises into the brightening day.

But, for some time, he sits, as she catches insects above him, slowly drifting away.

She is almost out of sight before he takes off, and powers up, long wings flexing under his power. Above him Swifts are spaced across the sky. For another minute, at full throttle, he heads upwards at forty degrees, intent on something in the distance. Below, Swallows are alarming, but realise his purpose does not include them, and they settle again to fences and wires.

A group of Martins are ahead of him, still unaware of his approach. He continues upward until he has got above them, and begins to level out, still working.

Now they see him, and they spurt away, quickly at full speed, in a loose group – specks against the sky – and he follows. As he starts a shallow dive and whips his wings – their tips almost touching above and below him – accelerating him towards the Martins, which dive for the ground, gravity-assisted, in an attempt to escape him. The group begin to scatter as he chooses one as his target.

By now they are two miles away, the Martin invisible in the distance, and the Hobby, now vertical, rockets towards the ground, disappearing behind a barn and are lost.

Along the river and all is warm and quiet. The water is risen from rains of late, but flows sedately, if swiftly, between its muddy banks. Cows come down to drink at the river's beach, where the mud shows footprints from many nocturnal drinkers. A Roe Deer's cloven hoof has sunk into the soft silt, and Badgers' broad feet have pressed. Herons' and Moorhens' toes walk along the shore, as if still present. And the tiny pattern of a Weasel's feet, have been printed daintily by the bank.

A Little Grebe submerges itself and rises upstream, immediately diving again and gone for good.

The Sand Martin colony still holds a few active nest holes – but most of them are empty now; parents slip inside quickly with crops full of food, and emerge to skim the skies again.

A Green Woodpecker is on the bank top, busily digging for ants. Above, the dark bulky nests of the heronry sit empty, their season over. A Buzzard takes off in protest from the beeches and flies upstream to the next copse. Moorhens, white tails showing against the marshy meadow, run for cover as it passes, and Mistle Thrushes rattle in alarm. Across the river a Kestrel hovers into the breeze, then drops out of sight onto something in the juncus below. By the creek, not far left, a Kingfisher sits on a fence post and stares at the stagnant, weed-covered water.

Then, in a shallow V formation, five Whimbrel fly west, downstream, rapid wingbeats taking them out of sight too soon.

Ragworts and thistles are alive with insects: Burnets and a single Cinnabar Moth jostle with bees and butterflies: Gatekeepers, Large Whites, and Tortoiseshells – their zebra-striped antennae tilting independently – and a Ringlet are all feeding, moving from flower to flower. One thistle holds a Small Copper and a Small Skipper, which sip side by side, nervously flicking their tiny wings at each other's presence.

New molehills pepper the meadow, marching along the banks and across the fields, great mounds of dark, still-wet earth poking above the buttercups. On the top of one sits a Skylark, singing half-heartedly – perhaps a practising youngster. Goldfinches and Linnets flit above the meadows and into the alders, calling and swirling as they land. Beyond, a Crow is chasing a Sparrowhawk, keeping close to its tail as it heads for the cover of a wood. The hawk, on half-closed wings slices between the leaves, and the Crow banks away.

At the ox-bow lake, beneath the alders, a Green Sandpiper, recently returned from northern breeding grounds, is wading the shallows, picking prettily at the surface: dark, spangled back above its white belly.

Somewhere above, a Goldcrest whispers, as it moves around the canopy, hidden in leaves larger than itself. A Holly Blue flickers pale through the dappled light, and lands to disappear in an ivy.

The woods are quiet: only the knocking of a Great spotted Woodpecker echoes over the root-rutted paths.

But the pull insists. And, so, back along the canal to the Hobby site.

There is chaos at the nest tree. A family of Crows and two Magpies are in the tree, and the adjacent sycamore. The Hobby pair is trying to drive them away, but is outnumbered. The falcons, screaming in anger, dive repeatedly at the corvids, but, as one gives way the others return. There seems to be no particular purpose in their presence: perhaps a cache of prey has been found, but they are reluctant to move on.

For an hour the Hobbies fend off intruding Crows and curious Magpies, not able to dislodge the menace, tirelessly rounding on their tormentors. Then, as if they have had enough, the corvids move off, leaving the falcons to their peace.

For a while they sit, at the tree's topmost branches, near to each other, facing west.

Then, the female dives from her perch and goes straight for the ground, plucks something from the field and rises with it back to the tree, her prey too small to see within her grasp. She raises her talons and eats, her ankle against the tree for support. And now, as if the morsel has whetted her appetite she begins to call to her mate, and takes to the air.

She heads off west, but turns back to him, still on the tree, flies over him and stoops a shallow arc that almost connects with his head, and away again. He follows, and as they rise, he tries to catch her up, quickening his pace in a short spurt of speed, but she responds and keeps ahead of him, as if in a race. As they head up and away, they keep up this competition in a show of speed and flying prowess: an awesome display of their skills.

Soon they are up amongst some Swifts, already running for their lives, streaking at speed across the sky. Within another minute the falcons are miles distant and simply vanish into the glare of the sun out west.

Below the nest, now, twenty Grey Partridges, almost all young, creep along the field's edge at a quarter of a mile an hour. For half an hour they are still visible, still moving, under the hedge's shadow. They pass a Hare, crouching by the fence, just skirting around it as they head towards the river.

A Chaffinch sits on the nest tree and sings. Hours seem to pass as the sun goes down, when, from the east, in the opposite direction that they had disappeared, the Hobbies return. They do not appear to have prey, and do not go to the nest, their foray unsuccessful, it seems.

As dusk begins to settle, the Hares come out to graze on the meadow's weeds, loping along steadily, ears aloft, then crouching to feed. One nearby crunches noisily on some green stem.

Then, a dozen Golden Plover drop in silently from the east, land in the field and settle for the night.

As bats stir and light fades, the Little Owl is silhouetted on the cottage roof, calling an alarmed *'keeoo'* into the dark.

The Golden Plover are still there this morning, stirring in the new day, sparkling golden spangles as the sun hits their mantles. Some sit, others stand. Three show worn adult plumages in various states: dark necks and bellies, some still black, others turning grey. The rest are juveniles in fresh pale gold and pale bellies. They begin to stride amongst the stubble, bending to pick at invertebrates.

And the Hobbies are absent, but two heads poke from the rim of the nest, snapping at bluebottles.

Along the hedge, a Lesser Whitethroat is making its way through the hawthorn, picking at torpid insects in the cool of the morning. A Song Thrush carries a snail to the fence, then flies away as a Little Owl loops along the line, back to its tree, holding a mouse.

A trio of Skylarks, calls rippling, drop down and land by the plovers, and become immediately invisible beneath the grass.

Suddenly, with the Hobby-specific cries of the Swallows, the pair is returning. The male is in front, carrying a large item of prey, a bloody slab already half-eaten hanging from his claws, as his mate homes in on him, with begging cries.

She flies beneath him, and, in perfect timing, he drops the prey and she catches it, carrying on straight to her tree. They land separately. He sits, staring south, the sun on his left, catching his feathers in a halo. She tears at the meal and eats for a few minutes, then takes the rest to the nest.

For the first time, she does not feed her chicks, but drops the prey to them – and one of them snatches it to feed itself. Prey and chick disappear from view as it feeds.

Swallows are swooping in the shade of the hedgerow, just below the nest tree as the falcons sit. The Hobbies ignore them, the Swallows seem unaware.

The morning warms, and with it the insects rise. After another hour the Hobbies circle up on the day's first thermals, wings at full stretch to catch the rising current, slowly ascending without effort, until a hundred feet up, where they start to feed, snatching insects every minute or so and eating as they fly.

They are drifting as they hunt, but remain relatively close to each other, perhaps a thousand feet up now, talons extending from time to time in easy catches, curving and diving, or speeding upwards for a few seconds to grasp an insect, stalling on the catch and allowing themselves to fall as they eat, continuing on in the vastness of their sky.

Then, in the distance, two more Hobbies can be seen. They too are insect-catching together. This pair is, perhaps, a mile or two to the north of our Hobbies, on their own territory, and each pair, knowing their boundaries, tolerate the presence of the other.

The Hobbies continue to drift and rise, until, at a mile high and more than a mile away, they are too far to be seen.

Back on earth the warm day has brought out the butterflies. August has ended the breeding season for many birds, but for the butterflies, the most species are on the wing now.

Leaving the nest site behind, to a flower-filled little valley, sheltered between copses, a stream running through, and full of flowers. Thistles are alive with insects: Painted Ladies, Peacocks and Red Admirals the gaudiest, but the browns more plentiful: Meadow Browns, Gatekeepers and a couple of Wall Browns compete with Small and Large Whites – adults of both are of second broods – and the meadow is a sea of butterflies. Honey Bees and Bumbles, Hoverflies and late-summer Wasps all compete for the bounty. On the cow-chopped turf one or two Common Blues flicker through, disappearing as they land and close their wings: only at close quarters are they visible as blue upperwings are hidden and the lovely marbled speckle of their underwing camouflages them.

Speckled Woods in the shade of trees descend to feed on the flowers and a single Small Heath puts in an appearance.

The day turns from warm at midday to hot in the afternoon. Brambles scramble across the meadow to trip the careless foot and blackberries begin to ripen in the sun. Ants scurry, heated on sun-baked soil, carrying eggs from a disturbed nest to another home, tiny ivory globules in their mandibles, held aloft as their column snakes through the short grasses and vetches.

Above the stream, Banded Demoiselles flutter gently, heart-stopping in their beauty, and a Southern Hawker, zigzagging past, pauses to greet, face to face, then on its way again, blues and black spots blurring as it speeds, over irises and nettles.

Then, in one of the ashes in the copse, a small flicker catches the eye. A bright tail moves: a Common Redstart, a young bird on its way south, has stopped in this little valley. It sits on the lowest branch, large dark eye watching, red tail quivering, and sallies out into the sun to take an insect.

127

For just a day or more it will remain here, on its way to Africa for the first time.

Ladybirds unfurl gossamer wings from the gems of their shells, lifting off into the heat, tiny black legs dangling, looking for mates.

Under the trees, in rain-softened leaf litter, a family of Pygmy Shrews is diving beneath the flaky rot in search of woodlice and worms. The leaves boil around their frenzied activity, as tiny bodies wriggle, noses swivelling on the scent of prey, short legs pushing them under the surface, sniffing and snuffling like miniature Moles. A Robin, in the branches above, watches, cocking its tail at this unusual phenomenon, waiting on the opportunity of a meal for itself.

From the shade of the trees and out into fields: the sun strikes from a clear sky, the world gasping for air. Under the hedge a Fox lies in shade, broad tail wrapped around its body. Its eyes seem closed, but their slight slit betrays his alertness. Black whiskers twitch and an ear swivels, then, in an instant, he has uncoiled and slipped through the hawthorns to the field beyond. Rabbits sprint along under the hedgerow, white tails flashing, then go to ground into foot-worn burrows. The Fox's progress is signalled its whole way: birds springing from the hedge and along, hovering above the Fox; alarms from finches and Blackbirds punch out into thickened air. A Magpie descends to investigate, rattling its machine-gun call and raising the long oar of its tail as it hops on the hedge, cocking its head in search of the danger. Its colours shine in the dazzling day: bottle greens and blues in iridescence as it moves, ice white flanks and ebony blacks, glossy in the bright.

This commotion heads away along the long hedge, and the Fox shakes off its followers to hide away on some other ambush.

In the distance, a Buzzard, tilting heavily on a thermal, is struggling to rise as it carries a Rabbit, which dangles like a lumpen rag from its claws. It manages to gain height, and turns to take its prey to a further tree.

By the farm, the Swallows are gathered: now, with three broods fledged, their number has multiplied and the wires and eaves are busy. Their calls echo under the barns' stone arches, stuffing the hot air trapped in the yard. The adult males still sing: bright gapes opening and closing as the sound escapes, the long dark needles of their tail streamers vibrating at their efforts, creamy throats pulsing.

Suddenly they all lift into the air, *'wheets'* sounding as they swirl and spiral around the barnyard. A Hobby is amongst them, around the buildings, its low approach unseen, long wings whipping on the turn, following the whirlpool of Swallows around the barns and up as they try for the sky.

The falcon follows a group of them as they dash over the rooves, hugging the building and down into the yard beyond, then out into the meadows, through the herd of cows, squeezing between, and off into the open. Now the Hobby, untrammelled by obstacles, in level flight, accelerates at one Swallow to within inches, but suddenly pulls up vertically and arcs away, looping over the trees beyond as the Swallow escapes.

For the remainder of the afternoon there is no further sign of the Hobbies; not in the trees, not in the air, nor at the nest. On the oak leaves, near the nest, at the sun-washed tops, tiny movements, almost too small to snag the eye, can just be seen. Purple Hairstreaks are crawling and flitting as they feed and find mates. The light sparks iridescence from their upper wing, and, briefly as they bask, the purple shows, then extinguishes to black at the change of angle. Most of the time their pale underwings show, and, when close enough, the two orange spots.

One butterfly descends – perching on a lower tree, turning as it tastes the honeydew. But this is not a Purple Hairstreak – its dark wing shows no iridescence – and the under wing is darker, with a faint silver line ending in a 'W'. Its hind wing also has a dark orange wavy edge: this is a White-letter Hairstreak. There are no elms, its food tree, anywhere, but – it is here.

Evening: and the Little Owl already on its pole, next to its nest tree on the corner of the lane, perched against a Chalkhill Blue sky. A full moon pushes against a single cloud in the western sky.

Between the hedges the flick of Swallows and cows' tails takes the eye to meadows and down to the wood. Jackdaws are already heading east to roost beyond the river, and – on the pylons and power lines – a hundred Rooks are gathering before darkness falls.

A last Kestrel, a gentle push of breeze behind it, glides into the dusk, as Tawny Owls begin to moan in bass, below the *'jink jink jink'* of Blackbirds settling for the night.

Shadows bleed and the darkest birds disappear into the fall of the night. Only the moon, half-risen, shines on. Its light lights up a line of cumuli to the south, creamy creases like folded buttercream piled on the plate of the earth.

In the moonlight, all the shadows silver-grey, the grasses grey-green. The moon's bright dish sails along the surface of the canal, out towards the river. Toads crawl and slugs emerge, silvering a trail across the towpath, heading to the water to drink.

The night cools, and across the sky from the moon's too-bright show, stars spin on the dome of the heavens.

The meadows are spot-lit; dark woods at their back. Night time is another country, familiar, yet strange.

A Little Owl calls with a long hoot. A Heron, unseen, answers.

Then, out from its nest box by the creek, a Barn Owl emerges and fills the night. Creamy wings flicker slowly as it quarters the ground, large head leading, large feet, sometimes dangling, at the rear.

Turning at the meadow's corner, around the hedge, and along the creek, it patrols, pausing and continuing, hovering and continuing, on around the field and over the hedge, heading this way.

Head-on, large dark eyes watching ahead, keen ears always listening, the owl keeps on coming, closer and closer. Now the fawn markings show on its upper wings, now the grey spangles; the white heart-headed owl suddenly brings itself to a halt, flaps silently, uncannily silently, then drops into the grass, head-first, claws out to pounce, on a Vole.

It lifts from the meadow, a Vole beneath its big, white-feathered legs, and turns to the nest box, low in the huge and spreading oak, lands first on a broad branch, looks around, then goes to its nest.

Beyond, in the meadow, two ghost-white wings are moving away: its mate is out hunting too. This fading form floats low, out over the canal, disappearing beyond, down into the depths of the unfathomable night.

Back, by the way of the canal's curving path, the moon shines so brightly that spiders' eyes appear as stars in the grass, and shadows of slate-blue slabs fall across the silvered sea of the land.

Above the dazzling dot of Jupiter, Orion stretches across the sky.

A warm bluster is blowing, over the meadows and woods, pushing at the hedges, ruffling the pond. Clouds scud and the risen sun dodges between. Rain has fallen briefly overnight, and glistens still, but the lane has already dried.

Butterflies skip the breezes and poke probosces into blooms bending in the blow. And in the fast and bending air, aerial feeders loop and jink for flies: Swifts dark against the sky and hirundines pale against the woods. The slow strobe of sun and shade turns the world from blaze to cave, the adapting eye busy.

Of a sudden, the House Martins concentrate and turn from feeding to flight. Swifts dissolve and Swallows dissipate – the crowded sky empty.

A line of a Hobby moving at speed stripes the blue and streaks toward the wood, across the wind on kinked blades, tilting towards a victim. And faster still, until, in darkened distance, he is gone.

Over to the south, after a breathless minute, there: his distant speck speeds away east. Gone once more.

THE EMPTIED SKY BEGINS
TO FILL AGAIN

THE sun shines; the wind still pushes ships of clouds; the world carries on.

In the big field the Golden Plover are still strolling, backs brightening and darkening under the fast-changing light. A Hare nibbles around them, ears aloft. A flock of Collared Doves flies down to join them, putting up Linnets, which swirl and resettle, and a single Stock Dove glides down, pearl-grey, lovely in the shadow light.

Then, a Sparrowhawk rises on the rush of updraft above the copse, and Swallows spin around it, calling alarms. Predator and prey dance and turn, angling for advantage. Now, the hawk, on a sudden sprint, goes for one particular Swallow and, on a zip-wire, slides down the wind. The Swallow escapes and the dance continues.

In the distance now, a falcon becomes visible and is closing in on a knot of birds: a Peregrine approaches. It circles. The breeze brings it closer. The Sparrowhawk dives for cover, the Swallows watch the falcon now.

The Peregrine wings along the treetops and turns, heading over the river, Crows cawing in protest. Swallows settle to their own prey, and sing again.

Between hedges as the day warms, butterflies begin to swarm on ragwort and thistle. Goldfinches and Linnets are busy on seed heads, Bumblebees buzz-bombing.

The Little Owl, out from its oak-hole, rounds the corner and hides in another oak's niche. A Grey Wagtail drops from the blue with a single 'stick', long ribbon tail behind, to a little runnel flowing through juncus.

A grasshopper's chirrups, and starts another nearby in a tiny cogged chain of sounds, bicycling along the lane to a Kestrel's hovering-pose above. A Common Hawker – a small blue and black jewelled lozenge – helicopters deftly low against the nettles.

The noonday sun shines on and the cumuli's shadows slide silently, dark cloaks slipping pools of darkness as they undulate over the rippling land.

At the Hobbies' nest, for a long time nothing shows, when, suddenly, as a Magpie comes to sit on the tree top, the female falcon flies in, carrying something white in her bill – perhaps a House Martin. She flies to the nest and drops the meal, then attacks the Magpie. She is silent, but the Magpie knows her intent, and makes off, the Hobby on its tail.

She returns to the nest, her movements largely hidden by foliage, moving around and, perhaps, feeding the young.

Then, off again, and with her the male: both rising towards the Swifts up high. But, before they have gone more than a few hundred yards, they turn back towards the ground, diving a shallow driving line. Ahead of them, and below, is a Sparrowhawk, and it is carrying prey.

At first the hawk appears unaware, and continues towards the wood, then suddenly sees the approaching Hobbies, now only yards behind, and almost level, and catching it up rapidly. The male Hobby comes in slightly above the hawk, and in front of his mate, and his distraction gives the female, approaching fast now from below, the advantage she needs. She suddenly quickens her flight with three rapid wingbeats, and rolls as she slices under the hawk.

So fast is her move, that her talons extend in a blink, and she snatches the prey from the hawk and is ahead of it in a blur, already out of the roll and speeding away, her mate above in parallel above her. The hawk wobbles for a second, then continues, empty-handed, her hard-won meal taken in a flash.

The falcons turn, back towards the nest, the female goes straight in as the male circles twice, displaying with whirring wings, then heads for the skies once more.

Above him, out west, a huge cloud darkens and is already shedding a fine muslin of rain, which billows pearl-grey as it falls. He slices into the squall, rising inexorably, towards the wind-whipped Swifts above. He dwindles as the distance and height takes him, and dives into the rainfall and disappears. Above, the Swifts spin around the bulk of the cloud top, mere specks: more gnat-like than avian. Somewhere in the cumulus the Hobby is still rising towards them, cloaked by cloud.

The darkening air is now crowded with cloud, and only the eastern sky and the hills below it, shine above a closing lid of grey. A wall of rain broadens to the west, slanting on the increasing wind.

Skylarks are dropping into the fields, and with them are Meadow Pipits, calls falling with them, pre-empting the rain beyond. A line of Cormorants straggles eastwards, yawing and pitching in the breeze, wing tips almost touching as they swerve. The western horizon drowns.

In the paddock, Pied Wagtails skitter, tails catching the wind like sails, turning them like weather vanes to the blow. The horses are restless, tails swept along their flanks, as they turn away from the weather. A line of Sparrows: Tree and House, horizontal on the grey rails of the fence, hunch as they grip the worn wood, then head off for the shelter of the barn.

A sudden shaft of sunlight, like a searchlight on a dark sea, rakes rapidly across the land, shines brightly and then shuts off.

Then the rain hits like a steam train, whistling in, all steam and sound, shaking the ground, sparks spitting, dark and menacing, thundering through without halting, carrying squalls, like carriages, behind.

Rain all morning and the grey clouds a sea, the same from every shore of the hills. Rain all morning, and the world in hiding, waiting.

Then, the lift. Now the great clouds towering and a blue break of promise.

House Martins condense against the sky, and Swifts and Swallows with them. Now the birds break from shelter and the sun suddenly warm. Curlews, invisible, call from up high. Meadow Pipits are drying in the lane. Bullfinches bob to fruits in the scrub.

By the copse, the Jackdaws alarm and are thrown into the void where the hirundines suddenly knot in a tight shoal, moving as one on a panicked tide, swirling and swarming, calling warnings, unsure of where to escape to; what to escape from.

Across the field, against the wood, a Hobby is speeding towards the river, dipping towards the water as it quickens pace, eyes on something ahead, now at distance and against the dark. Now just a line imagined, and gone.

Rain all morning and only one bright patch but to stun.

An afternoon of contrast. The promised blue materialises and the clouds depart gradually.

In the wood there is a bird wave passing: Nuthatches, young Coal and Blue Tits, Goldcrests, two Treecreepers, young Willow Warblers and Whitethroats: this throng passing quickly, a wave of calls reaching a small crescendo and then falling away, hissing through the trees; then silence. The whole wood empty once more.

And consternation at the Hobby site: a group of Magpies are again laying siege to the nest. The female corkscrews around, trying to attack several at once, trying in vain to see them off, but they will not go. Like a pack of Hyenas around a Lion, they circle, chivvy, threaten, move in and retreat as the Hobby goes for every one of them. But, she is outnumbered and her nest is surrounded on all sides.

Then, as one Magpie takes off, giving her a clear opportunity, she flies at it, and so quickly, the Magpie has no chance of evading her. She grasps it and grapples it to the ground, landing on top of it, the Magpie on its back, wings half-spread, head up trying to peck her. But she hangs on to it, her own wings mantling the Magpie, keeping her balance on the struggling bird.

Several of the Magpies come down to investigate; hopping around the falcon, watching as one their kind is held in submission. The Hobby lets go and attacks another Magpie, the first getting back up and flying away, and with that they all scatter and she flies back to her nest.

In the calm that follows, a Crossbill, calling *jip jip* flies right over the tree, away to the east.

In the post-rain dampness of the field, eighteen Mistle Thrushes are hopping in a loose flock, listening for worms coaxed to the surface by the wet.

Above them, a flock of over a hundred Black-headed Gulls are catching insects in a circling group, taking them in their bills as they fly. A Kestrel has joined them, and, Hobby-like, it fly-catches too.

Then, from the far edge of the field, dozens of Lapwings rise up in panic. The Mistle Thrushes, rattling alarms, head for the trees, and the gulls scatter.

A Peregrine is speeding in, and now twists at a Wood Pigeon trying to rise ahead of it. The Peregrine goes under the pigeon and grabs it from below, both feet out to grasp the belly of the bird, which suddenly lurches off course – the falcon continuing its line with just a jink at the kill.

The Peregrine goes to ground straight away, mantling its prey. It is being watched. Two Crows fly down to investigate, landing a few yards from the falcon. The Peregrine gathers itself and lifts the pigeon, flying heavily, but rising steadily, to the pylon, perching on the second tier of horizontal spars with its prey.

As it begins to eat, the Lapwings are still high up, circling the field, and then turning away to the north. The gulls have gone.

Not far away, at the next farm, the House Martins, seemingly unaffected by the drama, are mating and singing. They have young still under the eaves in their nests, but are ready to lay again. This will be their fourth brood of the season.

Beyond, at the flash, Red-eyed Damselflies sit on the lily pads, sunning themselves as the sun heads towards the horizon. A family of Sedge Warblers clamber on the rushes, into the willows and beyond to the oaks, keeping low. The Swans have four cygnets, well-grown and smudged brown, long necks snaking below the water for weeds.

Brown Hawkers pass back and forth beside the reeds, amber wings catching the low sun as they turn, and two juvenile Song Thrushes dip for water snails in the shallows, as a Snipe, disturbed by their presence, rises from the marshy edge and towers away silently.

A single Sand Martin slips by the water and continues south, barely pausing as it passes.

As evening falls, the Hobby nest is quiet, calm restored after the attack. The female is in the sycamore, looking into the setting sun.

Back along the lane, in the near distance, two Hobbies are hunting, from their sizes they are male and female, the latter an intruder on the territory, yet tolerated by the male: perhaps his daughter.

They spot a Swift passing below them, on its way south, and they go for it, falling from their height and gaining speed visibly. As they pass behind the poplars by the canal, the hunt is yet unresolved, but prey and pursuers are gone.

In the near dark a Little Owl alarms as a Kestrel hovers, still hunting as the moon rises.

Along the lane a Hedgehog meanders: a spiky bowling ball sniffing for snails.

Just before nightfall a single shooting star whips across the sky and leaves it dark.

At the nest today, a change: one chick is very much visible, its head – with a distinct dark mask now showing – looks out over the rim; and below, it is flapping short wings as it exercises, the effort causing its head to move slightly. Another dark head just shows behind the first. The parents are away, or perching out of sight.

The chick continues this for some time, then disappears into the bowl of the nest, morning exercises done.

Below, in the field, three Golden Plover are sitting with a score or so of Lapwings. Nearby a small group of gulls – Common and Lesser Black-backed – stand; all are facing east, into the morning sun.

A thin scrape of cirrus smears the blue sky, and a slight breeze comes from the east. To the west, the large disc of the moon, its edge taken off on one side, is setting.

The hedge seems alive: a dozen Blackbirds, three Song Thrushes, at least a couple of Yellowhammers, two Robins and a Wren are all in, on, or under it. Young Rabbits chase each other around the old gnarled trunks of the hawthorn, on well-worn, grass-free tracks. Bramble berries are taking on colour now: tight green budding fruits turning pink, red and even ripe black. The haws themselves are showing – as yet still green, but beginning to ripen. In the oaks above, young acorns are starting to brown: tanning in the sun.

And, the first butterfly of the day is a Clouded Yellow: a rare visitor. It floats past, orange-yellow: a piece of rising sun, flaked and fallen. As it flies along the hedgerow, two Large Whites take off to investigate, chasing briefly, then realising their mistake.

Then, like an apparition, a far larger rare visitor appears above the nest tree: a Marsh Harrier – from its size, a male – cream-headed, long, dark brown wings held just aloft in a shallow V, heading in from the north, low – almost at tree top height – head down, searching the ground below for prey.

Suddenly the Rabbits have vanished. The harrier continues south, long tail disappearing over the canal and beyond.

The auguries appear to be good for the day: but later will be proved wrong.

A bright yellow juvenile Willow Warbler is in the sycamore, adjacent to the nest tree. It flicks through the foliage, the leaves now spotted heavily with black-brown marks – spots of age that will cover them more and more as summer fades – delicately picking aphids from the undersides of the leaves, peering under them and occasionally hovering very briefly to seize the insects.

A Nuthatch is at the apex, peeling out a loud ringing call which reaches along the hedgerow, all the way to the river, and is answered from there by another. It takes to the air and heads off that way, chestnut under tail coverts showing as it goes.

Two Hares suddenly sprint from the open field to the hedge – for no apparent reason. They squeeze through the hedge and gallop across the next meadow, tails tucked under their rumps, heels kicking as they go.

Two Buzzards display – looping great vertical loops in the sky, stalling at the top of each to dive back, down on closed wings, then on the up, open winged and flapping back to height. At each summit a mewl cries out from the sky. Underwings flash as they turn.

A Blackcap makes its way slowly along the hedge, making brief appearances every few yards, then back under cover of leaf.

Up above, the House Martins are scattered loosely across the near sky, calls raining like grit. A few Swifts pass them at greater speed, tilting on a curve as they all head east.

Now, all the Lapwings are up, 'peeee-wits' squealing as they rise. The Golden Plover are with them, all in a tight group, rising fast. A Sparrowhawk circles just above them, leisurely rounding as they spiral on up. They get above the hawk, and follow its drift as their formation loosens, no longer in danger from a stoop. Below, as the Sparrowhawk continues, Starlings rise and flee. House Sparrows flock back to the cover of hedges and Swallows distance themselves across the sky.

Below, two Migrant Hawkers are fighting over a territory along the hedge. A Holly Blue finds a patch of holly and settles, silver undersides shining silkily as it closes its wings.

For some time after the Sparrowhawk's departure the Lapwings and Plovers remain in the air, gradually drifting down to the meadow only once they are certain the predator is gone. Heads stretch in nervous twitches after they land, a few last concerned calls crying out.

Then, in come the Hobbies. The female leads, carrying something; the male, presumably, having just handed it over, follows closely. They both land in the sycamore, at opposite points. He almost immediately takes off again, in typical fashion: powering up into the vast stretch of the sky. She has quietly dropped to the nest and her shadow can be seen dishing out a few morsels, then she is out again, but just to perch and preen, swivelling and fanning her tail to reach each feather in turn, primping them with her hooked bill, dark eyes always watching the distance.

By the lane's bend, two young Little Owls are hidden in their oak, cryptically camouflaged in oak-bark colours. They remain branch-still, barely a blink giving them away. They stare, confident in cover, dapple shade helping their cause. A Treecreeper shimmies up the trunk, continuing out under a branch, creeping and probing, silvery-white belly catching the early light, passing the Little Owls, neither seeing the other, then at the out-most twig, flies to the base of the next oak to spiral up and around that, heading up to the top of this on a twisting, circuitous route, often out of sight behind the branch. A thin hissing call escapes from its needle-like mandibles as it goes.

In bright and beautiful contrast to these bark-coloured birds, a Bullfinch in pinks and blacks, lands on the hedge and shows itself off to the day.

High cirrus silvers the sky now, scattering light in blinding intensity. Swifts, way up, move across this glare, blurring in the dazzle of air. Lower down, House Martins patrol, swimming in a loose shoal, triangular wings like pectoral fins, rounded fish-heads gulping flies as their school passes.

Out at the steeple, a Peregrine has taken off and now heads this way, picking up speed slowly, gradually, deliberately. The birds have seen it and start to run. But, on its tail, the male Hobby is giving chase, catching it up even as it speeds. Now they are closer their relative sizes are more apparent. The Peregrine is an adult female: though her wingspan is only half as much again as his, her weight is at least four times the Hobby's.

She circles up, broad wings stretched, catching an updraft, gaining height quickly. The Hobby follows, below the Peregrine, and they rise. Suddenly, her wings flexed more sleekly, the Peregrine stoops at the Hobby, closing her wings as she drops like a bomb towards him. He darts out of her path, now just above her, as she turns on an upward arc, her moment taking her back towards him.

Now she powers upwards towards the Hobby, which responds in kind, both heading at forty-five degrees. Her advantage of the arc closes her on the Hobby, and she reaches striking distance, but, just as she does, he jinks up vertically and she goes under him, huge claws raking fresh air.

But she hasn't given up, and rounds on the Hobby, beginning to chase him down. They both begin a long rapid dive, both quickening along the same line, rocketing back towards the earth.

Again, the Peregrine makes ground on her intended prey, closing up to his tail, starting to deploy those deadly talons as he swerves to one side, his slightness giving him the ability to outmanoeuvre, and the Peregrine misses again. Now both begin to climb again, only yards apart, the Peregrine using all her strength to try to gain on the Hobby, which now turns and falls back, the Peregrine following.

Another stoop: this a shallow line, the Hobby whipping his flexing wings as she rows her broader ones towards him. Again, he jinks at the last, twisting away, and she, unable to stay with him, takes a longer curve: but still she won't give up.

He is heading for the sky now, accelerating away on a steep climb, making ground on the Peregrine. But still she goes for him, and they both rise, high against the glare. Once more, as she reaches the Hobby, she tries to grab him; once again he avoids her claws, and with a twist and a spurt of speed he goes away from her, streaking across the sky, and the Peregrine gives up the unequal chase.

The dogfight has taken them both to some distance, and now the Hobby continues away westward, the Peregrine heading east. The sky, emptied of birds, is a void, but the vacuum sucks them back from the four corners, and the stopped day continues, breathing again.

Into a crease of wooded land, hidden in the fold of fields. Beech and birch, ash and oak, sweet chestnut and rowan – berries already red: a secret haunt. And, just above the meadow, pocked with Vole holes and patched in vetch, a dozen different insects busy and buzzing, sipping from scented blooms.

At the wood's edge a Spotted Flycatcher family perches on birches, the young still speckly, but already adept. The juveniles follow the adults from treetops to shrubs, and butter-yellow Willow Warblers forage around them.

A bunch of bright Bullfinches, just out from the vase, bob across the gap, calling softly. The chime of Siskins strikes from the sky and a charm of Goldfinches flash yellow wings against the fluffy thistle heads now gone to seed. A Robin and a Nuthatch sit together in an oak: a mismatched pair.

The day, from warm to hot, trapped in this little bowl of flowers, heats the air to wobble upward, giving Buzzards purchase to circle the rim and escape to the hill behind. Swallows sing. A Great spotted Woodpecker calls from the trees, then the sun-started Grasshopper's ratchet rasps from the grass, where a Small Copper tastes a fresh blade, turning the jewelled cog of its wings to the sun.

Down to a lush, light green, ferny gully where the stream gurgles and splashes; a Wren with a maggot runs along the wall like a mouse. In a marshy field thick with sedge and thistle, a Common Hawker is hunting, skimming blooms and dodging in dapples. Ghostly Large Whites flap their sheets: tiny yachts tacking across the ocean of the meadow.

Rumps of House Martins blink dots against the dark leaves, as a Kestrel, peering down from his air-perch, watches the tiny caverns dug by Voles: waiting, waiting, as his cruciform figure hangs on the breeze.

A Roe Deer, startled, crashes from the copse, splashing up the water-logged bank, and vanishes.

At the Hobby nest the female has just landed, carrying a Goldfinch under her. She lands in the sycamore and bends to take it in her bill, then goes to the nest. Two heads are already showing, and now a third, whiter than the others, peeks above the edge. She tears small pieces from the prey and, bending to her brood, carefully shares the meal. The chicks wait their turn patiently, gulping down the feathery morsels, disappearing from view as they take their share. The adult turns, in shadow beneath the canopy, and slips away towards the back of the tree. Only the nest rim remains to be seen.

Above, in the heat haze of the afternoon, a hundred and fifty Black-headed Gulls are catching flying ants, and now, she takes off – rising quickly – and joins them to circle and snatch her prey from the air.

Strangely, as if sensing her mode, Swifts join the crowd of gulls and, ignored by the falcon, snap up the ants from the sky.

In the paddock, the Little Owl young are active by the stable, catching their own invertebrates as an adult watches for danger from the fence post. A horse, hooves in the air, dusts its back: a cloud of bone dry soil drifting. Dung flies dance amongst the moist mounds and Pied Wagtails stride the turf.

In the nettle-banked corner, Peacocks and Tortoiseshells flutter and Rabbits stretch in the heat, close enough to burrows should a Buzzard's silhouette suddenly darken the pale of the sky. The sun, having crossed the canal, now begins its arc to the west.

Swallows line the wires, sitting close along the lines, preening and twittering as evening begins.

Tree Sparrows and their young, line up along the gutter of the cottage, and sit on the sun-facing tiles of its roof, resting after a day of foraging, chirps echoing from the small stone building.

Out towards the hills in the north-east a dark horizon suggests a change of weather to come.

A few morning clouds and a cooler breeze start the day, but they are quick to pass, and dissipate as the morning warms.

Two chicks are exercising at the nest, flapping their wings. The other remains below, just sticking its head up once or twice. All are dark-faced now, the older two beginning to lose the downy appearance, as their juvenile feathers push through. Even the youngest shows a dark mask, and is obviously growing, under the careful eye of its mother. After a while the activity stops, but two or three heads show above the nest from time to time.

Along the canal, Brown Hawkers hawk the bankside vegetation, clattering wings against the stems as they home in on insects. A Brown Rat runs along the towpath, then jumps into the water, clambering out at a pipe jutting from the canal side, and darts inside. A Magpie flies down from the tree nearby to investigate, but the rat has gone.

A row of poplars behind the boatyard are the tallest trees in the vicinity, and, out of the blue, two Tree Pipits, pausing on migration, land at the topmost twigs of one. One calls twice: *'speeze speeze'* and confirms their identity, then, within a minute they are gone, off again to the south, rising high.

A trio of Grey Partridge cross the lane to the field beyond, then, with whirring wings, fly to the far corner. A Kestrel is walking – picking up beetles – in the same field, and a male Yellow Wagtail calls from a water trough to his mate below.

As the day warms, clouds, at first on the horizon out west, continue to close and grow. By midday a purple wall of cloud begins to crest, like a breaker reaching the shallows. The sun lights it up, and blackens the over-towering tops with shadow: paper charred at the edges. A fitful breeze blows back and forth, bending the poplars, as their leaves shimmer against the dark bank of cloud.

A small but steady stream of Swifts is heading south, at first high up, but as the weather closes, they are getting lower. The consistency of their direction shows them to be at the start of their autumn migration. Before the rain, perhaps two or three hundred have gone south.

Big, cold, face-wetting blobs of rain start to fall, well-spaced at first, as the sun continues to shine, as if it might stop. But soon the spots are closer, heavier and persistent. The clouds curl around the sun, a fiery rim standing at their edge like an unmoving bolt of jagged lightning, blinding against their burnt orange flanks.

For an hour the day darkens and rods of rain race from the sky. Under the arch of the humpback bridge a curtain of rain splashes up from the towpath, almost reaching the opposite side of this shelter. The canal's surface boils as the temperature falls.

Then, as if switched off by some gigantic hand, the rain stops. Within ten minutes the sun screams out from behind the cloak of cloud, sunbeams clashing like brass against the ground, the thunderous wave of cumulonimbus rolls on east, now backlit plum-toned, its juices squeezed dry.

Everywhere the gurgles of draining water, the small splashes of dripping trees, and the electric sparkle of wetted surfaces, persists for a while. Wisps of water vapour from sun-facing fences rise, soon dissipating and disappearing. Horses' flanks steam, as their manes drip.

Swallows take to the evening air, as flies rise again.

An hour later, after an absence of almost the entire day, the male Hobby flies in, a Swift, plucked from the storm, trailing from his talons. His mate greets him, a hundred yards out, takes his prey and turns to her nest. He follows and they land side by side at the tree's top. As she feeds herself and plucks the primaries from the prey, he preens, shaking the last of the rain from his feathers.

For almost an hour he sits, watching his world as the sun dips. His mate has taken the Swift to her young and slipped away.

Swifts jink a kinked path against the wind's push, angling at flies, slicing their knives through the huge cake of air.

A mistaken Swallow alarms just once, and into the pregnant pause, a Kestrel skims by, trying for a bee with a half-hearted snap, before turning on the breeze to stop above the meadow, peering at potential Voles.

Now the Hobbies are heading up and away, making for the clouds, dwindling to two tiny specks in minutes. As they turn, still rising, the cloud swallows them up and they are gone.

The wind blows in the evening. Cloud tops redden, as colours fade from the land, and sail like giant hot air balloons, lit up by their burners into darkness increasing.

The Kestrel still hangs, hoping on the last light to bring out his prey, keen eyes dark-adapting as the last light fails.

A Noctule Bat flies a quick and direct line across the meadow, and Pipistrelles start to twist out into the night, from daytime crevices.

Somewhere, in the deep and secret sky, two Hobbies are hunting, unseen.

In the big field, the Hobby pair is perching on the pylon. Both are on the central spars of the body of the structure, the male higher than the female. Two Crows sit at the apex.

In the field a family of Yellow Wagtails are striding in the weedy stubble. Stock Doves in pairs, too, are feeding there. A few Lapwings sit.

All appears calm. Morning Swallows swoop low, the insects still to rise high. Above, the sky seems empty of birds.

At the lane, a Magpie flies down from the telegraph pole to the hedge top, looking down intently, hops along, peering at the base of the thorns. Suddenly, three Bank Voles run from the verge and scurry across the lane. As they do so the Magpie launches itself from the hedge and flies at them, skimming the road and catching up to one of them.

The Magpie, in flight, dips its beak and grasps the Vole, and as it does so, turns a somersault – head going over, body following, still grasping the Vole. As it rolls upright, the Magpie plants its feet on the lane and takes to the air, carrying its catch, all in one fluid movement.

It takes the prey back to the post's top and puts it between its feet, then hammers at it with its bill, killing it. Now, transferring the vole back to its bill, it flies off to the copse, disappearing into the trees.

The air is so clear this morning it intoxicates on its intake, so clear that the distant hills seem closer, distant features are picked out, distant clouds sharp-edged. The heavens are a mid-blue, high white clouds dot the near sky, dizzying perspective crowding them towards the horizon.

Two (perhaps four) miles distant, two Hobbies are crossing the void, west to east. The pair on the pylon, who had been watching, now take to the air themselves, at first dropping towards the field, then circling back towards the pylon, starting to rise. As they do so, the male, at first behind, puts on speed and overtakes his mate. Now she accelerates and passes him, and he responds with yet more speed, as they continue upward together.

Within a minute, the farm below them, they both make a sudden arc and dive towards the buildings. A shoal of House Martins flees in front of them, desperately trying to keep ahead, but they are caught unaware and have no height advantage. The falcons, now sometimes hidden from view behind the farm buildings, arc around in co-ordinated attacks, looping up and around – first one, then the other, as if attached by elastic – each drawing the other rapidly back to the other's origin, impossibly fast, and progressing with the running flock.

For a moment both are out of sight, then, up they come, winging back to the pylon. As they near, the female's extra burden is visible: she carries some prey. He follows in her wake, and they land on the girders. For a few minutes they are still, looking out from their vantage, then she begins to eat.

The Crows have watched their return, and now descend from their towering perch to land by the falcons. They do not approach too closely.

The female Hobby takes off and heads straight for the nest, one of the Crows following, but her mate is on its tail, easily catching up, and makes to strike the larger bird, forcing it to swerve his outstretched talons.

Its momentum lost, the Crow gives up its pursuit, and turns back to the pylon. The male Hobby follows it and they land simultaneously several spars apart.

At the nest, the female drops the House Martin, checks on her chicks momentarily, and then goes straight back to her mate. They sit in the sunshine, custard claws just showing beneath their bellies.

Below, in the field, the Yellow Wagtails are still strutting amongst the straw.

Hares' ears poke out above the weeds, and, at the field's edge, poppies nod amongst the daisies.

Butterflies float the soft breezes, and finding mates, spiral to join on the grasses. Butterflies soak up the sun, fan wings, then, when warm enough, close them. Butterflies on the brambles, taste the ripening fruits. Buzzards up above, spread themselves to catch the blue upwellings of the afternoon's air.

Swifts are heading south: very high up – specks drifting across the high dome of the sky, dreaming of Africa.

In the hedge, three young Blackbirds, short tailed, speckly brown and spikey with down, wait to be fed, quietly squeaking, bright gapes showing, blinking at their new world.

Now, from the south, a Peregrine glides over like a missile and makes straight for the pylon. The Crows, cawing in alarm, drop from their pylon perch and go for the riverside trees. The falcon lands where they had been sitting, the Hobbies directly underneath. The Hobbies crane their necks at the threat above, but do not move. For twenty minutes the Peregrine sits: solid, bulky, dark-hooded, its big talons wrapped on the angle of the girder. The Stock Doves have gone from the field below.

Suddenly it takes off, heading towards the church spire, where the Jackdaws, though their nesting season is behind them, still perch. The falcon gets over half way to the spire when the Jackdaws see it, head-on. Immediately, with their alarms echoing, they dive from the stonework and head away, the Peregrine in pursuit, now accelerating directly at the flock.

The Jackdaws and their predator disappear over the rise, the Peregrine's long wings working as it goes. On that horizon a hundred Wood Pigeons flee in every direction, signalling the falcon's route.

At the pylon its spars are now empty – and half a mile distant the Hobbies are up – powering away towards the drifting Swifts. Half way up, they circle, rounding on insects instead, catching several each, still rising on thermals. The up currents take them higher and ever higher, until amongst the clouds, where they turn and begin to hunt: two lines in parallel speeding to the north, shrinking in the distances.

Back at the nest, their well-fed chicks are flapping their growing wings. Their turn will come.

Across the river, a combine harvester and attendant tractors and trailers have entered the large wheat field, its harvesting delayed by rain, the crop part-flattened by the storms. The machines – organised now – line up and the harvesting begins.

The wheat grain begins to spew from the harvester, arcing into the adjacent trailer, as it crawls across the field, a dust cloud hanging in the air behind. A neat bare tract of cut falls behind as it goes, stubble and hay bales standing where the wheat has lately been. As this tract lengthens, the birds descend.

A flock of Black-headed Gulls follow the wake, dipping into the sea behind the combine, picking insects on the wing, or dropping to the stalks below.

Now, a Buzzard flies in, looking for mammals and invertebrates uncovered and injured by the cut, strutting and flying to follow the machine, busily feeding amongst the gulls. Crows and Rooks spiral in from the trees, joining the Buzzard, and soon the field is filled with birds.

Swallows follow, darting ahead and behind, looping at driven insects, hovering above, waiting for the next; never still.

Gradually the wheat is gathered, its myriad rows shrinking as the combine cuts, turns and comes back on itself. The shorn parts increase, and still the birds come in, scattering across the field to glean the bounty.

A Hare suddenly breaks from diminishing cover and sprints across the spikes of straw, keeping low, ears flattened, to the hedge. The Buzzard flap-runs to snatch a running Vole, and, with Crows in attendance, sets about eating it, tail rising to balance as it tears at the prey with its bill, holding it between its talons. The Crows watch and then give up, as the Buzzard swallows the last.

Chaffinches and Yellowhammers, Tree and House Sparrows, Linnets and Goldfinches have come to pick spilt grain from the yellow straw rows, keeping to the hedge side for now, as tractors come and go. A

Kestrel lands close by, briefly putting the small birds back to the hedge, and feeds as it walks.

Two hours pass, the birds are sated, and dot the half-bare field, resting in the hot dust. Two trailers, brim-full of grain, stand at the corner, waiting to be collected, the combine halted temporarily.

The Buzzard, crop bulging from its feeding, takes off at a run and flaps heavily to the trees, into the deep green shade. From the hedge, two Whitethroats drop into the wheat stalks and pick the fallen flies between, as the finches and buntings move out further from cover during the lull. A Willow Warbler joins the Whitethroats, flicking and catching, disappearing between the forest of stubble, reappearing to balance on their tops.

Above, the House Martins swirl above the field, swarming in a shoal, turning and returning, netting the sea of air, filling themselves in easy glides and swoops, blue-black backs glinting in the glare, white bellies moon-like against the field.

The machines start up again, roaring into life and shattering the calm, dust clouds drifting as they crawl across the crop. The standing wheat continues to shrink. Two more Hares gallop from the stalk, racing to cover. The gulls rise up from resting to begin to follow the combine again, and more drop from the blue.

The wheat becomes an island, shrinking to the last few turns of the combine, and now the Voles are visible as they start to run into the open, then turn back into cover in panic. The Kestrel, now hovering on the flank of the huge harvester, starts to stoop, then stops, mid-air as its prey hides again.

As the last lap takes the remaining wheat, and the combine clears the last vestige of refuge, the final Hare streaks from the crop and flees to the hedge. Now the Voles have nowhere to hide, and the Kestrel takes one as it scampers away in vain. The falcon takes it to a telegraph pole to eat.

Suddenly, from nowhere, a Hobby leaps the hedge, hugging the field's surface as it arcs down and along, and too late, the finches rise before it. The Hobby sees the finches, just yards in front, scattering and fleeing as fast as they can, and, with an almost casual twist and tilt, takes a Linnet in a rising loop, turning upside-down as it follows the finch, then turns as it rights itself, making for the pylon across the river.

As this happens the House Martins, evaporate into the haze, zipping away from the Hobby, and Swallows make for the sky, as quick as their blurring wings can take them. Only the Rooks and Crows, like black scraps, dot the pale, newly-shaved face of the field.

The machines move off, their huge and noisy bulks, even redder now, towards the settling sun. The dust lingers, its amber-afterglow absorbing the shafts of low light, above the raw and riven stalks.

It is morning. After a vigil by the Hobby nest and nothing showing, suddenly there is activity.

A chick emerges from the cup of the nest and, standing and flapping stubby wings for a while, it then gets up onto the nest's rim, and though partly-obscured by foliage, is in view.

Its head is almost entirely feathered now, with just a hint of down sticking, punk-like, from its crown. Even its dark moustaches show on its cheeks. And its mantle, mostly dark too, can be seen, the feathers of the wings, though still with plenty of white surrounding them, are growing longer. The youngster is no longer the white downy chick it was.

Now, as it exercises, the extent of the wing feathers is apparent. Though still far from full grown, the primaries can clearly be seen, extending from the downy cover of their coverts. As they flap, the lift generated causes the bird to rise, still grasping firmly to the nest, anchoring itself from tipping from the rim.

Below, at first just one, then two, dark heads show in the nest, as the siblings move around, perhaps exercising too, one facing north, the other south. Half an hour later the first one drops back into the cup of the nest, and joins the others: three heads just above the rim.

From the morning sky, now, a Hobby is dropping from the west. It is the female, and she is carrying a Blackbird, gliding and flapping down on a straight line towards the sycamore, coming in below the crown and rising at the last, slowing on the steep curve, to perch near the top.

Behind a branch her movements suggest she is plucking and eating. Ten minutes pass. Then, slipping from the sycamore, she enters the back of the oak, to show at the parapet of her nest, the remains of her prey in her bill.

Three heads look up and turn her way, and, for the first time, their voices carry across the field, loud in the morning's quiet. She drops the Blackbird to her young and watches for a while, then dissolves away to cover. For half an hour, heads appear from time to time, above the rim of the nest, then disappear below.

At the corner of the lane, a single Little Owl is showing, sitting, one-legged on a lichen-covered limb, high in the oak. A Chiffchaff skitters around it, calling alarms, daring to approach to within a foot or two, then away again, wings flicking, tail pumping. This activity attracts a Yellow-hammer, which comes to sit close to the owl, watching, silently. And now a Great Tit joins in the alarms, 'tink-tink-tinks' loud and insistent. A Chaffinch flies in, perching on the tree's top, searching for the danger.

As the Chiffchaff departs, a Blackbird replaces it, and now a trio of House Sparrows, from the paddock, come to investigate. And, still the Little Owl sits, implacable and unmoved, as its magnet continues to draw in more birds.

A Whitethroat, a Wren and a Robin are now in the oak, ticking and chirring at the owl. Four Long-tailed Tits, pause their foraging along the hedge to add to the commotion, small trills and burps of indignation sounding. Tree Sparrows join the Chaffinch at the top, fidgeting and peering at the noise below them.

The throng continues to build, until perhaps thirty or more strong. The birds, intent on the Owl, do not see the approach of the next bird.

In from the sun, to hide in its blinding, dropping like a winged brick, a Sparrowhawk plummets straight at the oak. So fast has his approach been, and so distracted by the Owl, the birds do not see the hawk until he opens his wings and hangs his talons to slow his descent. But, by now he is just feet away, and has chosen a target. Like a silent bomb exploding, the oak flings off its birds in every direction, the air around filling in a shock wave of fleeing prey. But the Sparrowhawk has already made a kill, taking the Chaffinch from the tree only inches from its perch, and its momentum has driven it and the Chaffinch within the crown. Now, it extricates itself from the oak and flies away, carrying the Chaffinch, eyes already dead, with it.

The Little Owl has gone too.

High-pitched screams are ringing out from the Hobby tree. Both adults are there, flying around it in tight, rapid circles, knifing into the foliage and out again. Two shadows move near the nest: Crows are very close to it. The falcons continue to attack, furious at the corvids, which won't budge.

One Crow then emerges from the nest tree and is carrying something – a small bird perhaps. The female falcon gives chase and the Crow speeds away. The other drops from the tree and follows.

The Hobbies return to their tree and land. Perhaps they have just been robbed.

For an hour or so they remain near the nest, moving to the sycamore and the tree beyond, then they take off together and head for the skies. Ten minutes later the female returns, but her mate is still up high, on another hunt.

Ninety minutes goes by, with only bright butterflies to delight, until the male returns.

She spots him, way off, high up, and takes off from the tree, on a powering line to meet him. Swallows alarm at her departure, and the sparrows whir to the hedge, but she ignores everything and continues, at a shallow angle, which she begins to steepen.

Out across the canal and over the next field, she is diminished by the distance, and now the speck of him is visible. They meet high up, circling around each other as they both head for the nest tree. Now he starts to dive, increasing speed as she follows. Back over the canal, at steeple height, still falling towards the nest, she quickens her pace, now screaming at him, catches him up as he drops some small prey to her – right overhead.

She takes the Blue Tit and continues, knifes into the nest tree to deliver the meal, angling her long wings towards her body as she disappears into the leaves. He glides over the tree, circles it twice, a quick display-quiver of wingbeats as he does so, then lands on the sycamore.

She is quickly beside him, and they sit close together, on their lookout.

A small movement from one of the young is all to be seen at the nest.

The sky begins to colour: turquoise turning to purple, to oranges, to reds. Smoky browns obscure the reds as the sun dips, before the colours fade, then the smoke of night billows out across the sky.

Two falcons watch, still.

Bats begin to hunt as the stars pierce the black.

Now, just one falcon is silhouetted on the tree.

Sunrise at the nest site: clouds out west, pale egg-blue sky to the east, the sun peeking between the woods, casting shadows to lie long across the field, and striping a lick of pale paint on the trees.

A "kee-kee-kee-kee-kee" rings out from the nest tree: the female is calling to her mate; a signal to hunt.

Both lift off, heading south-west, into the breeze, thirty degrees of slope, the sun lighting them up as they go. At five or six hundred feet up, the hunt begins.

Keeping some fifty feet apart, they circle and glide, sometimes accelerating towards Swifts, which keep their distance. Then they drift away, now merely specks in the sky. Suddenly, turning downwind, they're off at speed, on a shallow slope. As they approach they continually row their long wings, always accelerating as they lose more height, faster and faster still, still quickening as they pass overhead, at well above a hundred miles per hour, perhaps much, much more.

But this is just a warm up, a bit of play.

They circle again and drift downwind, now well east of the nest tree. Their line takes them into the distance and below the tree line. Gone.

Ten minutes later the female is back on the sycamore – sneaking in unseen again. She is not alone for long.

Two Jays, moving along the hedgerow trees, have reached the nest tree, and now the female falcon goes for them, slicing around them, through the bigger gaps, as the Jays hide themselves in the smaller branches and leaf clusters. For ten minutes the chase carries on, she unable to shift the Jays, which simply return at the end of each of her sallies.

Then, tiring of the attention, the Jays give up and go to the sycamore, continuing on to the next, and the Hobby, satisfied, settles down to her perch again.

The warmth brings out the butterflies, fluttering along the hedge line, tasting brambles and grasses, floating on the welcoming air, flickering in the dappled shade, gliding along the far side of summer.

The young Rabbits are growing fast, and chase around the hedge base, in one field and the next, never far from cover, scurrying back to burrows at any hint of danger.

Bees are busy in the clover, always on the move, taking flight across the meadow, to the next bloom. Hares sit; ears aloft, half asleep.

From the trees by the river, young Buzzards' begging calls roll out into the air.

In the Little Owl oak, a quiet movement, subtle and almost unnoticed: a shift of shadow. There. Again. A small bird is making its way through the leaves, silent, discreet. A minute passes. Again, a hint of something. A quick flight across the oak, then gone again. Just once, it shows, giving a glimpse. It's a Marsh Tit. A glossy black cap, neat black bib, a pale, just two-toned cheek, then away and gone, without a sound.

Above, on the wires, the hirundines are starting to line up, evenly spaced. Their numbers have almost peaked at the end of the season. They are in condition and getting ready for the long migration to southern Africa; for many, for the first time. Within a month most will have gone, and the Hobbies will follow.

Now, up high, Swifts are passing south, draining from the emptying sky, feeding as they go. Their journey already begun. The female watches them, her preferred prey, but does not go after them. After some time, she takes to the air and circles for insects, lazily drifting and swooping in easy fashion.

Below, Bullfinches undulate down from the copse and come to the hedge: a family group of five, the male standing out, showing off in pinks and piedness, amongst the others' browns. Low whistles pipe icing of sounds over the hawthorn as they progress along, low amongst the brambles and thistles, taking tiny seeds and an occasional caterpillar.

A Blackcap is feeding a youngster there, too. The young bird sits and waits as its parent works in the hedge, collecting grubs, its brown-capped head just peeking from the budding berries. A Willow Warbler suddenly sings, recalling spring to the end of summer.

A Kestrel has joined the Hobby, and they circle the same thermal, without antagonism, sharing the sky and its insects for a while, before gradually drifting apart.

The Hobby's flight takes her higher now, pushed eastwards on the breeze; then she transforms herself with a flexing of her wings and becomes a true hunter. Now, she powers upward, turning into the wind, knifing through its push with the blades of her long sharp wings. Soon she is as high as the passing Swifts, still heading south in small, loose groups.

She bides her time, high up and keeping station, head into the wind, not needing to flap, waiting for her moment: choosing her prey. Ten minutes pass. She is even higher now; the Swifts underneath her. Then she stoops.

With a sudden twist of her shoulders she turns to the south and heads downslope, beginning to flap her wings in increasing depth, until they almost touch above and beneath her, her speed rapid and rapidly increasing, now whipping her primaries faster as she steepens her fall, and the Swift she has chosen gets closer.

The Swift has seen her and is flying at its top speed, falling towards the earth to avoid her, but she follows, closing in, as the Swift starts to spiral and jink in a desperate attempt to shake her off. But she still shortens the gap, watching its intent, cutting off its escape routes as it tries to arc back to the skies, forcing it to remain below her.

They spiral in awesome speed, the ground rushing up to meet them now, as the Swift twists and she flick-flack follows, almost catching it twice as she goes. Then the Swift makes a last manoeuvre, arcs up and sideways at once, she sliding past at greater speed, turning after it, and now gaining on it again, reaches it and takes it, the two scythe-winged forms joining as she pulls up vertically, arcs a loop that corkscrews her level, and begins to fly back to the nest.

With the Swift under her tail, held aerodynamically in her talons, she wings back to the pylon, still at speed, where she glides in, decelerating at the last, and perches, the bulkiness of her prey at her feet. Within a minute her mate lands nearby, obviously having seen her return. He watches as she begins to eat and feathers drop from the girder to the field far below.

Swallows, below them, fly by, seemingly unaware. But he has seen them.

Now, he drives from his perch and, suddenly at speed, drops towards the Swallows. They see him, and scatter across the field, in uncoordinated flights, as he arcs at one, low against the stubble, but misses as it sidesteps his outstretched claw, and he slices past, giving up the hunt immediately, as if indifferent.

Now his mate takes the Swift's remains back to the nest, and he follows, their lines in parallel; he above. She goes directly in to the nest, while he lands above, at the top of the tree. After a minute she is out, and sitting on top of the sycamore. A Buzzard comes past, almost brushing her, but, unusually, she ignores it, allowing it to continue, away from her young.

In the newly-harvested wheat field across the river, beyond the pylon, the birds are flocking. A hundred or so Rooks and several Crows are pecking at the exposed ground, Black-headed Gulls are walking and flying alternatively, snapping at insects, Lesser Black-backs in similar fashion. Twenty or more Pied Wagtails flicker, squabbling over new-found feeding territories in the field, and Yellow Wagtails walk amongst the stalk rows, occasionally sallying up to catch a fly. A herd of Wood Pigeons waddles fatly.

Two Buzzards are striding at the back, picking invertebrates in this new resource, and a Kestrel hovers just above. Finches and buntings fly to and from the cover of the hedges, barely starting to feed before spooking at nothing, back to safety. Then, back out in two and threes, until forty or fifty creep over the ground, picking spilt grain.

Skylarks, too, cryptic but just visible, keep their heads down, running over the striped mounds of the old furrows, down to the tiny valleys between.

And two or three hundred Starlings swirling in one flock, rise and turn, rise and turn, like an animated carpet, flying up and landing again, covering a portion of the field with the dark rug of their numbers.

Blackbirds chase Song Thrushes along the hedged border, and Robins drop from the lookout of the thorn to the field to grab a morsel, and back as if on delayed elastic, to watch once more.

A small group of warblers: four Whitethroats, two Blackcaps, and three Willow Warblers, pick and hover amongst the stubble and weeds, flicking and snapping.

Hares sit and nibble, watching for danger, hunkered down in the remnants of the cover.

Suddenly a small commotion starts at the corner of the field, by the gate. A Stoat has just emerged through the gap and bounds in a low looping gallop along the hedge, stopping every few yards to stretch up and look around for prey, and for danger.

Yellowhammers and Chaffinches flee back to the safety of the hedge top, watching the Stoat; the Blackbirds start an uninterrupted alarm, which is taken up by others in a bright chain of sound as they follow from a safe distance.

The Stoat has smelt Rabbit. Now, disappearing into the cover of the verge, it moves rapidly along the hedgerow. Ahead, a small group of young Rabbits nibble, heads down, unaware of the approach of the predator. They are out in the open, amongst the scant cover of wheat stalks as the Stoat emerges and runs at them.

The Rabbits seem confused; some run, but circle back, others freeze, rooted to the spot. The Stoat approaches slowly. The Rabbits stare, petrified.

Now, the Stoat starts to leap and swerve, zigzagging as it goes, towards and then away from its prey. One Rabbit runs. The Stoat ignores it. Two in front are rooted to the spot, only turning their heads to watch the cavorting Stoat, which gradually shortens its distance between them, still leaping and rolling as it comes ever closer.

Now, within two feet of one, the Stoat makes a direct dash at the Rabbit, which does not move, and grabs it by the neck. Though a youngster, the Rabbit is bigger and heavier than its predator, and only now does it try to run. Carrying the Stoat with it, the Rabbit begins to sprint, but the Stoat twists around its neck – its short, black-tipped tail quivering quickly in the move – and sinks its teeth into its throat, and the Rabbit slows to a halt. For a while the two are locked together, the Stoat partly under its victim, then, the Rabbit seems to sigh and collapses to the ground.

The Stoat takes a proper hold of the now-dead Rabbit and, with huge effort, starts to drag it towards the hedge. The other Rabbit looks on, still on the same spot. The Stoat and its prey pass close by, the Stoat pauses, dropping the Rabbit, as if considering making another kill. The Rabbit stares back and still remains unable to run.

For a time-stopped moment the Stoat and Rabbit stand, considering each other, then the Stoat picks up its prey again and drags it back to cover. As it disappears, the inevitable Magpie drops to the hedge to see what the activity is, but the Stoat has gone, down a convenient burrow, to feast.

For another five minutes the Rabbit sits in stupor, then finally rouses itself and runs away.

As it does so a 'cronk' drops from the sky, as a Raven flies in and lands on the pylon at the field's corner, staring down at the throng below. A Buzzard lifts from the field and heads for the trees, and the Raven dives at it, calling its 'cronks' as it falls to it, flipping upside down and back again as it goes. The Buzzard turns on its back and presents its formidable talons to the Raven, mewling in protest at its antagonist. The Raven climbs back to the pylon and the Buzzard continues to the copse.

The smell of drying hay wafts from the bales and wheat stalks as bees buzz over the cut, searching for flowers newly exposed. And the butterflies have found the field too, flickering amongst the birds and bees.

Above, in the deep blue ocean of the sky, a dark arrow flies across: a Hobby is heading for its nest.

Two Cormorants circle, looking down at the river beside the field, trying to find a gap to land in through the trees. Heavily, they lift back up and head off to fish elsewhere.

A flock of twenty Grey Partridges marches under the gate, looking for cover, necks stretched, then crouching and creeping into the stubble. All but two are young birds, either two broods of one, or two families joined up. Slowly they make their way through the field, picking delicately as they go, only their backs showing, except for a sentinel parent, standing out to watch for danger. A Hare, unmoving, watches as they pass by. They move behind a hay bale and one adult hops up on top, black belly patch showing, on lookout duty. As they move away he joins them, slipping back to cover, and they all evaporate into the wobble of haze rippling up from the hot land.

Back at the Hobbies' nest a great deal of activity can just be glimpsed through the oak's leaves. On the rim of the nest, two young Hobbies are flapping their wings vigorously, just far enough apart not to clash. The third chick's head pokes out from the nest cup, watching its siblings as they exercise.

For forty minutes more this carries on, when their activity is interrupted.

Appearing like a phantom at the nest, an adult lands, carrying a large prey item; perhaps a Swallow. The young all stop their flapping as the food is given to one, which takes it to the base of the nest to eat. Three heads just above the parapet – one dipping down to feed on the Swallow – the others watching.

As the day comes to a close, the young settle to the nest, the adults elsewhere, unseen.

It is already warm, even before sunrise. The swell of bulging clouds seems to sag so soon, laden as they are with wet air. The hidden sun strikes their tops, setting them alight in orange and yellow, their overhanging summits shadowing their flanks.

Migrant Hawkers, high above the hedge, are already hunting, the midges thick in the moist air: clouds of them coalesce and disperse, the swarms darkening and fading as they do. White butterflies flap limply, like damp pieces of cloth. Bees swim, rather than fly – the air like soup.

The Swallows are low, finding easy flies in the rich thickness of the air, slipping along, gapes opening as they swerve, fattening further. The horizon's light catches them and they shine silkily blue above, orange breasts glowing and plump creamy bellies rounding their figures as they porpoise over fences, hedges and down into ditches, whipping the flippers of their wings: reef fish along the coral.

An early grasshopper begins to rasp from the meadow, just as the dazzling edge of the rising sun wobbles over the hills out east. Then the air begins to stir. Warm and gentle wafts barely moving the leaf, push at the swarms of midges, and they sway like kelp in the current, rippling in response.

Clouds, at first wholly white, crowd the sky, now their tops spread and darken: cauliflowers starting to rot. The barrage of them drifts slowly northward, billowing in full fatness, and their bellies begin to rumble.

Between them, around them, in the narrow chasms of the overhanging cliffs of cloud, Swifts, glinting in the tilt, slice through, pale throats bulging with flies: a packed lunch carried with them against leaner times ahead.

Then, from the white cliff edges, two dark scimitar blades strike: the Hobby pair is speeding toward the Swifts.

The male is ahead and above his mate, and above a group of four or five Swifts, she is just below. As he accelerates the Swifts speed up too, but the female Hobby outpaces them all, beginning to rise towards them as she does so. Sandwiched between the two falcons, the Swifts break their loose formation, jerking upwards and down again, as they spot the male above, taking them into her path.

Now, one arches downwards, passing the female on her rise, and the male dives from above, an incredible spurt of speed hurtling him towards the Swift. She, now above, continues to rise for two more seconds, watching her mate below.

The Swift swerves out of the way of the male, rising in a rapid jinking flick, the falcon now underneath him. That is what the female has waited for. Now she arcs and dives at the Swift, which, in desperation, heads groundward again. But his manoeuvres have slowed him just a little and she is closing in rapidly, turning the blades of her wings to the earth, head down and plummeting.

She makes to take the Swift as she passes, but again it dodges in a flick, and she misses, now under him. The Swift swerves away from her, and she lets it go, but her mate is now on another loop that speeds him at the hapless Swift which sees his bullet-like approach, and turns back.

She spirals around and the Swift responds, their double helix described in the sky, then she gets above him, almost in reach, but again allows a gap. As she does this, the Swift trying to keep an eye on her, her mate makes another lightning strike and hits his prey with a deadly bolt. The Swift is knocked, and spins, and before it turns again, she has taken it on her pass, and tucks it under her as they both turn back northward and head for the nest.

As they reach the nest site, the first rumble of thunder barrels out from the clouds, rolling like a cannon ball across the sky.

On his way to the sycamore the male Hobby swerves down and casually catches a Migrant Hawker over the hedge, and eats it as he glides the final few yards. His mate lands on the nearer tree and trims the Swift of its primaries, eats its head and takes the body to the nest, and her young. Three dark-masked heads move as she flies in, and Bluebottles circle at her disturbance. Within the minute she is out from the tree and goes to sit with her mate. They look out at the darkening, cloud-filled sky, as another throb booms and a flash of a lightning sheet turns the black cloud silver-white.

To the north, the receding clouds drop a dark curtain of rain across the river, but the southern sky is already brightening in the slight and warm breeze. The storm, now out towards the hills, puts on a spectacle: flashes of light sparking in growing number and duration, floodlighting the sulphur and black wall of cloud, thunder like dynamite's explosions from a distant quarry.

From the edge of the nest, one large, and mostly-feathered chick, watches the display as one of its siblings continues to feed.

On the pylon in the newly-cropped field across the river, a Peregrine sits, half-asleep, hunched: a pale blob against the dark sky. Unaware, dozens of Rooks and scores of Wood Pigeons strut across the stubble below. The wagtails, buntings and finches are gleaning grain near the safety of the hedge, and several Tree Sparrows – perhaps all youngsters of three or four broods of a single pair, dot the hawthorns. Starling numbers are down from yesterday – but fifty or more stride around, thrusting bills into the soil.

Suddenly all these smaller birds rise up as one. The Starlings join up and bunch to a tight ball. The others dive for cover to the thorns. A Sparrowhawk's dark silhouette is crossing the field like a running shadow, skimming the stalks, her breast almost touching the cut tops.

She heads straight for the hedge and plunges in, half disappearing within, long legs probing the foliage, wings flapping against the leaf. A flurry of finch and sparrow bursts out from the far side and the Sparrowhawk, in a flash-turn leaps the hedge and follows, disappearing beyond as she goes for the prey, broad wings whirring in a short spurt of speed.

For a while the Starlings circle above, then drift away to feed at another field.

The Peregrine, unaffected by the passing storm, slumbers on.

At the river a Heron, having hunted motionless for two hours at the same spot, though appearing to doze, suddenly uncoils its snake-like neck and stabs at the water, snake-strike fast, and comes up with a sizeable fish. It stands for a while as the fish wags its tail, trying in vain to wriggle from the grasp, but the Heron's vice-like bill holds it firm.

After a few more minutes the fish has been subdued, and the Heron lifts its head, opens the grip on the fish and, with a single jerk, takes it, head down, and swallows. A bulge stretches the Heron's neck, which ripples along as the fish slides down. Its patient hunt successful, the Heron lifts from the bank with a jump, and flaps heavily away on huge broad wings, long legs under it, feet jutting behind its tail, turns and heads away over the trees.

Behind, from the field, all the Wood Pigeons have risen in a clattering cloud. The Peregrine is no longer on the pylon. Though flying, it seems not to be hunting, and ignores the pigeons, making off northward, towards the dark clouds disappearing on the horizon. For a while the pigeons swirl, then finally glide back down to their feeding. As they land, a Hare gallops away, stiff-legged, ears aloft, and heads for the hedge.

In the paddock a flock of Linnets feeds under the horses' hooves. Tree Sparrows join them. Only their movements give away their presence, cryptic colours hiding them as they pause. But, even so, from its tree, the unseen Little Owl sees them; but they are too far away. A pair of Yellow Wagtails is fly-catching around the water trough, where four Collared Doves come down to drink.

The afternoon is hot, and despite the passing storm, is still and humid. The horses' flanks twitch, trying to shift crawling flies, thick on their hides. Their dusty tails flick ineffectively. One or two roll in the dry dirt, and Pied Wagtails flicker around them, snapping at the insects.

In the weedy corner, a Buzzard sits on the fence. Two Magpies try to chivvy it away, hopping around it, chattering rattles: a hail of bullets aimed its way. The Buzzard ignores them, barely moving. A Song Thrush has a snail, and emerges from the nettle patch, carrying it by the shell's edge, to a small stone fallen from the wall, and smashes the snail three or four times, shifts its grip and repeats. The shattered shell comes away and the Song Thrush swallows the considerable ball of wet, still squirming, flesh.

Then, from the Hobbies' nest, the young are calling out, as one of the parents slips in to deliver another meal to one of them.

One now gets up at the nest's edge, and begins to exercise, its dark feathers now more prominent than the loose down remnants that waft as it flaps its wings. It walks the parapet as it continues, balancing and clinging on to the twigs of the nest, disappearing behind the foliage that obscures the bulk of its home.

For an hour it carries on, almost unstopping, flapping away vigorously.

Then a 'keer keer keeer' sounds softly from the tree and, after a minute, the adults take to the air.

The female takes the lead, heading horizontally away west, her mate following at first, then catching her and passing. In a minute of steady flight, they land on the pylon's girders, and look out across their territory.

Swifts are sparser in the sky now; soon only one or two late passage birds will go through, on their way south. The sky seems empty without their continual presence. The falcons search the clouds for familiar specks, but other prey are still plentiful.

Two Buzzards circle in the late afternoon lift, warm air still rising in invisible bubbles. A flock of House Martins pause in their hunting to swirl around the Buzzards, huge in comparison to their diminutive forms, and the Hobbies, always watching, launch from the pylon.

Making for the same thermal to aid their rise, the falcons spiral upward towards the Martins, but before long, the prey are heading off, speeding away from the Hobbies. With a shift of pace, the pair accelerates and power upwards, the Martins now high and distant.

The Hobbies continue to go after the fleeing Martins, now almost invisible in the distance, then, they too dwindle and, still in pursuit after three more miles, finally vanish.

As another afternoon turns to evening the falcons are up in the cubic miles of their sky.

A slight breeze blows cooler the next morning, the air fresher, though still warm. Not a cloud mars the pale sky, from horizon to horizon. As the sun gathers itself for launch on the eastern horizon the Hobby chicks are, as yet, invisible in the nest.

The Swallows wait for the flies, which are just rising from night-time stall, and sit on the wires, fidgeting before the off, as if waiting for the flag.

A Fox trots across the meadow, fully out in the early light, back to its den in the wood. Hares, on hind legs, watch from safe distances, ears along their backs, front paws drooping limply in front.

Sparrows, late risers, chirp from eaves and watch as the sun pours over the horizon, like molten iron from the crucible, setting the earth alight.

A female Kestrel dives from hovering, thumping into the grass, but comes up empty-handed and perches itself back on the slow-moving air, having to work in so little wind, body almost vertical as its wings pump to hold it still. Five minutes go, then the Kestrel scribes a small circle, and stops a few yards further along the verge. For a few seconds more she continues to hold station, only twenty feet high, then plummets to the ground, and this time stays down to kill.

She lifts with a mouse, to the nearest tree, and sits, her prey held under one foot. She is so close that her black claws show clearly against the faded grey of the branch, the glint in her eye is the far-off sun's reflection.

Now the Swallows are up, swooshing silently over the fields, and rising gradually with the fly.

Black-headed Gulls begin to drop in from roosts out west, on angled wings, turning back into the breeze before touchdown. The adults are already losing the brown hoods of their breeding plumages, and the immature taking on their first-winter garb. More come in, until forty or fifty are walking in the field, prodding and picking.

This small crowd of gulls is gradually approaching the field's edge, when, like a stone, a hidden Buzzard drops from the nearest ash tree, and thumps down onto an immature gull, immediately pinning it to the ground.

With a deafening din of alarms screeching out, the remaining gulls fly up in terror, spiralling up as fast as they can, as the victim vainly tries to flap from under the Buzzard, which has its wings half-spread for balance. For the next hour the Buzzard sits and eats, feathers spreading around the now-dead gull. A pair of Crows approach and harass, and Magpies watch from the ash. A Great spotted Woodpecker flies up from the fence post to the tree and alarms at the Buzzard below, raising hackles and crown feathers, as it shuffles up and down its branch.

The Buzzard's crop is distended, and it has eaten as much as it can, before it decides to leave its exposed position for the cover and shade of the trees, leaving behind a bowl of bright plumage, which disperses in the breeze. The Crows hop onto the remains and pick at the carcass, but there is little left for them to feast upon.

Out west, a filament of cloud is drawn along the horizon: a single line written at the foot of the page.

There is movement at the Hobbies' nest.

A young bird, from the nest rim, jumps across a short gap and lands on the nearest branch. It stands there, swaying slightly and tries to turn back, awkwardly shuffling around. Another chick emerges onto the nest's top and stands to watch its sibling, its head rotating and swivelling, as if in disbelief.

Now a third head peers out over the parapet at the activity beyond, stretching to see as the first youngster takes a leap back to the nest, over-judging the distance and nearly falling in. The two on the rim now begin to exercise, clashing wings at first, before spacing out a little. They look sturdy and powerful now, their wings growing longer, their down receding as it is replaced by dark feather.

Across, from the pylon, both parents are approaching. The male is carrying something which he transfers to his bill; his mate follows. He flies to the nest tree, at the back, then emerges through the gap at the crowded nest's edge with his prey. The two young stop flapping and call to him, crouching, necks stretched. But he ignores them and bends to the head of the third youngster and hands over a large morsel.

For a minute or so there are three at the nest's spattered ledge, then the adult slips away to the sycamore, and joins his mate.

A butterfly-filled hour passes as morning becomes afternoon. One or two Buzzards dot the clear sky, and a Sparrowhawk circles above the paddock. Three Cormorants wing their way eastwards, trying to form a formation with too few.

The Hobby young have settled back to the cup of the nest. Out west the line of cloud has grown, nearing like an incoming wave, still far distant.

Now, to the north, a single Swift is heading this way, and as it nears, the Hobbies take to the sky. They head away from the Swift, steadily rising, and as it passes they are still way below it. But they are only start-ing, and now, the Swift in front of them, they speed faster, on a direct heading at their intended prey. As they reach the same height, they are now two miles to the south, and still they rise. Swift and falcons dwindle to specks, then the specks shrink, until only imagined in the eye.

Along the canal and past the copse, where the meadow is thronged by butterflies. An Emperor Dragonfly flashes by, blue and green blur-ring along its line. At the hedge, Long-tailed Tits – a group of a dozen or more, tails poking from the blackthorn and cherry, leapfrogging along the length towards the water's edge.

A Nuthatch rings out from the treetops, drowning out the faintest whisper of two Goldcrests. A Brown Hawker patrols the towpath, spiralling above the bridge to avoid the short sunless tunnel. Young Coal Tits and Blue Tits cling to leaf clusters and pick from undersides of foliage, and a Chiffchaff, with a metal ring on its left leg, calls a short whistle from a bramble.

A Brimstone billows past: a tiny ship under full sail, fluttering gently into the wood. On the ivy covering the bridge, the flowers are swarming with honeybees and hoverflies, and a Holly Blue basks on the vertical sunny side, head down, creeping along a single leaf.

Suddenly in a neon flash, a Kingfisher, fast and silent, zips under the arch and out into the light and beyond, rounding the curve of the canal – past brightly painted, geranium-planted narrowboats – and is gone.

A Yellowhammer calls from a single shrub in the meadow's centre, as a Whitethroat pokes its head from the thorns, then turns back and disappears within.

The young rowan trees' berries are ripe, and on one, a Mistle Thrush stands guard over the larder, flying at a Blackbird daring to land in its tree, rattling a warning, as it flashes pale outer tail feathers as it rounds on the intruder.

A Green Woodpecker flies from the copse into the meadow. It is searching for ants on the ground, probing between the plants into small mounds, lapping up the grubs beneath with its long tongue. Its green back hides it well, only its red-capped head giving it away as it lifts to check for danger, before digging again. As it probes, the lime-yellow rump shows, as it holds its tail against the ground for purchase. Then, suddenly spooked, it flies off, bounding in long heavy undulations back to the trees, visible briefly, then moving into leafy cover.

Vole holes dot the lush grasses, but only once does a single short scurry sound from one run, as a Vole darts back, unseen, to cover. Goldfinches balance on dandelion clocks and pick the tiny seeds from the filamentous plumes, which cling to their short conical bills as they eat. Small tinkling notes trickle down the wind as they move to another cluster, flashing yellows and whites as they go.

At the edge of the canal a Frog is trying to climb out of the water at the vertical stone bank, front legs scrabbling ineffectively as it thrashes its webbed feet behind. A Mallard swims by and the Frog ducks underwater, the frog-coloured surface hiding it immediately.

The poplars flutter in a sudden gust of wind, and at once the world seems cooler.

Out west the nearing cloud bank has become a dark wall, now filling over a quarter of that quadrant of the sky. There is a faint hint of the smell of rain on the wind.

Now, a dozen Swifts swoop over, as low as the poplar tops, and two Sand Martins pass south with them. A few minutes later more Swifts slant in from up high, anticipating the closing of the weather, turning eastwards on the wind, away from the rain to come.

A Little Owl alarms from the boatyard just as the first cloud obscures the westering sun.

Thirty or so Lapwings, following the canal's course, wing over to the east, as if trying to outrun the incoming weather.

When it comes, the rain starts almost as a drizzle. Now the sky is charcoal-grey, two-thirds of its dome obscured by the cresting wave of cloud. Dusk falls early, and the rain starts to persist, growing heavier gradually, and the world grows cold, fanned by an increasing wind that slants the downpour at forty-five degrees.

The evening is drowned out in the insistent hum and throb of wind and rain, and night falls as the last bright crescent of the sky is closed by the leaden lid of the stratocumulus.

Neither moon nor stars penetrate the clouds until almost dawn.

By sunrise the next day the rain has gone, the clouds remaining only eastwards, with a few blowing in the wind overhead. The world has cooled considerably – the aftermath of the cold front from the evening before – and a steady westerly streams in.

In the big stubble field there is much activity. A flock of Lapwings, already strutting, are joined by three Curlews: dropping down, long curved bills showing the way. And a few Oystercatchers are back to add further to the variety and a splash of red.

Rooks and Crows and Jackdaws herd together and slowly progress across the field, heads down, mostly into the wind; and, as they turn, their skirts blow and fan. The rain-softened soil has opened a whole new habitat for feeding, and all these bills probe and pull at newly-available food. A hundred fat Wood Pigeons waddle amongst the stalks and pick at seeds.

The Swallows seem energised after the last few days, and rise after the wind-blown flies. Above, amongst the scudding clouds, House Martins swirl.

In the paddock, the horses are skittish, relieved at the wetting and reduced heat. Wagtails are busy, running and launching out after insects, tails blowing angles in the breeze. Two Little Owl young peer down from their oak at the House Sparrows on the fence. A Dunnock sings and a Great Tit calls. A ripple of Skylark blows down from above. Two, three, Buzzards tilt in the wind, on the easy lift.

The sun appears, white-bright from over the low line of cloud drifting away to the east, and blinds as it catches the wet lane, skimming off to light the undersides of the overhanging leaf. Vapour starts to rise from the tarmac and blows away down the wind.

Suddenly a Hobby is alarming, as a Buzzard slices in over the nest, and as it continues, the falcon flies at it, almost touching its bulk with a rapier parry, twisting away to attack again. But the Buzzard is quickly gone, windward, yawing and tacking against the blowing. The Hobby circles back to its nest tree and lands, bending forward for balance against the breeze.

Some of the flocks get up and swirl around at the Buzzard's passing, but re-settle quickly to their feeding. Two Hares chase across the wet weed, running a wide arc that takes them back to the beginning. A Siskin, calling brightly, whisks overhead, wind-assisted, as Meadow Pipits parachute down to join the crowds.

At the Hobby nest, as light lances through the leaves, there is nothing to be seen at first. Then a brown head of one of the young appears. After a while it clambers out to the nest rim and peers out at the rising sun. Two more heads move around below, silhouetted against the spotlight sun.

Above the river, two Swans are heading west, low over the trees, huge and pale, under-lit yellow-white, long necks leading as they flap deeply to lift their weight.

Now one of the adult Hobbies, the female, from a hidden perch, sets off across the field. The flock below continues to feed as she passes overhead, heading for the pylon, on which she lands. Only nearby Swallows alarm briefly at her flight, then resume their hunt as the falcon lands again.

At the nest, the youngster jumps out onto a branch, out of sight amongst the foliage. Then, some minutes later, only its shadow visible, moves to another limb. One of the other young is on the nest top now, and begins its morning exercises, the sun lighting it up well. It looks more adult-like now, less dumpy, longer in dark feather, just the odd tuft of down persisting here and there.

The female has left the pylon.

Swifts are still heading south, fewer in number now, passing high overhead in the clearing sky. But at the farm the House Martins are still busy with their breeding season. They still have young in the nest, and young from the previous brood try their chance, begging from commuting parents as they return to the nest-bound chicks.

Tree Sparrows along the hedges and Linnets in the verges move along in bounding flocks as a horse and rider clop down the lane. At the corner they turn, flying back to their origin at the other end of the hedge, as the horse goes through the gate. Above, a pair of Collared Doves coo – like comb and paper whistles – sound out loudly and fly along the paddock. A bright Yellowhammer drops in to drink from the trough by the metal gate, dipping delicately and lifting his yellow head to swallow: three more times and he is done, then he drops to the paddock, hopping around muddy patches, searching for seed.

A Blackbird alarms and flies to the hedge, flicking his tail, alert at some unseen danger. The Yellowhammer squats flat for a while, then continues to feed.

Butterflies flicker over the verge now the sun has warmed the world. Green-veined Whites and Speckled Woods, Tortoiseshells and Peacocks, and a single Red Admiral search for sustenance and swirl: pattern and colour, multiplying the beauty of the day.

From the trees by the river, two Buzzards glide to the field, the squawks of Jays protesting sending them on their way. As they settle in the stubble, the flocks move away, rolling up like a shaken carpet, to land at a safe distance, as the Buzzards begin to stride on wide, feathered legs.

Now, Swallows are alarming, circling to the south, grouping in a swarm, on the rise. Over the river a Hobby is after House Martins, a flock in front fleeing northward, the falcon on their tails. Predator and prey disappear beyond the trees, more Swallows rising from the further farms there, showing the direction of the hunt.

Back at the nest, two youngsters are on the nest edge, flapping away, facing north and south. A Magpie comes in, hopping around the perimeter of the activity, but the Hobbies ignore it and continue their exercises. Bluebottles circle the season-worn nest, now flecked liberally with white droppings, and the young Hobbies stop to snap as they pass.

Suddenly a young Blue Tit appears on the nest, watching the Hobbies for a second, absolutely still, then vanishes quickly. The young Hobbies, their workout done, settle on the nest rim to watch the world, peering out through the gaps in the foliage to the land and sky beyond.

Then, the adult male flies in, his shadow arriving at the back. The youngsters start to beg from him, but he sits for a while, looking at the nest, a House Martin's remains held in his bill. Then he moves out of sight and delivers the meal to the young bird somewhere nearby in the tree. The others watch their sibling, pointing to his position, as their father flies off again, disappearing to the back of the oak.

At the deep ditch by the field's corner, its narrow surface covered with pond weed, a Heron hunches, half-asleep, as two young Reed Buntings perch above, on the bulrushes and on the irises, bounding from one to the next, white-edged tails fanning, flicking, then they drop to the water's edge and disappear into the sedge.

Across, near the barn where it was born, a young Kestrel hovers, looking down on rusted ploughs and harrows, which are half-hidden by the nettles thrusting rank between. Nervous Linnets watch from weed tops, one eye on the falcon, as they feed, keeping quiet so as not to draw attention.

House Sparrows, at dry margins, are dust-bathing in the paddock, while Pied Wagtails flicker around puddles, still muddy wet from the rain. Swallows sit on the wooden fence line, watching Goldfinches twittering on thistle-tops, and Rabbits stretch, sunbathing by the nettle patch near their burrows. Beyond, by the canal's low, stony embankment, dandelions dot the mosses. A Brown Hawker skims just above the flowers, swerving at flies as it progresses, leaping the hedge to vanish below its line.

Everything is calm, when suddenly the Swallows twist away from their fence perch, Goldfinches spiral into the panicked air, and Wagtails rise to join the Swallow swarm alarming upward. The House Sparrows go to the cover of the hedge, as the scythe-like shape of a Hobby slices in from over the canal. As she passes, directly overhead, a Swallow's limp shape can just be seen, below her tail.

She goes straight to her nest. The flocks of frightened birds begin to re-settle to paddock and fence and field.

At the nest the visible young are in its cup, and the Swallow has been delivered to one of them. She stands at the nest's rim for a while, watching her young, then turns and moves to the sycamore, perching at its top, scalpel-sharp, obsidian eyes watching the world. She preens briefly, and pulls a feather from her claw. It drifts downwind, its filaments weighted by a tiny, dry drop of blood.

In the field below, the Wood Pigeons, their morning feeding done, lift off heavily to the trees to digest, crops bulging. The Lapwings are asleep, heads turned to their bottle green backs, head-plumes wafting, as they sit amongst the stubble. The Rooks have already moved on, the Curlews, too, have gone.

A score of noisy young Starlings helter-skelter down to the field and begin probing the softened earth, opening beaks to separate soil and snapping up invertebrates and their larvae. The Hobby has seen them; they are oblivious of her watch point position. She allows them to close the gap between them, heads down unwisely.

She launches from the sycamore. Two long fast wingbeats and then she stoops at the flock below.

She is only yards away when the first alarm sounds, and it is a Swallow's. The Starlings have heard it anyway, and now rise and ball as the falcon circles them, going underneath the flock and behind them, turning a tight arc as they spin to the sky. She twists around and, now above, dives at the Starlings, which flash away from her speeding approach, their wings co-ordinating in the manoeuvre, like a fish shoal from a shark.

She puts on all her speed at them, suddenly right up to the bait ball in a flash, almost touching the nearest one, then turns vertically in a blink and her speed fires her towards the sky. The Starlings seem unsure what to do, as the falcon, at first going away from them, makes a hairpin turn at the apex of her rise, and accelerates towards them again, turning on her back for half a second in the twist.

She drops towards the Starlings, reaching them again in a moment, turns to her side, claws out, then suddenly arcs away, flying at a Swallow passing in the opposite direction, getting to within striking distance in seconds. Once more she chooses not to make a kill, and slides past the panicked swallow which twists one way as she goes the other. Her speed takes her, without further effort, back to her sycamore, where she glides in to land at the same branch.

And, out across the field, a group of Starlings are still flying away.

The Lapwings, still in the stubble, are awake now.

An hour later the male is on his approach, and she takes off to intercept him. They meet, half a mile out, five hundred feet high, and she turns to match his speed as he accelerates downslope towards their nest. He has some prey – as he nears it is, apparently, a House Sparrow. She wants it from him and calls to him, but he keeps it for another hundred yards, then lets it drop, as he rises, dangling his feet.

She sees it fall, turning over, head-down in its drop, and meets it in her level flight, legs extended to catch it, and takes it to the oak. He turns to the pylon behind him now, and lands near the top.

At the nest two young are out in the tree, but close by. They see her impending arrival and call to her, and she answers, swerving in to land inside the oak. A third head in the nest watches her land.

She delivers the Sparrow and is quickly away again, flying across to join her mate on the metal giant at the far side of the field.

And the bees are buzzing round the dandelions and daises; there's a warm wind blowing through woods and the fields; there's a Yellowhammer calling from the top of hedge now and a Buzzard tilts and flashes as it flies above it all.

At the pond the electric blue dots of the Blue-tailed Damsels float above the lilies; and Brown Hawkers skim the water, where Great-crested Grebes surface with silver fish, burnt-orange frills fringing their heads, and Coots dive for pond weeds below the glossy surface, wobbling the sun's reflection like a boat on the sea. A Heron is hunched by the willows at the edge and Sedge Warblers climb into the afternoon light; a Moorhen is calling as a Swallow swooshes in and takes a drink, sipping the sun, her bottle-blue wings held above, her creamy belly reflects a fish below the surface, swimming in time until it dives at the Swallow's rise.

Ringlets flicker down from the hedges and lay their eggs at the bases of the grasses, the eyes of their underwings blinking as they flutter. Speckled Woods spiral in corkscrew combat from the oaks of the copse, and Meadow Browns in clouds dance across the lushness of the marshy pastures; Emerald Damselflies lift suddenly from the irises, float-flying softly, slowly, tissue-wings dissolving in their whirring, bodies shining green sheens in the dappled shade of the green sword leaves, landing soon again, pale blue tail segments showing in the sunlight. Below, big brass and copper-coloured snails cling, sleeping on the iris stems, deep in the shade and moistness, away from Song Thrushes' searches.

Minnows rise and plunge back to shallow deeps, and Sticklebacks stand guard in tiny territories, and the faint glow of orange flanks shows below the pond's green soupy surface. Whirligig Beetles coruscate – tiny bronze pebbles dimpling the surface – spinning madly like mercury droplets on tilted glass. Water Boatmen row across the underside, a single set of oars sculling steadily, on the hunt for aquatic invertebrates.

And in the shallows a Palmate Newt rests in a sun shaft sneaking through the foliage, on a waterlogged leafy shelf, its broad flat tail curled at its flank.

And, at last, a Kingfisher calls to split the silence and slices a bolt of blue across the pond, coming to a dazzling finish on a darkly shaded stump, jutting out over the water's margin.

Evening slides around the land, the sun beginning to blind out west. Greens become dark, blackening the eastern edges of the wood, hedges' shadows lean, long across the meadow and even the pale stubble stalks turn from gold to ash. Bird calls reach out, louder in the late of the day, enmeshing the land in long lines of sound.

The last Cormorants of the day head back east, their poaching finished until tomorrow. Their Pterodactyl outlines: skinny, angular wings black against the paler sky.

The pied shapes of seven Magpies enter the woods, only their whites showing against the trees, and disappear within, the last cackling calls rattling back from ratchet throats.

The stubble field has emptied of birds and the paddocks are quiet; a Grey Wagtail's sharp needle call pricks the calm as it flies along the canal's length, as a single Swift skims the evening air.

The breeze drops with the dipping sun as the western sky begins to burn, yellow furnaces with tongues of orange flame, charcoal at the horizon's grate.

Above the pylon, Rooks and Jackdaws are heading for roosts. A single Hobby, at the apex, stares out into the evening light. At the corner, by the copse, a Little Owl is chasing the shadowy form of a Tawny Owl, out too early. The Tawny Owl, wings bowed, glides back to the trees – the Little Owl on its tail – which then turns, its job done, and undulates back to the telegraph pole to wait for moths, just beginning to emerge into the darkening air.

Blackbirds start to "pink, pink" as they settle for the night.

A Yellowhammer calls, just once.

The Hobby, down from the pylon, is above the field, a dark scythe re-cutting the stubble, catching insects as it glides slowly, grabbing at rising moths and eating them on the wing. It makes its way across and back again, working the field. As the tide of shadows pools across the land, the falcon's silhouette fades and blurs, but it is still out there, in the dusk, hunting on.

Now the first bats flicker out into the dark sky, the Little Owls are calling, short whistles bouncing across the night. A Grey Partridge sings a half song from an invisible corner of the field, underscored by the low mournful hoot of the Tawny Owl.

Somewhere above, a Hobby flies on, hunting in the darkness now, for bats.

Dawn: two Hobbies on the pylon, one plucking and eating some prey, too distant to identify. The day is almost still, but a smudge of cloud smears the sky.

Both the falcons take off together, one with the remains of the prey. They are coming this way, towards the nest. The male has the food, and he goes in on a curve, at the front of the tree, and lands facing away, at the near side. Three heads bob up to his arrival, calling to him, and he bends and drops the prey to one, standing to watch for several minutes.

His mate circles the nest tree, just above the crown, then swoops at a Magpie, which has approached at the signs of activity, and chases it off. She returns as her mate exits the tree, out of the back, and they fly off towards the river, disappearing behind the cover of the tree line.

Rooks are cawing from their roost, setting off on the day's foraging, deep-flapping wings in a slight display.

Mistle Thrushes drop into the field – two dozen together – and start to hunt in a loose group, blotched breasts above the straw. Three Hares sprint across the stubble, almost touching nose to tail, and sink out of sight over the hump.

A Buzzard is already striding at the field's edge, bending to bite at every other step. Behind, unseen in the cover of the trees, a Roe Deer barks, the sound carries way out, even to the canal, its shock wave echoing off the embankment.

Two Herons, overhead, battle each other and call sharp 'kranks' as they clash wings, long legs dangling for balance, losing height until almost at the ground, then part and go their separate ways.

A watery sun rises, blotted by the cloud scrape.

Skylarks are calling: rippling the air as they fall from the sky, landing amongst the Mistle Thrushes, and immediately disappearing below the weeds.

Swallows start to line up on the wires – a dotted arc laden with birds – pegs without the washing. House Martins join them, two strands now full. Behind, in the paddock, all is quiet. All except for a single Wheatear, showing off its fresh autumn plumage. It stands, almost upright, then runs to snatch a fly from the nearly-bare ground, turns and hops to a dry dung mound, white rump flashing briefly. Two leaf-chewing Rabbits watch from their nettle patch.

In their oak, three Little Owls catch the morning light, turning their heads away, false eyes looking back from their napes. Their lichen-coloured mantles flatten them into the lichen-covered bark.

One squats suddenly and peers upwards as a Kestrel passes overhead – a small alarm squeezes from its mouth. The others eye the falcon as it lands on the telegraph pole nearby. Some of the Swallows take off and swirl as the Kestrel goes by, but circle to land quickly.

The sun continues its rise. A Willow Warbler flies into the hedge, already bursting with Goldfinches. A Nuthatch rings from the wood. From the barn, a Starling at the corner of the roof, calls a perfect imitation of a Curlew.

Then, a Meadow Pipit calls rapidly, twice, and the Swallows explode from the wires, firing off in all directions, alarms filling the lane. They swirl in loops and eights, uncertain of the direction of the danger, as a Hobby fills the sky. It is the female, and she has come across the field from the far side of the trees, skimming the stubble to leap the hedge at the lane where the Swallows were perching. Up from nowhere, from the hugging ground, a deadly curve described, the blades of her wings slashing as she rises in a tight arc that takes her up.

Now she is among them.

A tornado of birds twists around; Goldfinches and House Sparrows trying to keep with the Swallows and Martins, two Greenfinches and several Linnets have been sucked into the dust storm that spirals. And through the eye the Hobby stabs, missing on her first attempt, claws raking the air beside the cheek of a Swallow, then turns, back into the shoal of birds.

On her turn the flock scatters, cohesion gone, and birds break off in every direction. But she has her eye on the slowest, selecting it unerringly from the crowd. With a whiplash of wings, she is back amongst the prey, and takes one out so quickly that she has travelled fifty feet before her success is apparent.

Now, clutching a young House Sparrow, already heading the way she has come, she continues at speed back to the sycamore.

The dilute sun shines on the shattered remains of the morning.

At the nest tree one of her brood, the youngest, is on the nest rim. The other two are out in the oak, sitting nearby, almost entirely hidden in the leaves. All of them scream to be fed, and turn to face her as she lands.

It is still only early morning, and two of her young have been fed.

The youngest, on the nest, begins its exercises, flapping away as one of its siblings, now fully out of sight, feeds itself, somewhere in the oak.

A tiny breeze, just enough to turn the leaves, takes the Sparrow's feathers away from the tree.

For another hour or so the exercising youngster continues, on and off, to build its strength. Then, as one of its siblings hops back to the nest, wings flapping for balance, they both settle on the parapet and doze, as Bluebottles circle them.

There is little difference between them, and they appear to be the same size. The same tufts of down detract from the dark feathers covering them, the same jut of primaries at their backs.

Only now are the Swallows drifting back to the wires.

High up, two Swifts are heading south.

Above the woods, a Kestrel and a Sparrowhawk are sparring, clashing with talons and tipped wings, the two youngsters returning to the fight as each finishes a bout, first one, then the other antagonising, and testing strength and agility. After a minute they part, honours even, and go on their different paths.

Down beyond the river the brambles are ready with berries, scrambling prickly and plump. Red Admirals sit and taste, proboscis coiling and uncoiling, Tippex-tipped antennae held aloft. The rowans are heavily pregnant, their branches bending under cherry-ripe fruit. Wood Pigeons cling to the boughs, bending precariously to gorge on the berries, flapping wings as they pluck, tails spread against the leaves.

New molehills rise above the turf, pushing a dotted line of miniature peaks that meanders between the briar patches. On top of one a Common Blue sits, bluebell-blue wings flattened to catch the pallid sun.

Under the edge of a brambly bank, a slight shift and the merest ruffle turn the head: a Grass Snake has just moved. It freezes for a moment, judging the danger, then slides into the thorny cover with barely a whisper, its dark sinuosity evaporating before the eye. Its shape persists in the mind, but it is no more.

Migrant Hawkers sail above, along lines diminishing and expanding, heads held just below the horizontal of their progress, like helicopters accelerating. From time to time they catch a gnat, munching as they go, tiny legs dropping from their mandibles to float to the ground.

Then, the Wood Pigeons clatter aloft, diving from the rowan trees, as the shape of a Peregrine is silhouetted overhead, black against the milk of the sky.

173

It heads for the pylon, out of sight beyond the copse.

Back along the canal, where a Mute Swan family swim, six in all, crowding the water as it narrows across the viaduct, carrying it above the river below. The embankment is thorny and flower full. As it curves, the Barn Owls' meadows come into view, marshy at the margins, ditches draining in geometric rectangles, hawthorn and blackthorn scrub at their banks. Two Herons stand sentinel, as Coot run for cover back to the water from their grazing on the turf.

A pair of Jays is flying from copse to copse, wide wings flapping haphazardly, as they drop downslope, white rumps into dark cover.

Across, on the opposite bank, the big Badgers' sett is obvious from this viewpoint, but no Foxes are out today. A group of Rabbits run around, at the base of the slope, keeping to the drier ground, above the waterlogged flats thick with juncus hummocks.

White butterflies, like blowing petals, skim the lush, thistle-thick meadows, and on the embankment Gatekeepers flicker, clashing occasionally with the Speckled Woods, down from the trees.

A Yellowhammer perches prettily on a gorse bush, paler yellow than the coconut-scented blooms. Linnets search under the scrub. Two Grey Wagtails take off from the towpath, rise over the bushes and dive to the river below.

The lines of pylons stretch from here across the land, straddling the canal: two highly visual lines converging, markers for wandering, high-flying birds.

At the copse the land rises to meet the curve of the canal, now bending towards the west, back towards the Hobby nest, two humpback bridges coming into view.

Yellow Wagtails are between the dark, mud-spattered cattle hooves, dashing at disturbed flies, running to keep up with the strolling cows. At the water trough, a Reed Bunting drops down from drinking and forages along the brambly field-edge, barely visible in its camouflage. Swallows loop around the herd, and out into the pasture, blue and cream, cream and blue as they turn, slippery in their swim.

Chaffinches perch with Tree Sparrows at the hedge leading down from the canal, along the lane to the Little Owls' corner. None is visible in the oak now.

The female Hobby is on the sycamore, looking out across the field, where, on the pylon, her mate is on the upper arm, and a Peregrine is at the apex. The Peregrine looks huge in comparison to the Hobby's small shape; it squats, feathers fluffed, dark-hooded head looking south. The Hobby is sleek, long wings scissoring at his tail, handsome head peering up at the Peregrine.

For a long, slow time the perching falcons are stationary, only their heads moving.

High up, small loose groups of Swifts are passing. The Hobbies see them, but remain.

The Peregrine, without preamble, stands and launches from the pylon. She is heading for the steeple, eyes on something beyond. In a level flight she gradually puts on speed, and, arrow-straight, is already half way across the big field, when, as if on cue, both Hobbies take off.

He follows the Peregrine's wake, steadily catching up, even on his rise. She converges on their paths and accelerates to close the gap, but the Peregrine simply keeps on southward, and is more than a mile distant as the Hobbies are joined, and satisfied with its distance, they turn to circle at the ridge beyond the church.

In the distance Crows and Jackdaws, Rooks and Wood Pigeons and a flock of Lapwing have risen before the Peregrine's approach, and the horizon fills with birds as the falcon disappears beyond the rise.

The Hobbies are now up high, spiralling around each other, playing in the air. Their diminishing forms rise ever upwards, until even the light glare of the sky begins to vanish them. As they turn towards the sun's position, you cannot watch.

Ten minutes later, a group of House Martins are heading north. And fast. From their velocity they are obviously fleeing a falcon. A minute passes, then the two Hobbies are visible, still as high, following the Martins, way below them, wings whipping steadily to keep them in station with their prey.

To the north, a dozen Swifts are coming this way. The falcons are two miles from them, but have seen them well before this. Hobby and Swift close quickly, and are a mile apart when the Swifts realise their path holds their nemesis.

The falcons already have a height advantage and, having judged the passage of previous Swifts, they have risen above the line of their migration. The Swifts have little choice: they turn back to the north, but the backtracking has scattered them.

The Hobbies fall upon three that are still grouped, as they select one to hunt. This small flock splits and each Swift is alone now.

In a well-practised tactic, the falcons, each in turn, arc down on the prey which, from instinct and in trying to gain speed, flies vertically towards the ground. First the male Hobby tries for the Swift, which evades his first attack, but the female, within a second, is already making her arc as her mate rises back to prepare for his next.

She closes the gap quickly as the Swift dives again, flying for all his worth, like an animated arrow flicking towards the ground. She reaches it and the two seem to join, the Swift subsumed by her larger, similar shape, then she rises, taking the Swift with her, and it flaps no more.

Her mate has followed, and he flickers around her. They are less than a hundred feet up and turn to the pylon, sliding in to land on the upper arm. Almost immediately she begins to feed on the Swift and its feathers begin to drop to the field below, to join others from the season.

As the late afternoon becomes evening she takes the remains to the nest – where her young are nearly fledged.

A dozen or more Grey Partridges run under the gate at the corner this morning, into the meadow beyond, skirting round the hedge base quickly, looking for cover. A Little Owl watches from the big hawthorns across the lane, sitting out in the early sun. But the birds have found it and it goes back to the oak to hide, before the mob becomes noisome.

Across the field the Hobbies' tree is quiet, not one falcon can be seen, but the low light casts deep shadows in the oak, and hides its dark contents well.

Opposite, above the pylon, fifty or so Lapwings are high up and circling, bunched and obviously spooked. But there is no cause for concern visible as they continue in consternation. A single Curlew, long-winged and rakish, is with them, keeping to the flock, hiding amongst them.

Now, the Grey Partridge suddenly rise and skim the pasture in a tight group, orange tails following them as they land at a run under the far hedge, by the canal's embankment.

A slight breeze blows from the north-east, a few small cotton-wool wads of clouds sail slowly by.

Swallows and Martins are up: perhaps two hundred dot the sky over the river. A few Swifts are higher up, all on a southerly journey, feeding as they go.

Two Hares nibble greens in the middle of the field, as a Nuthatch whistles from the trees beyond.

Thirty or so Jackdaws, calling as they come, drop from the church to the field and begin to forage around the Hares, which chew on, impassively – big brown eyes, each reflecting the turning sun.

A group of Black-headed Gulls slide in from the west and join the Jackdaws: a pied patch of birds now marches through the stubble. And now the Lapwings come down, tilting on bowed wings and calling softly in reassurance to each other. The Curlew, almost hidden in their crowd, stands taller now they have landed.

Then, above the river, all the hirundines start to turn one way, and bunch together. Three Hobbies are above them, heading for the nest tree. It is the pair and another female: an intruder is with them, and she is carrying some prey.

All three go to the oak, where the young are already calling – their screams loud in the morning air. A flurry of movement, too quick to observe: three adults and at least two young in shadow and dapples. Seconds later and the intruder exits, with the female on her heels, flying quickly back towards the river, the sky above it now devoid of birds.

The male is on the sycamore, and in the nest tree one of the youngsters is out above the nest, and then makes a short glide back, landing perfectly on the parapet. Another is to the right of the nest, well away from it. The third, for the moment is hidden.

The female returns, having seen off the food-providing intruder – certainly her daughter from last season – and lands in the sycamore.

Dark shapes in shadows move around in the oak. It seems that at least two of the young are out of the nest, perhaps all three – as the nest appears to be empty.

The female flies into the oak, hidden somewhere within, then flies back to her mate and begins to call to him, imploring him to hunt. For half an hour he ignores her pleadings and she goes quiet.

Rooks pass their position, winging down to join the throng of feeding birds, and, across the way, a Kestrel takes a recently taken Vole to the pylon. The Hobbies can see him, but he elicits no response in them.

The female swoops down to snatch a Silver Y Moth from the grass top, deftly holding it in flight as she returns to her perch. Having eaten, she starts to call to her mate again, and this time, after a few minutes, as the Little Owl alarms, they both set off to hunt. Rising over the earthbound flocks and above the Kestrel still on the pylon, their awesome power takes them quickly away.

Two minutes later, and almost three miles distant out west, now a few hundred feet high, their shapes dissolve into the blue.

Back in the oak, the sun now higher, the shadows shrunk somewhat, there are two young sitting on the same branch, just above the nest. Their down has almost gone, their colours showing: they look like Hobbies. A third youngster hops into view to their right, bobbing its head, judging distances, then flies a yard or two to another branch, out of sight again.

One of the visible young birds begins to flap, its wings hitting its sibling, but neither adjusts their positions. After a while it turns to face away and exercises some more, its primaries still battering against the other.

An hour goes by. Bluebottles circle the young Hobbies at the nest, and the falcons settle, starting to doze.

Another hour has almost passed before the parents return.

He has a Swallow under his tail, and as they approach the oak the female starts calling 'khhee, khee, ki ki ki'. He lets her take the Swallow in a deft aerial baton change, and, still calling, she slips into the tree, transferring the prey to her bill as she does so, finally quiet, and perches on the empty nest.

The young have started calling already, and one of them hop-glides to the nest and takes the Swallow from her, jumping into the bowl of the nest with it and disappears.

The other young are still screaming as she flies out to join her mate on the tree tops. The sun is out, the breeze has dropped and the two small falcons sit and preen as the humbug waistcoats of their breasts fluff out above their orange-red trousers. In the oak under them, calm and quiet returns to the tree.

She takes off and dives at a passing Migrant Hawker, and for once, misses as it side-steps her, zigzagging away. She glides back up to her perch.

From the field below, all the birds suddenly rise, the Lapwings calling, the Jackdaws louder. They spiral upward, the Rooks head for the woods. The gulls scatter and wing away over the canal, quickly. But whatever has caused the panic remains hidden from the lane, yet the birds have gone. As the Lapwings circle, higher now, the Jackdaws head for the church. An unseen Peregrine has passed this way.

Several Swifts are heading south, still far beyond the river, and the Hobbies set off, heading south too, the Swifts behind and above them. For now. A mile out they are level with the Swifts, still half a mile behind, and then they turn and circle higher. The Swifts see them and swerve off east, and the falcons follow, speeding towards them as they disappear beyond the trees.

After their departure the sky fills with Swallows and House Martins, returning from their escape flight from the Hobbies. They continue westwards, increasing the distance still further.

Twenty minutes later and the falcons return, but have not been successful, dropping in empty-handed. They overfly the nest site, checking for menaces, then continue to the pylon across the field.

Only now are the Lapwings coming back to land.

For some time, the Hobby pair sits on their pylon, watching and waiting, then they are gone. They have slipped away in seconds, to the west.

Half an hour in and they are on the way back, passing the pylon and heading for the nest. The female has some pied prey under her – possibly a House Martin. They reach the sycamore and land, the young screaming out at their approach, then a dark shape flies out of the oak and goes to the sycamore adjacent – it is one of the young – and on a maiden flight. It looks dark and stubby-winged in comparison to the adults, brown feathers and a sepia ground to the breast, but for all that it is a Hobby.

The female disappears within the sycamore with the prey – taking it to the youngster, its first foray away from its nest tree behind it.

The other two youngsters are out of sight for the moment, somewhere in the oak. The adults fly in and around, checking on them, then they are away across the field to the pylon again.

A Buzzard's movements are causing a flock of Wood Pigeons to take off and re-land in the field, keeping themselves a safe distance from the predator, as it changes position in the stubble.

Out to the west a breeze-blown bank of clouds is growing larger, and a shower of rain descends in the distance there. A Kestrel, now with some air under him, hovers at the field's corner, his black-banded grey tail spread, fan-wise.

Ahead of the weather, several large gulls are winging in on a glide. They drop down to the stubble field – several Great-Black-backs and a few Herring Gulls. Many are not full adults, and their varying browns and greys, blacks and whites ornament the field in a party-coloured pattern.

Gradually the clouds close in. Swifts, descending with the weather, head over in threes and fours. The falcons are up again.

Letting the wind take them up and easterly, they rise easily, without exertion, and drift up and away into the clearer sky out east, then, turning windward. They power back towards the clouds and into the rain, vanishing into darkness.

Rooks are heading to the stubble to feed, and, as the rain starts, the Wood Pigeons lift to the woods beyond. The Buzzard flaps further into the field as the gulls sit, heads westward.

Movement at the nest tree: a youngster has arrived back at the nest, and stands, peering around. Half an hour later it jumps off and glides to a branch nearby, out of sight again. The one in the sycamore now flies back to the oak, flapping rather awkwardly as it tries to steer itself into the tree.

Rain showers hit the oak from time to time, but there is no force in the wind, and plenty of shelter amongst the leaves.

At the corner, the Little Owl drops on a beetle, as it crosses the lane in the rain, and takes it back to its tree. The paddock Pied Wagtails are flickering around, snatching rain-nudged insects as summer showers begin to refill the puddles.

At the corner, near the canal, a Blackbird and a Song Thrush are bathing, stimulated by the rain.

Swallows swoop lower, around the horses and barns, as insects are brought down by the showers, until they suddenly alarm, just as the sun breaks out west.

The Hobbies have arrived back at the nest site, after ninety minutes of hunting, and return carrying a Swift. It is already part-plucked and part-eaten, on some unknown perch, and the remains are brought to the oak by the female, who flies inside to search for the dispersed youngsters.

The male sits on the sycamore, the sun low on his back, a rainbow behind him and three well-fed, fledged young in his tree.

As evening falls on a clearing sky, the Rooks, from their feeding, take off to head for their roost.

Bats start their night flights as the falcons head out for the pylon, their hunting still not done.

By the next morning, breezy and bright, the oldest youngster had already taken up its new position in the sycamore, the more open aspect of the tree allowing it greater flight room within its shelter. The others were somewhere in the oak, it was to turn out, but for now, they are hidden.

Swallows are rising, following flies into the warm air and the field is already filling – Rooks, Lapwings, Starlings and Wood Pigeons strolling, strutting and waddling as they breakfast amongst the stubble.

Four Cormorants wing overhead, swerving to avoid the Buzzard crossing their path, then off to the west. The Buzzard carries on, over and beyond the church. A large shape, mostly hidden by the girder angle of the pylon is probably a Peregrine, unseen by the crowd in the field, it seems.

A Green Woodpecker powers an undulation from the wood, heading across the river, as the male Hobby swings in from the north, over the riverside trees, carrying something in his talons. As he appears the young see him, and the begging cries ring out.

The one in the sycamore flies a few yards to meet the adult as he approaches the trees, but it is passed quickly as the male goes to the oak, and disappears inside. The youngster turns a small loop, flapping and steering with its tail, and goes to the oak, crash-landing half-way up in the outer branches, still calling out.

Twenty minutes passes before the male is out again, and he perches on the sycamore's top.

Half an hour more of quiet, then everything in the field is up, heading for the sky and the woods. The Peregrine is off from the pylon, and heading towards the Hobbies' trees. It is rising and already well above the tree tops, but, before it gets half way across the empty field, the female Hobby launches out from her hideaway and heads towards the approaching Peregrine.

As it goes overhead, she is still below the Peregrine, which carries on, away to the east. She swings around and gains on it, and she chases it off for another half mile. Then, satisfied that the danger has passed, she circles back, into the wind, gains height and heads off to hunt.

Her mate, meanwhile, has also left his perch tree and now he speeds towards her disappearing shape, gaining on her all the way. But she circles back and dives to the pylon, as if re-claiming it as her own.

Only a couple of Hares remain in the stubble below her watch point now, and the entire landscape seems devoid of birds. Her mate has been rising steadily above her, and now he turns to the north and glides away until out of sight.

Back at the nest site, two young Hobbies leave the oak and fly into the sycamore, both just visible within the canopy. For a few minutes they sit quietly, then one, begging calls crying out, takes off from the tree and goes to the ground, landing in the stubble.

Now it starts to walk and seems to be snatching at insects on the lying straw. A few minutes of this and then it takes off and returns to the tree, circling before landing adroitly on a horizontal branch.

Hours go by and the trees are quiet. Swallows and Martins are back over the meadow. The sky has cleared and the wind has dropped. Only one of the juvenile Hobbies is visible, and the pylon is suddenly empty of the female – she has sneaked away unseen.

It is almost evening before the male arrives back, and his approach has not been seen by his young. As he flies into the sycamore with a meal, one youngster flies to his landing spot. All three are crying out to him, and he is back out, minus the prey, in a minute. He circles just once and is away again, the begging calls diminishing as he goes.

Mist hangs between the hedges and in the hollows this morning, the first sign since June. The season is turning.

As the sun comes up the trees are quiet, and not a single Hobby is in sight. The mist dissipates quickly, though the air is still, and the slight cool of night time chill turns to warmth.

Now the young Hobbies are calling. Hunger rings from the oak. Then, as if condensing there, the male is on the tree top. His young have seen him, and their calls intensify, and though hidden, their presence is obvious from far away.

Away he goes, westward – and suddenly, there she is too – she follows him to the pylon and lands there as he continues, disappearing into the distance.

To the north, only half a mile or so away, another Hobby is stooping an arc at some prey, then heads off northward, beyond the trees across the river.

Just half an hour later and the male is back with prey – a Swallow or Martin – and she rises to meet him, taking the prey in mid-flight. She goes straight to the oak with it and two youngsters are out, flying towards her approach, for just a few yards. Both are blunt-winged and gingery compared to their mother. One goes to the ground, and the other loops around, back to the tree, calling to her as she disappears within.

One of her young gets the meal. The male has landed, briefly at the top of the sycamore, but is quickly away again, this time to the south, and within seconds she follows, catching him up as they both rise towards the canal. Swallows are underneath them now, and he accelerates briefly, then suddenly swerves and dives, disappearing just before he makes a kill.

Within seconds she has the Swallow from him and she heads for the pylon. There she plucks and eats briefly, then takes off back to the nest tree, calling to her young, whose cries meet hers across the field. This time she gets to the tree without being met, and jinks inside to deliver the meal to a second youngster.

The male has followed her back, and has only just landed, when she emerges and is calling to him, urging him to hunt again. She leads the way, out west, and he follows. She seems to have seen some prey beyond the pylon, and now speeds over it.

Now, she accelerates to an impressively fast rate and arcs towards the trees on the far side of the river where Swallows are above the meadow. Over the trees she dives a parabola at some Swallows, and, though they elude her attack, her mate is just behind her and, now he swerves in tightly towards one, forcing it back up into the clear air – and she has another lightning strike as the desperate Swallow dives to the field, skimming the grass, now out of sight, and, unseen, one of the Hobbies takes the Swallow and they return to the pylon again.

For some time, she just sits, the Swallow under her, then begins to eat. While she feeds, he has already gone away to hunt again.

She stays at the pylon for an hour, the Swallow eaten.

A warm afternoon wafts quietly in, only butterflies seem to move. The young Hobbies have settled out of sight, and remain quiet.

Two Hares suddenly stand up – fore paws in the air, ears back, both staring towards the river. By the hedge, Rabbits are running. Magpies hop along the hedge top, peering down at the field. But whatever has caused the consternation is hidden.

The Hobby has gone from the pylon. Ten minutes pass and the juvenile falcons are calling, one, or perhaps two are flying within the oak, mere shadows amongst the foliage. There appears to some sort of activity within the trees, but only sound emerges. Then, one youngster flies between the sycamore and the oak, a Magpie following. Then, a second, and a third Magpie are visible, and shadows chase inside the oak.

Now, pair of Crows, who are attracted by the commotion, are in the sycamore, and drop into the oak from there, cawing loudly. Two young Hobbies emerge from the branches, a Crow flying at one. Magpies chatter and circle.

One of the youngsters goes to the ground, a Magpie follows and sits facing the falcon, then attacks it head-on, a quick peck and away, as the

Hobby counters by jumping up after it, claws extended, then lands again in the straw.

The Hobby flies back to the sycamore, and the Magpie chases after it. Both disappear inside. The Crows are in the oak, calling out to each other and harassing the Hobbies, all largely hidden by the leaves.

For another hour this continues before the Magpies, tired of their aggravation, depart, flying away towards the river. As they disappear the female Hobby returns to the nest site, and has seen the Crows still in the oak. She dives inside, and a Crow flies out of the opposite side and away. A moment later its mate leaves the tree and they follow the Magpies along the hedge to the riverside wood.

The falcon has evaporated, and peace has returned to the trees.

Late afternoon and cumuli drift south, a blackberry-ripening season's-end sun slowly sinks towards tomorrow.

A hundred House Martins swim the shallows against the woods, all translucent and faded in the burn. Clouds float slowly, meringues in the bowl of the sky, and the air itself dazzles.

The deep gashes of shadows beneath the trees are ink-dark now, and a thousand gossamer threads sail across, catching the last of the light.

A Sparrowhawk spirals up, barely stirring the Martin shoal, and heads away, across the canal. A Heron coughs a warning as it glides to the water. A Siskin's peel falls, a strip of citrus sounding.

Now, every House Martin suddenly rises in a rush, as one, a knot of birds concentrated above the river, climbing fast and high. Now the hundred birds are just dots – one ball of prey packed closely.

And, there, their nemesis: a Hobby, high and fast: a deadly line, towards the sun, light glinting off the knives of its wings as, even now, it tilts in attack.

Four Swifts appear, fleeing the danger, rapid and dark, slicing the sparkle, as the Hobby and Martins race over the horizon.

The sun begins to set and a cool draft descends on the end of the day.

Meadow Pipits are passing overhead and Swifts are running south this morning; clouds are already thickening as the wind picks up. In the paddock the skittish horses are kicking up dust and disturbing the Sparrows – and a Little Owl is out on the fence rail, near to a post, inconspicuous in grey.

A Kestrel hovers by the canal, and thumps down to the ground, rising empty-handed to stand on the wind again, head-down and wings working.

Goldfinches move to a safe distance and sit on thistle tops until a passing Sparrowhawk puts them to the hawthorn hedge as a Blue Tit calls an alarm. Blackbirds, like shadows under the hedge, pull worms from the morning-damp soil.

Nothing moves in the Hobbies' oak, but a young falcon is visible in the sycamore, sitting in shadow, waiting patiently. A Heron calls as it glides, bow-winged, down to the canal. The Hobby watches it go.

Shadows slip along the stubble, dark tablecloths thrown over the field, blackening brown Hares resting in the greenery.

Two Collared Doves fly towards the oak just as the female Hobby arrives, and they swerve away quickly to the paddock. One of the juveniles has seen her, and calls from cover, as she sweeps away again, towards the river behind.

Two Buzzards are walking in the stubble, wide legs stepping as they peck at worms. Rooks keep their distance as they strut.

The Swallows are keeping low in the cool air, passing the hedgerow trees where the Hobbies are sitting, looping around the leeward side of the hedge, away to the corner and back again, blue backs cloud-darkened, pale bellies showing out in shadow.

One of the young falcons flies out from the oak, gliding down to the straw lying at the field's edge. The Swallows don't react – seemingly knowing that they are in no danger from it. The Hobby sits for a while, motionless, then walks to catch an insect on the ground. A curious Whitethroat, in the hedge, watches as the falcon catches another morsel, then flies back up to hide in the oak again.

Swallows continue to swoop.

For an hour or more, as shadows chase across the field, there is no change. But, then, up high, two Hobbies are hunting.

The similar shapes of Swift and Hobby are raking the sky, silhouettes speeding southward. The male falcon is just in front, and only twenty yards behind one Swift, two others just ahead. Within a minute this hunt passes beyond the horizon's ridge, and the hunted and hunters have gone.

The Kestrel has his Vole now, and circles to the barn to eat, the Goldfinches swarming around him as he goes. Pied Wagtails rise and drop back to the paddock and Jackdaws call brief warnings.

Two scythe-like shapes are approaching the pylon. One holds a Swift: the Hobbies have been successful. As they land there is a chorus of calling from the oak tree – the young have seen them.

But ten minutes pass before the female comes across the field, carrying the Swift with her. She is still a hundred yards away when two young-sters fly out to meet her, still screaming, and she passes them as they try to turn and keep with her, still not skilled enough to make aerial contact. All three fly into the oak, where the meal is handed over to one.

The male is still on the pylon, watching his family from his perch. His mate soon wings back to join him and they both call to each other as they meet. The sky darkens further as clouds close the canopy of the sky, rushing by to the south-east.

The juvenile Hobby carrying the Swift in its talons, comes out from the oak, and flies across the short gap to the sycamore, landing in full view on a big branch. There it begins to pluck and eat its meal as feathers fly away on the wind.

A heavy shower starts to slant in, and the leaves shake with the increased wind, the tops swaying against the slate sky. The young Hobby leaves the sycamore and joins its siblings in the better cover of the oak, some tatty remnants of the Swift still carried in its claws.

The pylon is empty. As rain comes down, both adult falcons are out of sight. It is evening before the rain eases to a stop, and the wind begins to turn more westerly.

Large gulls have dropped in to the field during the rains, and now they rise from sitting, shaking themselves off and take to kinder air, long wings climbing into the setting sun.

A hundred hirundines are in the evening air, making the most of the last of the day, in the lee of the woods by the river, where wind-blown flies congregate.

Against a reddened sky, a Hobby flies to the pylon, watching Rooks overhead, and eyes the Swallows and Martins by the wood. The Kestrel is still hovering by the lane, all on fire in the sunset's blaze.

As the Swallows head back to the barns the Hobby launches from its watch point, dropping to the field, where it brushes the stubble at eighty miles an hour, over the hedge and accelerating towards the farm, long wings cutting the dusk and taking it up amongst its prey, caught completely unawares as it gets amongst them.

The falcon arcs around the barns and upward, a Swallow just in front, as they disappear beyond the buildings, others twisting away as their alarms fill the farmyard, echoing into the sky.

As the sun reaches the red horizon and submerges beneath, begging calls ring from the oak, where another meal is dished out.

Across the blood-soaked western sky, a silhouette floats by: a Woodcock is flying out from the woods to feed in the field beyond the river. It drops in as the world darkens, long bill leading the way.

A Noctule Bat, black against black, at tree-top height, comes across the field and passes perilously close to the Hobby still in the oak.

Night falls with the colours all gone, and the Little Owl adorns the telegraph pole like a bulb on a shade-less standard lamp.

Early morning and the wind already dropped, with the clouds gradually clearing as the day begins to warm. The grasses and the lanes still wet with rains, the eastward hedge sides glistening as the sun slides above the trees.

Down at the river, Redpolls descend to the alders as a Moorhen slips to sallows, slips from shore to shallows, swimming to rushes and disappears.

Swallows suddenly silent, and just within the wood, close enough to touch, a Roe Deer freezes, one hoof raised, head turned head-on, its nose like a still-wet black pudding, tastes the sweet summer air.

The call of a passing Yellowhammer chips the silence; the Roe Deer starts and slinks into shadows between the trees.

Back in the meadows the first butterflies catch the light above the thistles. Berries, bright and autumn-ready shine from the hedges.

Above the bees' hum, a Vole's munches crunch from the hedge, inches away but invisible.

SUMMER LINGERS STILL

WITH a dozen Swallows on its tail, a Hobby is taking a Sparrow back to the nest, low and direct, the sun on her flank.

At the nest site the begging is subsiding, one juvenile Hobby is visible in the oak. The female is already leaving the tree and heading for the pylon, and one of her young is flying after her, but turns back from halfway across the field, as she goes to perch. Another youngster, mistaking its sibling for an adult, flies out to meet the one returning, and they almost collide as they pass. Both make it back to the oak, flying in with some grace and agility. The third youngster is in the sycamore now, and has the Sparrow. Out of sight, it begins to feed.

Buzzards call and lift from the woods, circling into the warm lift from the sun-dried stubble. A Kestrel joins the thermal and they all spiral together.

Dragonflies are on the hunt; a Brown Hawker and an Emperor Dragonfly skim past each other, overtaking in turn, along the hedge. Two or three Migrant Hawkers, way up, zigzag after midges. A Peacock and a Tortoiseshell corkscrew around each other and Meadow Browns ignore them as they pass.

Wood Pigeons seem to fill the field, herds of them slowly marching fatly, still finding food amongst the stubble.

Up above, a swarm of flying ants is attracting the Black-headed Gulls. They circle and swoop on the insects, feasting in the rising air, growing in number as others see the feeding flock and join from every direction. There are a hundred or so, gradually rising, a loose group manoeuvring: sharks amongst sprats.

A Hobby joins them, dropping in from way, way up, becoming focussed through the high haze, diving and climbing, clawing the ants from the air. For forty minutes the flock feeds, and then begins to disperse as the food runs low.

The Hobby suddenly closes its wings and, head-down, describes a plomb-line to the earth.

Two-thirds of the way down, his target is obvious: a flock of Linnets and Goldfinches in the field below. As they rise in panic, he twists on half-opened wings and adjusts his aim as he streaks towards the finches, starting his turn to follow their rise. His speed is so great, that, at their full throttle, he passes them as if they were standing still, slicing amongst them, flick-flacking to take one then another, but misses at each try, and has passed them all without a catch.

Now he loops upward, vertical, now upside down, now turning back towards the earth and the fleeing flock, flicking his long wings in a whirring blur as he rights himself, level again and closing in, again from behind. In another second he is with the flock once again, as a small group detaches from the flock, spinning upwards in a desperate spiral.

He follows.

With a single jink which seems to defy physics, the Hobby is on to the group and his feet reach out, talons closing around one unfortunate Linnet. He spins around to level flight and slows to a hundred or so as he eases away towards the nest tree.

He rises to tree top height as a youngster leaves the sycamore to greet him. Then, he drops the Linnet for his young as it approaches, but it falls to the ground, followed by the young Hobby, which has failed to catch it.

The others can be heard screaming away, and one flies out towards its father, then back to the oak as it realises he has nothing to hand over now.

On the straw, the Linnet is being plucked and eaten. A Black-headed Gull calls out as it passes overhead, watching the falcon below, but decides against robbery.

For an hour or more the male sits at the sycamore's crown, as butter-flies flicker along the summer afternoon. He then sets to preening, spending many minutes on feather maintenance, breast and belly first, tail and primaries last.

As the Wood Pigeons clatter up from their feeding, he heads off to the pylon, perching at the second spar, looking back towards his young.

For another hour he is alone, watching the skies. Then his mate flies in from the south and joins him on the pylon. She has only been there for a while when they both take to the air, powering up in their usual hunting mode, towards the western horizon.

From time to time, at the nest site, one or more juvenile Hobby takes to the air briefly, flying around the trees' canopies, keeping to the vicinity, but practicing their flying skills. And now, when two are together there is a hint of size difference between them. There is at least one female and one male, but there are never three together, to determine if the third is one or the other.

In the late afternoon, now the insects are plentiful, one of the young appears to try to catch something in the air, but the prey's size makes it impossible to see if it has been successful.

Two trees further, towards the gate at the corner, a Blackbird is protesting at a Little Owl. One of the young birds is perching out on a branch, and has been spotted. The Blackbird approaches and stands to challenge the owl, raising its tail and alarming loudly. The commotion begins to attract a Chaffinch or two, and a Greenfinch and a Wren have arrived to see what the fuss is about. The Little Owl squats, staring out at the reception for several minutes, then flies back to its oak, followed by a small crowd of birds. As the others disperse, the Blackbird continues its alarms, though the owl is out of sight.

The sun is only just up when the male flies back with prey.

This time two juveniles fly to meet him – a female leading a male, their slight size difference now apparent as they fly close together. As he reaches them he proffers the catch to the female and she takes it directly from his grasp, as he slows to almost a halt in mid-air, his legs extended down and forward to help the transfer.

There is a lot of noise from three or four birds as he makes the exchange, and the juvenile male follows him as he lands in the sycamore, still begging to him. Now the third youngster flies out from the oak and sweeps around the back of the trees, coming back after a three-tree flight, keeping silent as it goes. Pale feather edges of the juveniles catch the early light, giving them a scalloped appearance, and their translucent tail ends show as they fly away. But for all their tell-tale juvenile traits, they are Hobbies, and though their wings are still growing, their distinctive shape shows.

The adult is off again, as Swallows alarm around him, powering away to the pylon. One of the young starts to follow, but, after less than a minute, turns back to the nest site and swoops into the foliage.

Above the river a hundred Wood Pigeons rise and flee, scattering quickly, across the field and over the paddock and farm. A Peregrine appears, heading east, then it turns and approaches. For a few minutes it circles deliberately, as if choosing prey, or direction, then stoops a shallow dive to the pylon at the back of the nest site.

It is out of sight for a while, below the tree line, then suddenly, it is tanking across the field beyond the farm, just above the cows' backs as they return to the meadow from milking. A group of Rooks and Jackdaws are foraging around the water troughs by the canal side of the field, and have not seen the falcon's approach.

As it speeds in, even lower now, the flock in front sees the danger. Alarms explode as they jump for the sky, but it is far too late.

A Rook, only having risen six feet from the grass, is struck with force by the Peregrine as it smashes into it, knocking it spinning, probably already dead. The Rook spins like a rag thrown upward, as the Peregrine turns a tight circle and takes it from the air, adjusting for the considerable extra weight as it labours back up to the pylon, one of the Rook's wings flapping in the wind beneath it. Rooks and Jackdaws continue to exit the entire area – black specks dwindling to nothing.

It is some time before the panicked world begins to settle, and in their trees, the three juvenile Hobbies are safe, for now.

Midday: at the nest site everything is quiet. One juvenile can be seen, half-asleep in the sycamore; the other two out of sight.

The pylon is empty, too.

High up, from time to time, the last of the year's Swifts are crossing the sky, draining to the south, their number fewer and fewer.

On the wires by the paddock, Swallows are lining up. They too are dreaming of Africa, and will soon be on their way, as the last of their broods reach independence and the season is done. The Sand Martins are already gone, and only a straggler or two from further north will pass by now. But at the farm, the House Martins still have young in the nest, and some are still sitting on eggs, as they stretch their season to summer's end. Their numbers are still increasing, three broods already behind them, some with a forth in the nest.

But summer has long-since peaked and almost all the breeding done. Post-season movements are well under way, many already finished. Young have grown, flown, become independent, moved on. Singing has virtually ceased entirely – only the Wood Pigeons and Collared Doves still carry sticks for new nests. But, for the dragonflies there is plenty of time, yet, to breed, and at the ponds the egg-laying continues. And this is the time of butterflies – many second broods are on the wing – Large Whites and Small Whites fill the sunny afternoons, while the Meadow Browns still patrol the new grasses in the stubble. Red Admirals have months of flight left, and, as the fruits ripen, new foods will be available to them.

The ivy covering the humpback bridge swarms with life. Amongst the many Hoverflies and Honeybees are jewel-like beetles, shining green-bronze as they crawl. Commas and Tortoiseshells flicker around the flies, fighting for space, and a Holly Blue, like a tiny speck of sky, turns itself towards the sun. A Peacock, wings closed, angles itself on the arched wall, and a Speckled Wood drops in to join the crowded creeper.

Under the bridge now, a young Grey Wagtail, in custard yellow, white-edged tail see-sawing steadily, struts and runs at flies rising from the water.

Greenfinches are calling from the poplar tops as Goldfinches rise from the weeds in the boatyard: a Little Owl crouches in a pile of iron, squinting out from the dark interior of a rusted pipe, with a square flange flaring at its end.

Across the lane, three Grey Partridges squat by the water trough, greys and browns disguising them against the bare earth. Rabbits stretch out under the sunny side of the hedge as Linnets crawl between the scanty nettle patch gone to seed. A Rat is nibbling something it holds in its fore paws, whiskers twitching, a worm-like tail along the soil. A Song Thrush hops past, stopping to stare for a second, carrying a snail.

A Kestrel puts the Greenfinches to flight as it glides in to perch on the poplar's very topmost sprig, bending the bough as it closes its wings to settle; he peers down, and from its pipe the Little Owl rotates its head to stare back. From between the two predators, the Goldfinches bound away across the canal to safer foraging.

High up, among the cumuli, specks of House Martins are swarming and swirling, deciding on a direction to flee, turning south finally and running. Half a minute later, the shape of a Hobby appears in the blue gap between the clouds, following fast. It is gone in a minute – two miles distant now – beyond the ridge and the trees.

Back at the Hobby nest, the late afternoon has brought more activity. One of the juvenile falcons is on the ground under the oak, running after insects, Buzzard-like in its actions, picking morsels in its bill as it dips it to the straw.

Another youngster is flying around the trees, around and above the canopies, practising its turns and attempting to make a catch, snatching at insects on the wing. As it lands back in the oak, the third flies out and flies to the sycamore, lands briefly, then sets off again to glide to the next tree, where it sits out of sight again.

For another half hour the three young birds continue their activities, until their father returns.

For the first time, the three juveniles are in the air together, as they race towards the adult, which has some prey under him. Now the comparative sizes can be seen: there are two females and a male, the latter just a little smaller than his sisters. Their calls ring across the land.

The adult slows as he meets his young, bringing the prey out below him, letting it dangle as he almost hovers as the first juvenile reaches him, and she takes it in her talons and turns with it to the trees. Her siblings follow, and all three now chase back and fly into cover, two still screaming for the food.

The adult male doesn't land, but turns back and begins to accelerate away into the clouds again, his line straight and steep for minutes on end, wings working tirelessly and steadily until he is just dot in the blue.

For a long time after his departure the Swallows are absent, then they gradually drift back to the vicinity of the trees, and settle on the wires at the corner again.

An hour passes until, up high, a Hobby is drifting, catching insects; it looks like the female. She circles and swoops and thermals back up again, in her ease.

Suddenly she steams away to the west, and after a minute she is returning, lower now, and with her mate. He has made a kill and she chases him as he speeds back towards their nest.

When they are half-way across the field, two of the young fly out from the oak, calling to their parents. The adult female now passes under the male and he drops his catch to her, it falls for two seconds, then she takes it from the air as it tumbles.

This time the juvenile male is in front, leading his sister as they make for their mother, but, as he reaches her and tries to take the meal, she swerves past him and carries on to the oak, the young at her heals. All of them disappear within the canopy as the screams pierce the air around it.

Five minutes later the adult is flying out, back towards the pylon. Her mate has vanished.

Her upright shape on the metal spar is silhouetted now behind the sun, low to the west. Somewhere above, her mate is hunting once again.

As butterflies give way to moths, birds to bats, three well-fed juvenile Hobbies, perhaps, will settle for the night, though their father might, even now, bring another meal in the dark.

A knot of Lapwings is up high in a typical Peregrine reaction, the Wood Pigeons already out of sight elsewhere, but the falcon has already gone. Dark-bottomed clouds fill the sky. Linnets and Tree Sparrows bound along the hedges towards the corner.

A group of Starlings has displaced the Pied Wagtails in the paddock, and the horses are all gathered at one corner, nibbling each other's backs. A Buzzard at the canal side is keeping the Rabbits grounded in their burrows under the nettles.

And, in the sycamore, two juvenile Hobbies are sitting, dark in the morning light, low down at the lowest limbs, looking at the stubble below.

The other is in the field, sitting on the straw, just below the oak tree. A Magpie is in the hedge nearby, but flies away soon enough.

Somewhere behind, a Little Owl calls an alarm, then a Sparrowhawk arrives and all three young Hobbies fly up as it comes right past their trees. The four fly together for a few minutes, swerving around the trees, but none show any antagonism, though they are close enough to the hawk to grapple, and after a while, the Sparrowhawk leaves to hunt, and the Hobbies settle to the trees again.

For another hour and more there is no sign of the adults. The Lapwings have re-settled to the field, landing close to a Hare which sits, ears back, in the weeds.

To the west, rain slants down from a grey bank of cloud as the sun tries to shine between the crowded clouds to the east. Four Mallard overtake a Heron along the canal's course, rising gradually in tight formation; the Heron, barely buoyant, glides heavily back to the towpath.

Two Yellow Wagtails, put up by a Kestrel, rise up over the hedge and drop into the stubble field, briefly brightening the grey.

Now, as the Kestrel comes past their oak, the three Hobbies come out of the trees and, calling, follow the falcon, mistaking it for their parent. The Kestrel continues, heading off towards the river, and the juveniles turn back, two locking talons for a second in the air, and land back in their trees.

It is after midday when the female approaches with prey, her mate behind her, in from the east. She is carrying what looks to be a young

Starling, and nearly reaches the trees before her young see her, and, with loud calls, they launch towards her.

She is hidden behind the oak, flying in as the male goes to perch on the sycamore, dark juveniles around the trees, all trying to reach her first. In a minute the noise has subsided somewhat, one of the young carrying the Starling, pursued by a sibling, from one tree to the next, finally landing in the shadows.

Two Magpies appear from nowhere, but have barely landed when the female falcon dives at them, into the tree with wings against her, through a gap to find the Magpies, following into the branches and finally ejecting them onto the hedge below. She drives again and chases them away, and they give up the fight and make off along the hedge to look for the Little Owl.

She immediately goes to the pylon, scattering Swallows on her way, then veers off to the north, beginning to rise towards a shower darkening the sky that way. Her mate sits, eyeing the Swallows, when – from the rain – a Swift emerges and he takes off towards it.

He has been seen almost immediately – the Swift turning tail and racing back northwards – as he puts on all his power and follows, primaries glinting, gaining perceptibly as they rise into the falling rain, as the shower obscures them both.

Clouds scud and shadows sprint across the field, the sun blinking bright in spaces between, colours gone to greys in film-noir cinematography. The sky glowers, low and gloomy, letting fly with squalls that rock the trees.

Rooks and Crows and Jackdaws: black shapes moving, and Black-backed Gulls, dark-wings yawing as they coast across the field, the wind behind them.

For two hours more the showers continue, when, almost suddenly, the wind drops as the sun breaks, and the showers are distant. As if on cue a Hobby heads in from across the canal, slowly gliding and holding something beneath him.

Three juveniles head out to meet him, right across the corner of the field, over the lane towards the pond, as he dangles a small bird from his talons. One of them takes it from him, and turns, the others following, then one circles back to its father, calling to be fed. They fly together for a half-minute, then he rises and heads for the pylon, and the youngster heads back to the trees, which the others have just reached.

As the late afternoon sun warms the world, two juvenile Hobbies take to the air, rising above the trees, and start to insect-catch, appearing to take several each and eating on the wing. They rise with the prey, now perhaps a hundred feet up, they are joined by their mother, and the three circle together, feeding above their trees.

Back at the pylon, the male has gone.

From under the hedge, ten Grey Partridges creep into the stubble, as a small commotion happens above them. A Great spotted Woodpecker is alarming and crabbing sideways under a branch of an oak as a Little Owl crouches flat on the same bough, just above it. The Woodpecker pokes its dagger bill around the bark, towards the Owl, but the Owl doesn't move. The Woodpecker shuffles under the branch, completely hidden from the Owl and creeps around the other side, bobbing its head to catch a glimpse of it. For a while it stays absolutely still, then gets fed up of the attention and turns to fly off back to its own tree. The Woodpecker clambers around the branch and sits for a while where the Owl once tried to hide.

At the field's edge, Chaffinches and Yellowhammers attempt to fly-catch as they swap from picking seeds, while, behind in the near distance, two Kestrels shimmer against the low sun, stopping to hover on the slight breeze, then round the plump pillows of air to pause again.

A family of Buzzards, the warm waft lifting them lazily, circles the late day's air as one bends to tear at a Vole in its talons. Two Ravens drift in to join them, and they all sail along the ridge like surfers on the roll of an upswept wave.

As the sun starts to set, Stock Doves drop down to the stubble on dihedral wings, gliding an arc to the ground. A Hare, racing out from the woods, jumps over one, as it heads across to the lane.

The juvenile Hobbies have settled. Pied Wagtails are heading to roost, rising from the paddocks and over the farm to the safety of thorns.

As dusk slips a shadowed hand, gently across the land, the silhouettes of Swallows against the western sky skim along the lane towards the barns.

The adult Hobbies are on the pylon, watching the sun rise. The dew, like a silver sheet, drapes across the meadow below and a faint ghost of vapour hangs against the lee of hedge and wood.

There is a depth to the coolness of the morning, the longer nights draining the days' warming, the later sun only now taking the chill.

But the clear sky promises a fine day, and the Swallows and Martins are already starting to rise from gutter and fence and wire, as shadows slowly shorten.

Two Herons, calling at each other, drop towards the canal, grey wings drooping, legs dangling: two umbrellas falling from the sky. A Mistle Thrush is in the rowan, chirring at Blackbirds that dare to take its berries, and a Kestrel watches Linnets in the lane, from his telegraph pole perch.

One of the juvenile Hobbies drops to the damp straw beneath the oak and runs after a beetle, then sits and eats it, lifting one foot as it steadies itself on heel and tail.

All at once alarming Swallows are swarming along the hedge above the lane, and at the pylon, the Hobbies have taken to the sky. Together they rise, wings almost touching, heading south, the sun on their white cheeks, looking ahead where three Swifts are above them.

They are two miles away as they disappear over the horizon, the Swifts still in front.

Stock Doves and Wood Pigeons are in the field as the falcons return – he has a Swift as they streak in, she gaining on him as they fall towards the girders, but he keeps the prey as he lands, and she sits on the spar below, calling to him.

The juveniles have heard her, and seeing their parents on the pylon, they start to fly across the field, begging for the food as they go. The adult male stays where he is, plucking and feeding on the Swift.

Now, on a maiden voyage, the young fly all the way to the pylon, and the adult male flies out with the Swift's remains as they get close. One of the juvenile females takes it from him as they swarm around and she takes it to the ground under the giant structure, just out of sight below the field's humped middle. The other youngsters land on the girders and the family are all together, away from the nest site for the first time.

For almost an hour the adults sit, then they launch into the blue again, curving around to head across the river. One youngster follows for a few seconds, then loops round to go to the field where its sibling is still.

The third juvenile takes off, circling up from the ironwork, and begins to fly-catch in the warming morning, drifting back across the field slowly towards the nest site. Swallows seem unalarmed by its presence in their airspace, instinct telling them they are in no danger.

Half an hour later the adults come in from the east, and the juvenile in the air is closest as the male brings a small bird back from the hunt. The female lands on the sycamore as her mate continues and the youngster calls to him. They meet mid field and he hands over the prey, the juvenile taking it back to the oak to eat.

As the adult lands on the pylon the other juveniles rise from the field and one circles around him as the other lands nearby.

As midday comes to the field, the male is off again, flying over his mate still on the sycamore, who takes off to follow as he dives towards the barns. They disappear beyond, Swallows' alarms echoing around the farm, a swirl of Wagtails kicked up from the rooves.

During the afternoon the two juveniles at the pylon take to the air to catch insects, the slight breeze drifting them back towards their nest. Then there are three together for a while, the male showing his slighter build next to his sisters.

They are all perching in the trees as the adult male arrives back with a House Martin, and he flies over, heading for the pylon. They take off noisily, and follow him, and he accelerates away as they try to keep up, their shorter wings apparent.

As he reaches the spars he drops the Martin and the leading juvenile attempts to catch it, following it as it falls, but it reaches the ground before the catch is made. All three are on the field now, but the first takes the prey back up to the lowest girder, its siblings pursuing.

Out of the blue a Peregrine appears, and it is heading for the pylon like a bomb.

It dives towards the juvenile Hobbies which are too naïve to realise the danger they are in. All around, the sky fills with fleeing Wood Pigeons.

But, suddenly, from nowhere, the female Hobby is streaking at the Peregrine, and though still some way above, she is gaining rapidly. The Peregrine stoops, now below the pylon's top, heading for the juvenile Hobbies, but the female flies at it, like lightning, a blurred streak that reaches the Peregrine in another second. She meets the bigger falcon, which reacts with a swerve, looking over its shoulder as she attacks.

Now the male has joined in to battle the Peregrine, and the pair corkscrew around it, raking talons as it tries to avoid them both, its pursuit abandoned.

Now the Peregrine arcs away, rising as the Hobbies stay on its tail, hitting it in turn as it speeds off towards the church. The Hobbies follow it all the way, and as it attempts to land at the base of the steeple, they continue to drive at it, and it carries on to the south, and they return to their family on the pylon, spiralling around each other rapidly in their triumph.

As they reach the structure they loop upwards again, and rise high above, circling for minutes as they thermal, becoming specks in the glare. Thousands of feet below, one of their young feeds on the Martin, as the others take to the air to feed themselves.

The warm afternoon brings the butterflies, and the dragonflies: Migrant Hawkers are up catching midges – and the young Hobbies have bigger insects to try for, to hone their skills on.

Many attempts miss the target as the sharp-eyed Hawkers evade the outstretched talons of the juveniles, skimming away as the falcons try to snatch them from the sky. But each miss is a lesson learnt and before long they will have to feed themselves.

The female doesn't show again all afternoon. But, as the day draws to an end, her mate arrives with another meal, which looks like he has already eaten part of.

The juveniles meet him as he comes in from the west, rising up from the pylon, screaming the whole way. One gets to him first and takes the remains of a bird from him, the others following him to the pylon as he lands. One lands on the same spar and walks along it to him, but as it nears he takes off again, leaving it behind.

As the sun sets, the female flies in and lands on the pylon, and one of the juveniles flies to her, sitting close by until nearly dark, before heading back towards the nest for the night.

The whole Hobby family is at the nest site today, both adults perching at the tops, the juveniles on lower branches.

A Kestrel flies past the young and two of them fly after it for several seconds, calling. The adults ignore the Kestrel, but, as two Magpies fly into the oak, the female launches an attack, eventually driving them off.

With her spirits up, she rises now, calling softly to her mate, and they set off across the field. They pass the pylon and carry on over the next farm and its House Martin colony, still rising, then dwindle into the distance.

An hour passes. Two of the young are up, insect catching. The day is warm and the insects are rising. The other juvenile is in the field, sitting still. It stays there for another hour as its siblings circle. They drift higher and further, until almost above the river, swooping and gliding, then return to the site to hunt above their trees.

Then, from the east, in from the opposite direction he had gone, the adult male comes over, carrying a Goldfinch. The three juveniles fly after him, the two already in the air with the advantage, as the other tries to catch up. The all go to the pylon and the male lands there, still holding his catch. As they fly to him he launches again and hands the prey to one, which takes it to the ground to eat. The others follow: all three in the stubble now.

The adult is soon off again – and this time he doesn't return for the rest of the day.

As dusk falls the juveniles head back to the cover of the trees, their parents nowhere in sight.

Thunder clouds are already gathering. It is mid-morning and the young Hobbies are sitting in the stubble under the pylon. One of the adults is at the very top – possibly the female – and now sails away and starts to dive on Dragonflies.

As the first distant rumble of thunder sounds, the male arrives at the pylon, from the north, appearing over the river's trees. He has a small morsel – an insect perhaps – and flies towards the young. They fly up to greet him and one takes the offering and lands on the pylon.

The others go to him, and he speeds away, to the south. They follow. After several seconds he is circling and insect-catching and his young follow suit, the three of them patrolling the field as their mother drifts away, high up.

A young Sparrowhawk appears – circling up towards the falcons – and the Hobbies joust and spar with it, diving and looping, presenting talons and testing each other, once or twice stooping a short stoop and swerving away as they close. For five minutes the game continues, then the Sparrowhawk moves on and leaves the field to the falcons.

Huge clouds tower and build in the warmth, mushrooming, billowing in slow motion, darkening all the while. A line of them queues from the south-west to the north-east, and from one or two, rain falls and rainbows spark. A single Swift swerves between the cloud walls, but heading unerringly southward.

But only one heavy shower falls on the field, gone in forty minutes and the sky is already brightening as the thunderclouds, now overhead, steam steadily eastwards.

With the rain the fly-catching ends and the Hobbies are all out of sight.

Rooks descend to the wetted field, and a flock of Lapwings settle there too. Water vapour rises in the afternoon sunshine and the butterflies flicker over the field again.

From the far hedge a covey of Grey Partridges explodes into the field, skimming the stubble at full speed, bowed wings whirring as they arc towards cover at the corner. A Fox appears, runs along the hedge, scattering Rabbits, then disappears.

A minute later a Hare sprints from that side of the field and runs the entire length of it, not slowing until over the hump, settling on its haunches and watching back over its shoulders without turning its head. The Fox stays hidden.

It is evening when the female Hobby, having found a Swift at this late date, flies in with it. Her young are at the nest site and she delivers her meal. The juveniles greet her, but are fairly quiet, one of them taking the Swift, then she leaves for the pylon's silhouette and settles against the setting sun.

Young Tawny Owls are calling from the copse, but don't show, though two Little Owls perch up on the telegraph poles as the moths start to spiral.

August almost done and summer curls its brown-edged leaf; the late mornings' dew hangs on.

August is almost at an end, the young two weeks post-fledge. The weather remains warm, even hot in the afternoons, allowing them Dragonfly-catching practice. More and more often they are to be found at the pylon, only returning to the nest tree to roost.

Their wings are full-grown now and they resemble their parents in shape and size, and when high up insect-catching they are difficult to distinguish. During the next week they will cease to be fed by their parents, and feed exclusively on insects that they catch for themselves.

The parents become more and more absent now, hours and hours pass without their obvious presence, though their father is, for now, still bringing avian prey to them regularly, often hunting from early morning until after dark. The female, too, is still bringing food – though some of this is taken from her mate before she arrives.

The dew boils off the bramble bank, driven by the early morning sun. A Whitethroat chirrs its alarm as two pristine Sparrowhawks pass overhead, their presence predicted by ten Mistle Thrushes taking flight.

Fifty or more Jackdaws, put up by a passing Kestrel, settle again amongst the drying hay.

Five Buzzards find the first thermals and begin to spiral, while a flock of Long-tailed Tits flits by. Goldcrests call and Robins tick. Two Cormorants circle and continue east. Two late Sand Martins fly due south, and, a mile further, a Hobby draws the eye as it streaks obliquely towards some unseen prey, passing the half-moon and its craters before disappearing behind the trees of the horizon.

Cumuli bubble in the blue.

The day continues, sultry after its autumnal start; a Kestrel sits on top of a hay ridge now, its legs yellow against the dark golden straw. Swallows sing; a Nuthatch calls from the oak; a Wasp chews wood close by, its crunching audible in the stillness. A Holly Blue, underwing shining silvery, settles on a honeysuckle.

Blackbirds hack apples; a Small White butterflies by; a Blackcap 'tacks' from the brambles as a breeze brushes the poplars.

Two Herons, over very low, one squawking.

The day hots up. A Hobby approaches from the east, simultaneously another is calling overhead with its mate, the two now right above as the first turns south. All three are gone in seconds.

The sun reaches its zenith in an impossibly blue sky, all clouds gone.

A Yellow Wagtail calls as it passes.

September starts bright and warm and the three juveniles are again on the pylon, and so are the parents. For the first time in days the five are sitting together.

The female takes off, calling, and the young male joins her, and they rise together, the sky hazy above them. One of the females takes off and begins to hunt too, but much lower. She catches a few flies then circles up to join the other two, and they fly together for a while.

Suddenly the adult female accelerates away, and her son follows, looking quite the accomplished flier. They both disappear into the haze. This is his first foray into the wider world. The other juvenile continues to insect-catch for several minutes, rising steadily, when suddenly the young male is back with her.

They hunt together for a while until he goes to the pylon's top and perches: until now none of the juveniles has perched up as high, always sitting on the lower spars.

He is still there when the adult male comes in with a Starling and passes it to the youngster mid-air as he flies out to meet his father. But he doesn't eat, and a minute later the juvenile female flies down to him and lands, calls carrying across the field, and takes the Starling from him.

Now, from the east, the adult female comes in with prey. She is calling and at least one of the juveniles is too. She takes the meal from her mother and glides down to the ground to feed.

After a few minutes the young male drops from his girder to the field and goes to his sister, perhaps taking a morsel, before heading back to the pylon.

At the pool by the lane a pair of Teal – nervous by the shadowed edge – keep to cover. A family of Sedge Warblers are clambering around the irises and rushes, up into the overhanging willows, where Reed Buntings are sitting. And the water is a froth of activity: Migrant Hawkers and a Southern Hawker are mating and ovipositing in the shallows and onto the lilies, tails dipping below the water rhythmically, wings fanning. Common Darters skim by the margins and perch on the sedges, red bodies gleaming in the sun.

At the edge of the pond young Toads hide in the vegetation, like animated aggregate pebbles, crawling to hunting grounds nearby. A Brown Hawker whizzes by, wings yellow-translucent, glimmering as it tilts.

Along the lane's verges, Speckled Woods, Large whites and Red Admirals flicker, and a Brimstone flaps and glides under the hedgerow. Commas on the brambles, matching the turning leaves, open and close their wings in the sun. And two young Song Thrushes, not long from the nest, sit under the hawthorn, yellow gape-lines on their wide-eyed faces, stubby wings on stubby tails.

Meadow Pipits are passing overhead, thin calls falling from the bright. And, in the paddock, with a dozen Pied Wagtails, a passage White Wagtail shows its subtle differences as it hunts alongside the flock.

The sun sets beyond the pylon, and three young Hobbies become silhouettes: dark bronzes on the steel.

As dusk falls, two Snipe, zipping overhead, suddenly zigzag down to the pool, stiff, half-closed wings angled for the descent, long bills leading the way.

Pipistrelles corkscrew out into the gloom, flickering away into the night.

Across the field come two male Hobbies, one carrying prey. They are flying fast towards the pylon as the juveniles fly out to intercept them. At tree top height all five meet, and the prey is handed over mid-air – as a tangle of young try to take it, wheeling around as the intruder passes his catch – while being seen off simultaneously by the resident male. The intruder, undoubtedly his one year-old son.

The intruder flies away northward, the male seeing him off, as the juveniles squabble briefly over the food, one eventually taking it to a girder to feed, one of the others sitting beside it, begging from its own sibling.

The male returns and flies over the pylon, and his two unfed young join him in the air. They drift towards the nest tree as they catch insects, the three looking very similar now, in habits and shape.

Above, a pale line of Golden Plover, in a shallow chevron, hang in the sky, heads to the breeze, as if searching for a field to forage in. For many minutes their angle across the sky remains, before they head off westwards.

The blue sky bleaches to grey out west as the wind picks up, gradually, steadily.

Against the dark bank of the riverside trees, seven Jays emerge and undulate to the copse across the field, broad wings slapping silently. They dive into cover and are gone.

The House Martins are flocking around the farm: a Sparrowhawk is passing the buildings, slinking Fox-like by the barns, low, trying to hide, yet already discovered. Sparrows race to the trees and the hawk follows right in, forcing them to flee out of the other side.

As the Sparrowhawk accelerates out from the branches, a foolhardy Swallow follows, on its tail, an inch away. They all disappear beyond the barns.

The afternoon brings rains. It slants persistently, wind-blown wetness filling the world. After days of sunshine, suddenly the world is changed. Suddenly the butterflies are gone, suddenly the air is chill.

The rain continues, never heavy but non-stop, for another day and a half, two cold-fronts blowing eastwards, dragging low clouds across the sky, as the wind pushes the trees, and the first leaves of autumn tumble and lie wetly along the lane. The Hobbies are in hiding, their pylon empty, the Swallows nowhere to be found.

But the next day dawns bright, the wind already dropped, the world glistening like a new born.

And, there, on the pylon, as if never having been away, three juvenile Hobbies sit.

As the sun comes up, a Chiffchaff sings, as if it's spring.

The Swallows are back, still morning-low, sweeping the sleepy fly from the field top, slipping along the meadow, blue backs below the eye line; shining; beautiful.

A group of Lapwings are in the weeds, tugging at worms, pecking at beetles, striding the still-wet stubble.

Now, a family of Crows have found the falcons, and harass and harangue them on the pylon, strutting the spars and sidling up to them, forcing them to fly. The Hobbies merely move, arcing around the structure to land elsewhere, followed by the Crows at every turn. This goes on for some time, and then the Crows give up trying to move the falcons, flying off to the copse to crow from the tree tops.

A minute passes and the adult arrives, curving above the riverside trees with a Swallow dangling beneath him. His young fly up and tussle for the meal, two trying to take it between them to the pylon. He flies away immediately, off to the south, speeding on the rise until just a dot in the distance.

Fifteen minutes later and he is returning. Another item of prey is under him, tucked neatly this time, as he skims over the poplars towards his young. This time two come out to greet him, and as they reach him he lets the bird go. They go for it, diving at the falling lump, one managing to catch it just before it hits the ground, and takes it, low across the field, under the pylon to feed.

As its father heads away again, the remaining youngster follows, and for a minute they go together to the east, but as he gets beyond the farm, it turns and goes to the nest site to settle there.

Forty minutes, this time, before his return, back from the east and again another item of prey is under him. He is high above the nest tree when the juvenile launches out, trying to reach him as he heads towards the pylon.

The two meet up at the apex, and he passes the food to the third of his young, now having fed all three within an hour. He lands at the top as the youngster takes the prey to a low spar to feed.

The field fills with birds: Wood Pigeons by the score, Rooks by the dozen, Jackdaws, Stock Doves, Lapwings, Black-headed and Lesser Black-backed Gulls, all heads down, hunting, gleaning, picking.

And Yellowhammers and Linnets and migrating Meadow Pipits hide themselves between the tiny forest of stubble stalks, walking the rows, nibbling at seeds, running at flies.

The September sun shines on. The world is dry again, the rain put to the skies – small white clouds drifting across the duck-egg blue.

Now the Hobbies are up, rising with the insects, getting ever higher. The male has gone from the pylon, slipping away unnoticed. His young feed themselves now on less substantial but plentiful morsels. They are specks in the haze, darting and diving: small stoops onto small prey. As their hunting continues they separate across the sky, each seeking their own space in its vastness.

For them, these small forays will soon become globe-spanning journeys, taking them to Africa for the first time.

The juveniles are all up this morning – scattered across the cloud-dotted blue sky, catching insects.

The three are ranging widely now, but never out of sight if searched for long enough, returning to their field to re-group every quarter of an hour or so.

Now all three are loosely together when they are joined by a fourth falcon. For a second, as it drops lower towards them it appears to be another Hobby. But it is a male Peregrine, a juvenile bird, with similar colours – but considerably bigger than they.

They chase the Peregrine with spectacular flying prowess, easily out-flying the larger falcon, diving and twisting as it tries to evade them – circling and countering with its own stoops and arcs – but never with the advantage, and, outnumbered and out-flown, it speeds away southward, the Hobbies on its tail, keeping up with ease.

The chase has taken them more than half a mile away – and now they return to resume their leisurely insect-catching, over the copse and the riverside trees, passing the pylon as they drift.

Suddenly, in from the east, a female Hobby speeds in with some prey under her. The juveniles immediately give chase, screaming for the food, two of them nose to tail as they race after her. The third, from further out, is still closing as the leading juvenile takes the prey from her and heads for the field under the pylon, dropping down to feed.

The female continues her straight-line flight and fades away into the distance. Since their own mother has not fed them for some time now, this one seems to be a year-old intruder, practising for her next season, when she could have young of her own.

In the paddock two Wheatears, both adults, are showing off their colours as they hunt beetles, flashing white rumps before they land on turf clumps and fences. Three or four Meadow Pipits are nearby, creeping amongst the cropped grass like mice, as Pied Wagtails skitter brightly.

The Swallows are far fewer in number now. Their line on the wire shortening with the days, and high up, a steady stream of them is heading south.

Along the hedge, the cleavers are finished – their thousand dead stems sprawled like an old worn-out blanket draped over the thorns, and the verge is fluffy with thistle and dandelion heads. But, in the rows of stubble, the tiny bright violas still flower in profusion, and daisies still open to the sun.

Goldfinch and Linnet flocks bound above the field, dropping to seed heads and grain on the ground, tinkling like tiny bells as they move: whites, the golds and pinks melting into the meadow.

At the farm, the House Martins are still coming back, crops bulging, to nestling-full mud cups in the eaves, pied heads poking from within, the air still fly-flecked.

But the leaf is on the turn: brambles are tri-coloured as they age: green, red and gold, and the sycamores look sick with pox-marks – black dots turning each leaf to domino and dice.

Along the canal where the footpath leads down towards the river, the hedges are bright with berries. Rose hips and elderberries, haws and blackberries: signs of seasonal success and succession. A Red Admiral glides down to sun itself by the briars, as unseen Siskins' calls peel from above.

A Bullfinch whistles nearby as a Willow Warbler flickers in an appropriate willow, when, just yards away, a Stoat appears on the path ahead. It crosses to a concrete block and leaps onto it, running across and jumping down between two, then head-buts the block, moves on, runs across the path to the opposite side, head-bangs another block, twice. Running briefly out into the open again, it disappears under the brambles' shadows.

A juvenile female Sparrowhawk, harassed by Crows, flies a quick loop from the trees in front, its banded tail vanishing back to cover. Now an adult male Sparrowhawk, having seen her, flies straight into the same tree, and the two emerge in a second, the adult chasing the bigger juvenile, blue and brown along the hedge.

Kestrels are circling and hovering, Buzzards are up hunting; four of each.

Above them, migrating Skylarks and Meadow Pipits, tiny specks in the sky, are speeding south.

A young Great spotted Woodpecker, red-capped, shuffles up a trunk, watching as a Hobby flies towards the pylon beyond the woods.

Along the lane a Sparrowhawk is sitting in the road: an adult male. He skims the tarmac, just an inch above it, for a few yards and lands again. He sits, yellow-orange iris watching the hedges, where Sparrows cram themselves deep into the thorns. His head and mantle are hoary – flecked white – but, jutting from this old feather, a fresh set of neatly-edged primary feathers shows. Under him his thin yellow legs suddenly spring him from the lane and he flies a leap over the hedge, putting the Sparrows to flight, and he follows.

In the paddock, three Yellow Wagtails are picking insects from beneath a grazing horse's muzzle. A chestnut mare, her nose creased, soft lips brushing gently at the meadow, long and sparse orange whiskers catching the light, crops the short grass with audible tears, disturbing the insects for the Wagtails to snatch.

Linnets on the wire above, watch, occasionally calling their nasal music.

Out west, the clouds crowd the horizon, and two rainbows – multicoloured parentheses – shine from their edges. But above, only blue.

Above the pond, a Common Darter – miniature midge-assassin – zips over the bindweed strangling the brambles. And, at the next oak, a Little Owl, out from its usual perch, crouches at a bough-bend and squints at the sun, its back like bark. A Buzzard sits sentinel on the fence. Two Collared Doves balance, like tight-rope walkers, on the wires, with a trio of shining Greenfinches.

Then, from the field a flock rises: Skylarks, Yellowhammers, Meadow Pipits, Tree Sparrows and Chaffinches spin up and away. The finches and buntings head straight for the hedge, while the sparrows, the larks and pipits swirl into the air.

The adult male Hobby is heading over, low enough to spook the flock, as he heads to the pylon. His young gather as he approaches, rising now to the highest horizontal arm, landing before they reach him. Two of the juveniles land beside him, one to each side, and walk along the spar to him. The third circles the air by his perch.

But he has no prey for them, they are over three weeks old now, and his provision for them could soon cease. They fly after him as he disappears again, continuing to beg. Perhaps this visit was merely a lesson.

As September continues, the female is seldom seen; sometimes she is hunting high up with the young, but, for the most part she is absent. Soon she will leave them and head off back to her wintering grounds, migrating alone as she follows the Swallows to Africa.

As each day passes, any glimpse of her could be the last, then one of those absences will stretch until spring.

The early sun drums on the fence, driving a silver spout of water vapour to bend away upward into the clearing mist. Out along sweet chestnut-laden lanes, the blinding light from puddles strikes like a slap as a hedge-top Sparrowhawk launches and submerges below its line. Beyond, a Buzzard sits in the sunshine, pale breast pushed against the light.

Ten Grey Partridges strut to cover, under a Little Owl, stretched to press itself along a bough, trying to hide. Three Song Thrushes, silent, whip by and a flock of fourteen Lapwings drifts north. In the copse a Great spotted Woodpecker clings upside down to a branch, its scarlet vent blazing.

A Kestrel, from the barn, with a five-Swallow escort, flashes its underwing as it makes for the telegraph pole. The Swallows swerve away to hunt new flies.

A lone Raven, high and steady, heads across the river as acorn-raiding Jays flutter like huge butterflies from oak to oak.

Rising vapours take on colour as they coalesce, cinnamon against the blue. Turning leaves fall to the ground, rusty and spent.

In the paddock, lit by a million raindrops refracting dazzle from the early sun, horses graze quietly, almost studiously.

The crushed potato cumuli on the northern horizon have already faded from dawn's oranges to yellows, a shadow of rain like a dark skirt hanging below.

And, from the west, a Hobby in uninterrupted glide, in perpetual motion, though entirely still, is unendingly driven, coasting the lumped air pushing; then, sensing the curve, the wave ending, he slips beyond the breaker's fall to spin away, with a last glance, and with a barely discernible, deftest turn to his tail, the blinding sun caught forever in his eye.

There is a constant passage southward, pushing, this morning against a steady southerly breeze: Meadow Pipits, Swallows and House Martins. Four Siskins, calling as they go, separate themselves audibly from the Chaffinches overhead. Skylarks are everywhere, their calls falling from a blue sky.

Dazzling clouds with chasms of crease, fold themselves around the breeze, gigantic and magnificent, deafening in their silent sirens.

Buzzards wheel and catch the sun, and Kestrels, swapping poles, put passerines up from the wetted field.

Then, through a Black-headed Gull flock across the canal, a Merlin, fast and dark against the gulls, zigzags overhead, and all the small birds explode in every direction. The Merlin jinks towards a Meadow Pipit and misses, now low against the stubble, she veers towards the hedge, seeking finches, and skims the top to vanish on the other side.

Corvids carpet the stubble, flashing silver in the sunshine, moving restlessly.

And, not until late afternoon, does a single Hobby show, coming back to the pylon, followed by a second. Half an hour later the three juveniles are all on the ironwork, the metal turning molten in the evening light.

As the day fades, a Woodcock wings over, like a giant bat, flying out to feed in the night.

The ploughing has started in the big field beyond the river, and soon the Hobbies' pylon field will be turned over, ready for another crop. But the juveniles are, at this moment, a mile away, ranging further and further, and even now are thousands of feet up in the mid-September sky.

As they patrol and drift, catching Dragonflies now – such is their skill – from time to time, as Meadow Pipits and Swallows pass, they try their hunting prowess on this larger prey, but their attempts, so far at least, have been unsuccessful.

Out in the field – half in furrow, half tilled: wave and beach. And, in the wave of furrows are two hundred Lapwings, plovers paddling nervously, easy to wing at imagined dangers: shifting, flying, settling again to wade the pushing air.

Above, the waning moon, underbelly shadowed, sweeps slowly through blueing silver. Deep furrows head away in perspective-shrinking stripes, holding strips of water here and there – bright mercury, cold fire.

A dozen Linnets skip, chirruping around the hawthorns, ripe in berry, as Lapwings take to the air to circle nervously. A Hare sits, unblinking, hunched in the newly exposed earth, wise, flank to the sun, ears folded and tracked along its back.

A ripple of Skylarks bubbles above.

Dewy spider webs burn along the lane where Meadow Pipits and Skylarks compete. Two Jays on an autumn foray, flash rumps in the oak.

From the barn a Kestrel puts up a Grey Wagtail hunting sun-warmed flies on the roof slope. And out by the far hedge line amongst camouflaging tussocks, seven Grey Partridges shuffle imperceptibly, earth-coloured, ancient. These remnants remain.

Above, from the copse, a Buzzard launches a flight and flushes Stock Doves from the field. Swallows in loose groups skim south – low and blue. A Reed Bunting crosses their trajectory, a single call wheezing once.

Starling flocks flick and twist in the wind. A shuddering sky holds a rainbow in the sudden sun, ending at a flame-coloured chestnut, standing like a firework, silently spewing a spectrum.

On the field's horizon a tractor is sailing the furrows; plovers getting up to hang in the breeze: kites crowding the skies above the blowy beach. A Buzzard's cry is blown away: litter along the stand.

At the House Martin colony, all but the last of the lingerers have gone, with one or two occupied nests still active, the last youngsters almost ready to fly now.

Somewhere, up in the end-of-the-summer sky, three young Hobbies are still honing their hunting in the easy air. But, with their parents perhaps already gone, the instinct to leave grows within them, the shortening days a signal to go.

A gentle wind, a lover's hand, disturbs the skirts of the poplars. The welcome-warm sun fills the glass-clear air. Amber leaves launch to die diagonally along the shafts, where Red Admirals skim convolvulus flowers on the bramble tops.

Buzzards dance in the sky, buoyed on afternoon warmth, a foursome reel, below silver herring-backed and fritillary clouds, half a mile high. A Nuthatch's calls drip-droops from ash and lime; late Swallows hurry to the falling sun.

A Comma's jags jink in shade and in light; the last Wasp rasps its stripes from unseasoned wood. Somewhere a Collared Dove sings drunkenly.

Bound for the wood, the Woodpecker bounds against the summer's final blue, calling on the upbeat, flashing white and red, and a single solitary House Martin glides the lazy air, picking at the fly-blown breeze.

Out on the pylon, two silhouettes, ink against the page, stand looking south as their season ends.

Night falls, and the hissing sound of Redwings overhead insists: summer's end is signalled.

Dark dissolves slowly, pre-dawn ashy dank, dead cold embers of a damp night.

Robins begin their challenges to rivals still invisible, as Wrens blasts autumn songs from hedgerow hiding. The sky, murky and low-slung, from slate to merely grey, separates from the land.

A Heron glides down above the river, wings drooping archly, and a Kestrel's head, head-on from the ridge: apparitions in the mist.

The black velvet of a Blackbird slips to the verge and stops, head raised, listening. From above, the "seeps" of Redwings fall like fine drizzle.

As the day begins, a single Siskin meanders rapidly above, Chaffinches fall to the sycamore and a Coal Tit takes seeds to cache in stashes.

Gulls, just lighter than the grey, emerge and sail past silently.

With the full light, the mists, having whispered the seasons' shift, are gone.

Somewhere, from the new dawn's sky, the half-imagined begging call of a Hobby echoes across the land, like a memory of summer.

And across the stubble, the giant pylon, only now in view, stands stark and empty, every spar and every girder merely metal, no matter how hard I look.

POSTSCRIPT

THE Hobby activities described above are based on many years of personal observation.

While I lived in Lymm, Cheshire, Hobbies began breeding close by in about 2004. Their range had rapidly expanded from southern counties, reaching Cheshire around then. They had been heathland specialists in Britain, their stronghold for centuries had been Surry, Hampshire and Dorset. Then, for no known reason, they began breeding in farmland – and they are still expanding northward.

Finding the nest each year, which usually moves widely around their territory, was a challenge, as they are very discreet until the young are hatched.

Each day described above is a contraction based on of five years of activities: often a part day of watching was almost devoid of any sightings.

I was working full time for all of this time, though shift work meant I could visit the site at different parts of the day.

During those years the Hobby pair had five different nest sites, and their number of young were either two or three (with only one actually fledging one year).

The laying and fledging dates varied by nearly two weeks over these years, the latest fledging date being the 24th of August.

Various trials and tribulations occurred, and many incidents are not recorded above, nor have I mentioned there that three times the young were ringed under licence: no humans impose themselves on the world I describe, though, of course, there were a few.

I moved to Holmfirth, Yorkshire, in 2013, that year failing to find any nests locally, though Hobbies were in the area. Having moved again to South Yorkshire I was delighted to discover a local Hobby nest in my first season, and the parents fledged three young that year, two the second. Some of the above is described from there.

Time will tell, but I suspect that, in times to come, anyone reading this book will be struck by how many individual birds and what variety of birdlife abounded. This is not how things are, even now, in 2019. Even as I started recording sightings in that part of Cheshire, the last breeding Corn Buntings became extinct there, whereas previously several pairs could be heard singing. And, for now at least, there is a plan for HS2 to destroy almost entirely the Cheshire sites described above.

For years, many passages of the writing I've included in the book, has been online at Birdforum (www.birdforum.net) in threads I have posted there.